THE
NEW
WILD
WEST

THE
NEW
WILD
WEST

BLACK GOLD, FRACKING, AND LIFE
IN A NORTH DAKOTA BOOMTOWN

BLAIRE BRIODY

ST. MARTIN'S PRESS ✠ NEW YORK

THE NEW WILD WEST. Copyright © 2017 by Blaire Briody. All rights reserved. Printed in the United States of America. For information, address St. Martin's Press, 175 Fifth Avenue, New York, N.Y. 10010.

www.stmartins.com

Designed by Steven Seighman

Map of North Dakota by Rhys Davies

The Library of Congress Cataloging-in-Publication Data is available upon request.

ISBN 978-1-250-06492-9 (hardcover)
ISBN 978-1-4668-7152-6 (e-book)

Our books may be purchased in bulk for promotional, educational, or business use. Please contact your local bookseller or the Macmillan Corporate and Premium Sales Department at 1-800-221-7945, extension 5442, or by email at MacmillanSpecialMarkets@macmillan.com.

First Edition: September 2017

10 9 8 7 6 5 4 3 2 1

For my dad, Greg Briody

Memories are long in the western Dakotas. Maybe it's the winters, which give people time to brood, people who bear the pain of living in a harsh, unforgiving climate. . . . Hurts linger.

—Kathleen Norris, author of *Dakota: A Spiritual Geography*

CONTENTS

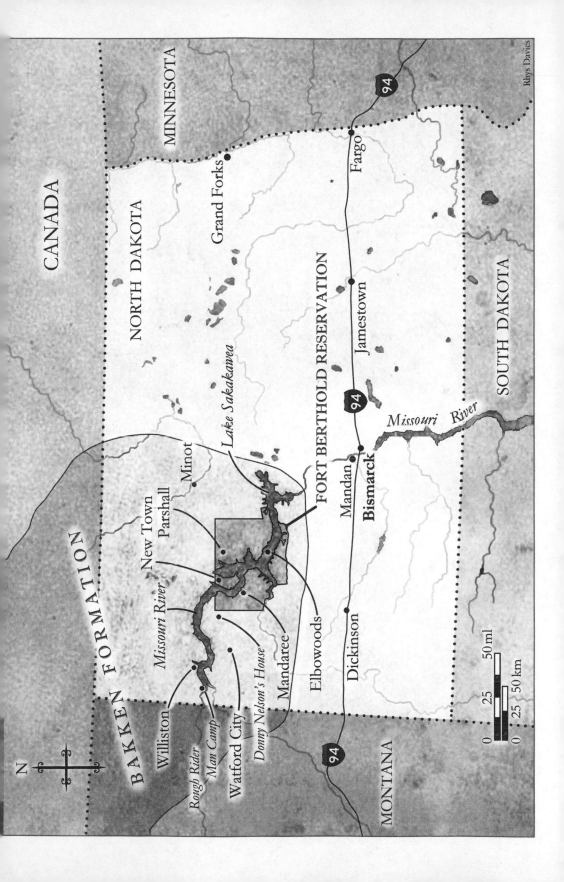

CANADA

MINNESOTA

NORTH DAKOTA

SOUTH DAKOTA

MONTANA

BAKKEN FORMATION

FORT BERTHOLD RESERVATION

94

94

94

Grand Forks

Fargo

Jamestown

Bismarck

Mandan

Dickinson

Minot

Parshall

New Town

Lake Sakakawea

Missouri River

Missouri River

Williston

Rough Rider

Man Camp

Watford City

Donny Nelson's House

Mandaree

Elbowoods

N

Rhys Davies

0   25   50 ml

0   25   50 km

WILLISTON VILLAGE RV RESORT

Welcome to the corner of Oil Avenue and Energy Street.

This is my home for the summer. It consists of a 2001 pop-up camper with 150 square feet of living space, a fold-up dining room table, and bathroom walls built only from particle board. I can see my neighbor's TV screen from my kitchen sink, and their 10-month-old daughter crying at the doorstep. Semi trucks rumble by every few minutes, kicking up dust and sending clouds of dirt into my eyes. Grassy plains stretch for miles on either side of the road.

I'm living in a trailer park on the outskirts of a town called Williston, North Dakota, about 60 miles south of the Canadian border, at the epicenter of one of the largest oil booms the United States has ever experienced.

Six years earlier, in 2007, this was a sleepy prairie town where it was unheard of to lock your doors at night, and the elementary school almost shut down because of declining enrollment. But in the past few years, the town's population has tripled as thousands of workers, mostly young men, have come looking for opportunity. Yesterday, the local paper reported that a woman was shot in the parking lot at Walmart. My trailer park landlord, a gristly woman in her late 40s, told me not to go out after sunset, and there've been rumors that there's been another rape downtown. "I always carry this on me," the 19-year-old girl working at the gas station tells me, gesturing to the knife strapped to her belt, the holster unhooked.

At a bar last night, a man I was talking with reached over and started touching my leg. I jumped up, paid the bill, and left, shaken. I had to walk past a crowd of burly oil workers standing outside smoking cigarettes. I felt their eyes on me as I hurried to my car.

Everyone I talked to warned me this place wasn't safe for a 29-year-old woman, but yet, I still came. I wanted to know what happens when a small town is transformed overnight into a bustling, nearly all-male metropolis. I wanted to see it for myself. So here I am.

THE
NEW
WILD
WEST

1. DONNY NELSON

On a sunny Monday afternoon in early September 2013, I sat in the passenger seat of Donny Nelson's dark blue Ford pickup truck, heading along a bumpy dirt road. Nelson drove and his small, shaggy dog, Lucky, perched on the leather divider between us. The clouds overhead extended for miles across the horizon, shifting and dancing along the curves of grassy hills.

A country singer crooned on the radio as Nelson stared out his window. He'd been explaining how he ended up with the oil rigs around his home. It had to do with mineral rights, and the fact that he didn't own what was below his property. We passed a pipeline construction site on the left. The side of the hill was carved out, revealing a wall of black dirt. Four yellow CAT excavators sat in a line like they were prepping for battle.

Nelson's farmland was one of the most beautiful parts of North Dakota I'd seen so far. I'd been living in oil country for two months, and my impression of the area was that it had become a wasteland. I'd seen more traffic, dust, and heavy industry than in any major metropolitan city I'd visited—in a state that, a mere three years before, had the third-lowest population in the United States. But this area of North Dakota was different. It was part of the Badlands—instead of flat prairie, rolling hills and eroded rock formations speckled the golden landscape. Theodore Roosevelt, who lived in North Dakota as a young man, once described the Badlands as "so fantastically broken in form and so bizarre in color as to seem hardly properly to belong to this earth."

As Nelson talked, he leaned forward in his seat, looking off into the distance. "Do you see that smoke?" he asked, pointing to the hills on the left. I saw nothing at first, but as I stared at the spot he was gesturing at, I saw gray smoke billowing up into the sunny sky.

Nelson drove faster, and Lucky sat up, sensing something was wrong.

"I definitely smell smoke," said Nelson. "It's right in the middle of my pasture."

We curved around a corner, and I held onto the door to keep from sliding. Nelson navigated the truck off the dirt road and onto the hilly pasture. My head almost hit the top of the cab. Finally we saw the source of the smoke: It was coming from an oil well site on Nelson's land.

Nelson pulled up and stepped out of his truck, and I followed. About six Hess employees stood around the singed grass, with one guy hosing it down. The smoke from the blackened patch floated up in thin strands into the blue sky.

One guy recognized Nelson and walked over. "Hi, Donny, sorry about this. A bulldozer hit a rock and created a spark. Luckily we saw it before it got too bad."

Nelson nodded, looking frustrated. He knew the guy, he told me later. He was a local. Nelson told them to update him if anything else happened, and we went on our way. "As you can see, nobody called the fire department," he said as we lifted ourselves back into the truck. I learned later that the fire was never reported and Nelson didn't receive compensation for the damage. Although he tried to be patient with the workers, knowing it wasn't always their fault, he wanted them to be respectful of his home. "If they didn't tell me about it, I'd make them pay," he said. "Because then you just get mad."

Nelson is 49 years old and owns about 8,000 acres of farmland, growing peas, oats, barley, durum, flax, and corn, and raises cattle, in what used to be in one of the most remote areas of the country. The entire 23,000-acre area he lives on has fewer than 10 families. Nelson went to elementary school with Wanda Leppell down the road, and almost every day he stops by the house of his neighbor Roger, whom he's known most of his life, to see how he's doing. When I visited Nelson, my GPS couldn't locate his address, so he gave me directions by providing the mile marker for his dirt road.

Nelson's grandfather came to North Dakota from Minnesota during the Homestead Act in the early 1900s. He took the train carrying a few suitcases of supplies to the small town of Tioga, 70 miles from Nelson's farm, and had to wait until the Missouri River froze over to cross it. "He came over this hill right behind my house," Nelson said, pointing, "and said, 'This is where I'm going to stay.'"

The original farm is along Clark Creek (Nelson pronounces it "Clark Crek"), which was discovered by explorers Lewis and Clark. Nelson grew up working on the farm. His father never had hired help, so as a small child, Nelson hauled water, pitched hay, and rode in his father's old Minneapolis-Moline tractor. His older brother did the tougher jobs. His father would strap his brother into a second tractor, stick it in gear, and tell him to turn off the key if he ran into any problems. "Everybody did stuff like that," said Nelson.

"We knew everybody. You didn't lock your doors. We had no traffic. That's what we liked and that's why we farmed out here and put up with the winters," he explained. "This was one of the most beautiful places. Everybody thinks their home is the most beautiful, but it was. It's a unique area and I'll never see it the same. I'm afraid future generations never will either."

Nelson drove up to a lookout point, and we stepped out of the truck. As we stood looking out onto the expansive hills, a blend of amber and burnt orange swirled as the prairie grasses waved in the wind. The clouds cast dark shadows onto the wheat fields, and we saw oil well after oil well, each one pumping up and down methodically—their black exteriors silhouetted as the sun dipped below the horizon. Because underneath our feet, two miles below the earth's surface, lay the Bakken Formation, a layer of shale rock that held some 170 billion barrels of oil trapped in its crevices and pores. It was the largest continuous oil accumulation the country had ever seen—and the United States had recently discovered how to tap into it.

2. A FORGOTTEN PLACE

When I first began researching this book, I knew little about the oil industry or North Dakota. I was working at a small online news site in New York City, mainly covering the aftermath of the 2008 recession and the housing crisis. Searching for energy wealth in sparsely populated land seemed like something out of a bygone era—a time when the United States cared little about the environment or those living off the land and simply sought acreage to claim or fossil fuels to extract. I had no idea how wrong I was. From where I was sitting in a Manhattan office building, North Dakota seemed like a forgotten state and oil, a forgotten American industry.

I learned about North Dakota's oil boom in 2012 after it was already well under way. News organizations like CNN and *Business Insider* were covering the boom, but other national media organizations hadn't caught on. I clicked on one story and stared at a photo of men living in Walmart's parking lot. They huddled in lawn chairs next to RVs or bundled up in their pickup trucks. I had read so much about the "tent cities" of the recession, but something about this was viscerally different. These people had jobs. North Dakota had the lowest unemployment rate in the country—how could they be living this way? They weren't refugees, fleeing from their homes because of war and destruction. They weren't immigrants, fleeing their countries because of corruption and poverty. They were, for the most part, American. Coming to a new land for opportunity. Surviving in a harsh environment to make a better life. Traveling in droves to compete for jobs and a livelihood. It all sounded so familiar—the Gold Rush, the Dust Bowl, the Westward Expansion. But in 2012? Really? For oil? I had assumed, perhaps naively, that things were different today. That you might lose your house or your job in a recession, but there were protections. Government programs like unemployment insurance and housing vouchers that were designed to help you rebuild your life in your current location. Of course there were a few exceptions, but those were exceptions, right? Not thousands of Americans becoming financial refugees and migrant laborers in order to achieve any monetary stability.

In many ways, North Dakota's boom represented a shift in the nature of blue-collar work in America. Manufacturing lost 6 million jobs between 2000 and 2009, and the construction industry shed another 2 million during the recession. As the economy recovered, economists touted the "tech boom" and "knowledge workers," but many blue-collar workers didn't have the resources, education, or desire to make this shift. After blue-collar workers were laid off by the millions from plants, factories, farms, and construction sites, the oil and gas industry, particularly in western North Dakota, emerged as a shining mecca.

As oil and gas boomtowns cropped up across America, blue-collar workers were becoming the new migrant laborers of the twenty-first century, following work wherever it took them and surviving in unstable environments. Most of those traveling to North Dakota had been beaten down by the Great Recession, had watched their stability, comfort, and income stripped away, and were looking for a second chance at the American Dream. North Dakota could give them that—if they could handle it.

The images of the men living at Walmart stayed with me. I discovered that people were migrating to North Dakota not just because of oil but because of the controversial practice of fracking, which had opened up new reserves. I was shocked I hadn't heard more about what was happening there. Whatever it was felt big. Gold Rush big. Why wasn't everyone talking about this?

In 2013, I left my job in New York and moved to Williston, North Dakota, over the summer to live in this new frontier and embed myself in the shale oil revolution. North Dakota felt like a world away from New York City, and almost everyone I knew thought I was crazy, but the move helped me understand a reality thousands of Americans faced. Those migrating to North Dakota were part of a population that seemed invisible to the liberal coastal cities where I'd been living. After spending a summer in Williston and returning several times over three years, I began to understand just how hidden the oil and gas industry, its workers, and those affected by drilling are from most of America. I didn't know I would hear stories so desperate and see living conditions so grim, I often had to remind myself I was standing on American soil.

North Dakota, a state that was all but forgotten, had put the United States back on the energy map. Oil companies discovered that by using hydraulic fracturing, or fracking, and horizontal drilling, they could unlock billions of barrels of oil in the state that were never accessible before. The state heralded the boom and published press release after press release on its economic growth. It appeared thousands of workers were achieving the American Dream—they risked it all to start a better life and worked hard, and many were rewarded with six-figure incomes. They provided for their families and maybe put a down payment on a home. But when you looked closer, this wasn't the whole story. Behind the positive spin lay a darker side of the boom.

Those living in North Dakota, on the front lines of the domestic oil war, watched their lives change forever. Small-town locals saw their beloved communities transform overnight into male-dominated cities. Farmers watched the land that had been in their families for 100 years plowed away to make room for more wells; Native Americans found toxic waste illegally dumped on their reservation; and laborers faced injury and death while living apart from their families. The government had cleared the way for the energy industry to set up with little regulation or oversight—and the people most affected felt silenced.

I chose Williston because it was the epitome of a modern-day boomtown. The living conditions were bleak, the schools overcrowded, the traffic maddening, law enforcement understaffed, housing limited and unaffordable, and city employees overwhelmed. Yet despite all of this, people still came by the thousands. Each new arrival traveled to the region to improve his or her life in some way, striving for stability and happiness in the midst of a chaotic oil town. Like many boomtowns before it, the city of Williston had two paths it could take—it could become a permanent hub, like Denver or San Francisco, or it could disappear into a ghost town, becoming yet another lesson in a history book.

To help me understand the boom, I closely followed the lives of Americans who represented different sectors of those affected by shale oil exploration: a farmer and his Native American neighbors who were forced to stand by and watch their land drilled; a 56-year-old grandmother who found herself single and broke after 28 years of marriage and became the only woman on a fracking crew; a stay-at-home mom who followed her husband to the Wild West and tried to raise children there; a church pastor struggling to maintain a community in his small town; and a homeless day laborer who slept in his car, hoping for a second chance at life.

In late 2014, oil prices took a nosedive, and North Dakota's boom did as expected. Many people left almost as quickly as they had come.

But where would they go? And what would happen to the locals left behind? The boom in North Dakota will have lasting effects on generations to come. Shale drilling has completely reshaped America's oil landscape, and though some companies struggle to survive with low oil prices, the oil itself isn't going anywhere. Many see the return to black gold as the beginning of a new era, particularly under Trump, with the United States rising to regain its world leadership status through home-grown oil. Oil companies work to increase drilling efficiency, producing oil at cheaper and cheaper prices to weather boom-and-bust cycles. To understand what footprint America's shale energy revolution and North Dakota's oil boom will leave on the U.S. fabric, we must start at the beginning.

3. WILLISTON

Picture any town or city in America, maybe your hometown, then imagine that the city's population doubles or triples in size in three short years. If it's anything like what happened to Williston beginning in 2009, first the housing fills up, with open rentals disappearing from the classifieds and only advertising by word of mouth. Landlords realize they can raise rents, yet demand only grows. Slumlords with dilapidated apartments, with cracked paint and rodent infestations, quadruple their rents, only to have dozens of people, including middle-class families with two kids and perfect credit, lining up to make an offer. Soon anyone without a high-paying job or a clean record has been squeezed out of the market. Tent cities crop up overnight, families park trailers on side streets and in backyards, workers idle in deserted parking lots and sleep in their cars. A group of six young guys split the rent for one room. The building frenzy begins but can't keep pace with the rush, and contractors capitalize on demand, raising their prices and contributing to the inflation.

Then the city realizes its infrastructure is being pushed to its breaking point. Schools don't have enough classrooms or teachers; contractors install more electrical, sewage, and water lines, but the city's system isn't designed to handle them. Tiny police departments whose officers once spent their days pulling cats out of trees and ticketing out-of-town speeders now work around the clock, responding to more and more calls, ignoring minor crimes and letting criminals back onto the streets after local jails reach capacity. Intersections that once rarely saw four cars at the same time now have lines of traffic stretching a half-mile long. Roads deteriorate faster than transportation crews can fix them. Grocery stores sell out of milk. Gas stations sell out of fuel. Small businesses can't find enough employees to staff their shops because although hundreds of workers are arriving every day, high-paying oil field jobs are everywhere, and living costs reach a point where no one, not even recent high school graduates, can afford to work for $8 an hour.

And all these changes happen while the rest of the country is in the midst of a deep recession. In hundreds of cities and towns across the country, families lose their homes and jobs. They have to pack up their dream home, the one they planned to pay off in 20 years. They gently box up their pictures and sell the furniture purchased on credit. They move into their parents' homes or rent apartments; others sleep in their cars or motel rooms, hoping their poor luck is only temporary. But many reach the lowest point they can imagine, and they know something has to change. They desperately want a way to return to the life they once had. They begin looking for a way—and a place—to start over.

4. TOM STAKES

Tom Stakes had arrived.

He felt triumphant. After two days, driving 1,300 miles, and a sleepless night at a truck stop in South Dakota, he was weary but energized. He had driven north along Highway 85, "the road to opportunity," as the mayor of Williston called it, past the multicolored bluffs and plateaus of Theodore Roosevelt National Park, past oceans of wheat fields, past RV parks that popped up along the prairie horizon, and past a giant white statue of Abraham Lincoln's head on the side of the highway. He crawled through a traffic jam in the smaller oil boomtown of Watford City and accelerated past 18-wheeler trucks filled with crude oil when the road widened. He finally pulled into Williston around 4 p.m.

It was a hot, early summer day in 2013 and the town of Williston, North Dakota, wasn't much to look at—a consistent cloud of dust filled the air, semi trucks were at every turn, and its downtown looked depressing with dilapidated brown-and-beige buildings from the 1950s and 1980s. But Stakes didn't come here for the town's looks—he came here for a job. The day was full of possibility. With only $20 left in his pocket, Tom Stakes was ready to start his new life.

His first stop: the bar.

Stakes drove his old white Chevy pickup down Main Street to the first one he saw, K K Korner Lounge, a dive bar known by the locals as KK's. It was located a block from the train station and across the street from two of Williston's strip clubs, Whispers and Heartbreakers. Stakes felt immediately at home in KK's—$1.50 beers, dim lighting, 1980s jukebox, green felt pool table, smooth mahogany bar speckled with water stain rings, and a backlit Budweiser sign in the corner flickering from a dying bulb—it was the type of bar he knew how to make friends in.

Stakes is an ex-preacher from Louisiana with long wispy white hair and a thick beard reaching past his neck. He's a man who can make friends anywhere—usually in bars, and while he's walking down the street, he might yell "Hey, how ya doin'!" or bum a smoke from a stranger and instantly become friends. Maintaining friendships, however, was more difficult for him. Stakes had friends all over the country—at a rehab center in New Mexico; at his former church congregation in Kenbridge, Virginia; on the streets of Atlanta, Georgia—but he no longer spoke to any of them. On the drive up to Williston, he picked up a hitchhiker who was headed the same way. The man had lived in Williston and told Stakes the best parking lots to sleep in where the cops wouldn't bother him.

At KK's that afternoon, Stakes asked everyone he met if they knew about available construction work, but they all shook their heads no. He walked around the corner to the day labor agency, Bakken Staffing, and registered to work.

That night, he slept in a well-lit parking lot across from Bakken Staffing and near the bars. The lot was flanked by a chain-link fence and, during the day, was used by employees of the National Guard. There were other men sleeping in their vehicles as well. They lined their cars up against the fence and draped clothes or blankets over windows to keep passersby from peering in.

The next morning, Bakken Staffing sent Stakes out on a job where he lifted and heaved furniture up four flights of stairs for eight hours. The work was hard on his 58-year-old body, and he quit after one day. "I was like, aw, man, this is too rough on me. I can't keep doin' this," he said in a singsongy Louisiana drawl. A few days later, he was offered a job sanding and staining a deck, but it was only for $10 an hour, the same wage he made back in New Mexico.

But Stakes wasn't deterred. He had a good feeling about Williston. He was already chummy with the owner of KK's, who went by "Shorty," and the bartenders were beginning to remember his name. Stakes hadn't had a stable home for more than 20 years—but maybe he was finally home.

Tom Stakes was one of hundreds of men arriving in the city that summer with few resources and no plan for housing. Some called themselves financial refugees, fleeing from the ashes of the Great Recession. The mayor estimated 20 new people arrived to town every day. Williston became known as the town the recession forgot. It had one of the lowest unemployment rates in the country, at 1 percent, whereas places such as Yuma, Arizona, and El Centro, California, had over 20 percent unemployment. Since the collapse of investment bank Lehman Brothers in 2008, the labor market had lost 8.8 million jobs, the most dramatic loss since the Great Depression. By 2011, 14 million people were unemployed—nearly half of whom had been out of a job for more than six months. Some 4 million people had lost their homes and more than 7 million Americans slid into poverty between 2008 and 2011. In the labor market, men had been disproportionately affected—three-quarters of those 8.8 million jobs lost in the recession were lost by men. The traditional male-dominated industries of manufacturing and construction were crumbling.

Thus, America's downtrodden set their sights on Williston. City officials adopted the American Dream narrative into their marketing strategy. Their town was "saving" people from recession-torn America and providing them with a fresh start. Of course the city wanted only the "right" kind of people to come to Williston—people who could buy the $400,000 homes being erected all over town and who could boost the city's budget shortfall. What it didn't want was more vagrants.

"People hear of this, and say 'I'm going up to Williston. They're giving money away,'" said Williston's mayor, Ward Koeser. "But then they come and have mental health issues. They're not employable, and we're not set up to handle vagrants and people living on the street. Before we never had it because of our winters. We don't have a social services network to deal with it."

Most newcomers would arrive to town with no plan for housing and quickly realize there was nowhere to go. Williston's hotels were full. The campgrounds were full. There was no hostel. There were no available apartments. There was no homeless shelter. Recent arrivals without a car pitched tents in a park across from the public library. Before long, the park was filled with two dozen tents every night. The tents were mostly occupied by men, but a few women and children slept there as well. Soon complaints from neighbors poured in. They objected to the noise, the rowdy, intoxicated men wandering around, and the trash and alcohol bottles strewn across the lawn. The city had recently upgraded a nearby playground with a teeter-totter in the shape of an oil well pumpjack for nearly half a million dollars, funded by oil companies; no locals wanted to take their children anywhere close to the park. People started calling it a "tent city"—only unlike the tent cities of the recession, these inhabitants had jobs.

After the city shut down the park encampment, some tent dwellers moved to a clearing across the railroad tracks near a wide, slow-moving tributary of the Missouri River, a section of town where few locals ventured. Others holed up in apartments, sleeping 6 to 10 people in a room. Newcomers with cars were the lucky ones—they'd drive around looking for a quiet parking lot with a restroom nearby. Walmart's lot had become the most popular. The store typically permitted overnight parking at most of its locations across the country, and it was never a problem in Williston before the boom. A few traveling trailers and long-distance truckers might park there, then head out the next morning. But in 2011, Williston's Walmart parking lot began to resemble a RV campground.

By early 2013, the number of individuals without a home (which included those sleeping in cars, tents, and trailers with no operating utilities) had grown to 2,069 in the state, a 200 percent increase since 2008. Of the documented homeless in North Dakota, 88 percent said they had come to seek employment. Despite the growing problem, Williston decided against building a homeless shelter—officials worried that if they built a shelter, more people from all over America would come. "People in Williston were forced to be transient," said Joshua Stansbury, who helped run the local Salvation Army. "They spent their last dollars getting up here and had nowhere to go."

Tom Stakes was one of them—he'd have to find a job soon if he wanted to survive. But like the many American dreamers who came before him, Stakes refused to believe he might not make it in an oil boomtown.

5. CHELSEA NIEHAUS

The first time Chelsea Niehaus saw Williston, North Dakota, was from the window of a train.

It was a cold morning in December 2012. Chelsea was traveling with her three-year-old son, Will. They had been on Amtrak all night, boarding in Indianapolis and transferring in Chicago. It was in Chicago that Chelsea noticed groups of oil field workers on the train with their industry-logo baseball caps and duffel bags. Chelsea and Will were two of some 54,000 passengers who rode this overnight train to the Bakken every year, a number that had more than doubled since the boom began.

They were there to visit Chelsea's boyfriend and Will's father, Jacob Klipsch. All three of them had lived together back in Louisville, Kentucky, but Jacob now lived more than 1,300 miles away. Instead of sleeping next to Chelsea in their four-bedroom, two-bath house, Jacob slept in a run-down camper—a 2004 Century Skyline fifth wheel—on a Native American reservation.

Chelsea held Will's tiny hand as they descended the steps to exit the train. She wore a sweater and a long wrap skirt with thermal underwear underneath, but she was not prepared for the cold when it hit her. She spotted Jacob standing at the train station, waiting for them. She hardly recognized him. His face was covered in a thick, fuzzy beard. She had never seen him with so much facial hair, but she liked it. He was beginning to look like a true oil worker, she thought.

Jacob hugged them and helped take their luggage from the porter. Chelsea sensed something different in him. He seemed more confident and secure as he talked excitedly and animatedly about his work. She hadn't seen this side of him for a while.

For this trip, Jacob didn't want them roughing it together in the trailer with his roommate, so Chelsea, Will, and Jacob planned to stay at the Super 8 Motel for $150 a night, one of the cheapest hotels in town. They hadn't traveled or stayed in a motel together since Will was a baby, but on this trip they could finally afford to do so without much worry. Jacob was making $19 an hour and about $6,400 a month with overtime pay—more money than he ever had in his life.

The excitement of their reunion didn't last long, however. As they drove away from the train station, Jacob broke some bad news to Chelsea—he had received a DUI the month before, and his court date was coming up. Chelsea didn't know how to react. She wasn't particularly surprised. Jacob had struggled with alcoholism for years, but she had hoped his time in North Dakota would teach him more responsibility. She was tired from her travels, so she swallowed her anger at hearing the news. She was determined to have a good trip together as a family.

Over four days, Jacob, Chelsea, and Will explored Williston and the surrounding area. They drove the 20 miles out to Lewis and Clark State Park on the upper edge of Lake Sakakawea, one of the largest man-made lakes in the world, with more than 1,200 miles of coastline—longer than the coasts of California and Oregon combined. The state park was named after the two explorers who camped there in 1805. A thin sheet of snow covered the prairie. Chelsea could see specks of light illuminating patches of land and realized they were all drilling rigs. Everything about the landscape was foreign to her—she'd never seen a sky so expansive. "God, it was flat . . . and the sky. It went on forever," she recalled. "I felt like I'd been flayed open for the whole world to see because there was nowhere to hide."

At night the temperature reached into the single digits—a bitter cold that seeped into her bones. They drove out to New Town, North Dakota, to see the trailer where Jacob lived. At his trailer park, about 20 old campers lined the dirt lot, dusted with snow. Trash and rusted equipment were strewn about. Jacob's musty Century Skyline fit right in. New Town was located on the edge of the Native American reservation, an area that had struggled with poverty for years. Chelsea was shocked at the desperation of it all. "It didn't feel like America," she said. "People living in campers with no water—I couldn't believe people were living this way in 2012."

Of Williston, Chelsea wasn't particularly impressed either. "It was a wide spot in the road with a Walmart," she said. Chelsea didn't know how long Jacob wanted to stay there, but she was excited they might not struggle financially anymore. Even taking such a trip to see him— with the costs of train travel, food, and the hotel—felt like a luxury. Jacob seemed in his element. She hoped maybe the DUI had taught him a lesson.

On the final day of their visit, as dusk hit the prairie, Jacob drove Chelsea and Will to the train station. Their train was delayed so they waited in the station for more than three hours. Other oil workers and their families sat with them on blue-cushioned chairs in the small waiting room. They watched oil tanker trains pass by—the increased train traffic from oil shipments was the cause of the delay. Jacob said he would try to visit home soon but couldn't tell her when that would be. Chelsea didn't know when she would see him again. Finally, it was time to go. Jacob hugged Chelsea good-bye. He hugged Will, but Will was too excited about the upcoming train ride to realize what was happening. Chelsea and Will walked up the stairs to the second floor of the double-decker train. They found their seats by the window, and Will pressed against the glass as they waved good-bye. . . . The train chugged and hissed out of the station.

For Chelsea, the idea of living in such a place was preposterous. She missed Jacob and wanted him home.

She had no idea that in less than six months, she would be joining him.

Chelsea Niehaus and Jacob Klipsch grew up in the same town of Vincennes, Indiana, and met during their sophomore year of high school. After high school, Jacob joined the Army, then attended Indiana University in Bloomington to study political science. But in 2008, he dropped out before receiving a degree.

With $40,000 in student loans and no marketable skills he could think of, Jacob began working in restaurants and doing construction. Chelsea, who had a bachelor's degree and an MBA from Kentucky's Bellarmine University, worked at a company called Clearwater Seafoods, a live lobster shipping company, and made about $36,000 a year. She had hoped to use her master's degree to find higher-paying work but struggled to do so during the recession.

She and Jacob moved into an apartment together in Louisville, Kentucky, but Jacob couldn't find steady work, and it was difficult to make ends meet. Then Chelsea became pregnant with Will. To provide for his growing family, Jacob worked almost nonstop. By early 2012, Will was two years old, and Jacob was working three jobs. During the day, he delivered seafood for about $250 a week, and at night, he delivered pizzas for minimum wage plus tips. When he had free time, which was rare, he picked up the occasional landscaping gig. But they were still behind on their bills most months. They were fighting a lot, Jacob was drinking more, and they were tired of living paycheck to paycheck. "I've never been so stressed out in my entire life," said Chelsea. "He was working himself to death, and the ends weren't meeting. He hated what he was doing; he was hating everything. I was like, 'Something has to change.'"

Jacob heard about the oil boom in North Dakota from a friend, then saw references about it on the news. He learned many oil companies liked to hire ex-military personnel. The industry seemed like a great fit for him. He applied online for jobs in the region while he was still at home but had no luck. Then he read that most employers hired through connections. To get those connections, he needed to be in town networking and applying in person.

Jacob arrived in Williston on October 1, 2012, at the age of 31, just as temperatures were dropping for the winter. At first, he slept in his truck and spent a few nights in the parking lot behind Concordia Lutheran Church with other newcomers—the church's pastor, Jay Reinke, allowed them to stay there. Every day, Jacob went to the local employment agency, sat at one of the computers, and applied for every job. He worked day-labor shifts at Bakken Staffing while he waited for replies and was offered a construction job within the first three days. He considered taking it, but he knew the building frenzy in Williston would eventually end and he'd be back where he started. He'd come for an oil job and decided to keep applying.

After a week of applying for jobs, he was hired as an oil field roustabout at Baker Consulting, where he would help build sites, install pipelines, and do maintenance at oil well sites for $17 an hour. The first week he worked 70 hours. With overtime, it added up to $1,445 a week. If he could maintain the schedule, he was looking to make nearly $70,000 that year—more than three times what he was making back in Kentucky. Jacob bought a used trailer for $1,800, parked it in a New Town lot for $400 a month, and moved in with a coworker named Steve to cut costs. At first it wasn't so bad, but then a holding tank that provided water to the RV park froze, and no one at the park had running water. He had to buy bottled water and shower at a truck station down the road.

Back home in Kentucky, Chelsea often worried about Jacob. She was unable to reach him for days at a time. Jacob worked long hours and tried to check in with Chelsea and Will when he could, but it was difficult. Cell phone reception was spotty. Jacob didn't have an internet connection in his trailer, so they could rarely Skype or email.

Chelsea and Will struggled to get by without Jacob. Will missed his dad terribly. "He was having separation anxiety," Chelsea said. "Every morning, without fail, he would cling to me. There was never a good morning when I dropped him off at preschool, and it wasn't getting better. He was scared to be separated from his family." Chelsea missed Jacob too and didn't want her son to be so far away from his dad. Chelsea liked their life in Kentucky—she had a full-time job, friends, a house, and their family just a few hours away in Indiana, but it wasn't the same without Jacob.

In April, Chelsea's job at the lobster company took a turn for the worse. The company was headquartered in Canada, and she said that the managers began blaming their shortcomings on her. They would call and ask to speak to her male colleague instead of her, she recalled, even though she had seniority. She felt disrespected and unsupported. At the same time, Will's separation anxiety worsened. Every day Chelsea fought with him about attending preschool. He would cling to her legs and cry, and she'd have to pry him off. She hated feeling like a single mother. She wanted to homeschool Will and help him adjust, but even with Jacob's higher salary, it would be a struggle to make the mortgage payment and cover Jacob's living expenses on his salary alone. If she quit her job and stayed home with Will, she would need to sell the house.

Their home was a 1,560-square-foot house built in 1931 on a quarter-acre lot. Chelsea was proud of the property and called it her Walnut Cottage, named after the street it was on. Though the house was far from her dream home, the roofline reminded her of the Creole Arcadian cottages she loved in New Orleans. In 2010, she had saved enough for a down payment and secured the loan by herself to be a first-time homeowner—a huge accomplishment in her mind. At $80,000, it seemed like a smart investment at the time, but the neighborhood was dicey, and during the recession it got worse. Middle-class families moved out and drugs took over. The value of her home didn't plummet, but it also didn't improve. By 2013, Chelsea hoped the market had recuperated. She talked to a real estate agent who thought she might be able to sell it for $100,000. Chelsea reasoned that if it sold, she and Will could move in with her parents or Jacob's and visit North Dakota more often. She decided to put the house on the market.

As she waited for potential buyers, she reached a breaking point at her job. In May, she gave her two-week notice and thought more seriously about her next step. She wanted more help taking care of Will. They could move into her parents' house, but her relationship with her mother was strained. Why not move to North Dakota for the summer? she thought. The summer weather wasn't bad, and they could be together as a family again. They could live in Jacob's trailer, or maybe find an apartment or a house to rent. Even though Chelsea loved Louisville—a city she'd been in for over 14 years—living in North Dakota sounded exciting. She liked travel and adventure. How bad could North Dakota be? She pitched the idea to Jacob. He agreed—it was lonely in the trailer. He'd been living in North Dakota for seven months, had no plans to leave, and wanted his family closer to him. His roommate agreed to move out, and Chelsea and Will began making arrangements to move to North Dakota.

The problem was, the house still hadn't sold. After Chelsea lowered the price, a few people looked at the property, but no one made an offer. Not knowing what else to do, she decided to vacate the property temporarily, hoping to sell it later. She sold their six chickens and rooster, pulled up her garden, gave away knickknacks and furniture to neighbors, and began packing. Jacob came home for vacation and planned to help Chelsea drive back to North Dakota.

On May 13, 2013, Chelsea and Jacob filled their 2004 Mitsubishi Outlander and piled belongings high on top of the car—a rolled-up rug, a plastic bin on top of a cooler, bags of clothes—all strapped together on the roof. Will and their 75-pound dog, Thor, a Great Pyrenees, crammed in the backseat. Chelsea looked around the empty house one last time and locked the door. She posted a photo of their packed car on Facebook with the caption: "Westward, er, Northward ho! Covered wagon is ready to go!"

That evening, they made it to Chicago and spent the night in a Super 8 motel. The next day, they drove through Wisconsin and Minnesota. They hoped to make it the rest of the way that evening, but they were running behind. Unsure of what condition the camper was in, Chelsea didn't want to arrive at the trailer park late at night. Would there be places for them to sleep or prepare food? Jacob wasn't known for keeping a tidy house. He told her he'd cleaned to prepare for their arrival, but still, she feared the worst. They stopped in Fargo for the night, slept at another Super 8, and drove through North Dakota the next day. Despite her worries, the mood in the car was hopeful and jovial. Will sat in his car seat and played "I Spy" with Chelsea during the long stretches of fields and farms. Thor put his head out the window to feel the wind on his fur. In the early afternoon, they finally pulled up to the J&J Lot trailer park in New Town.

Road-weary and exhausted, Chelsea stepped out of the car to survey her surroundings. The lot looked different without snow covering the ground, though a few melting patches remained. The lot was now covered with red-tinted sharp scoria gravel that could cut a person's feet if they wore sandals. As Jacob had promised, he'd straightened up the trailer's interior. Chelsea tried not to notice the grime and dust that covered the surfaces. Nothing some scrubbing wouldn't fix, she thought. It would do. She felt triumphant. They had arrived at their new home.

6. WILLISTON

Before I arrived in North Dakota, I had nightmares of the horrible things that could happen to me there. I read everything I could about the region's oil boom and heard stories of how women were targeted in the "oil patch" region. One night, I dreamed I was walking through a dark trailer park, past rows of four-wheeled dwellings parked on dusty gravel ground. Men sat on camp chairs around an open fire drinking beer. The night was pitch black. A dog barked in the distance. As I passed the men, they stopped talking and stared at me, watching my every move. I quickened my pace, feeling my breath shorten. I reached the end of the line of trailers and kept going, the flicker of fire light dimming behind me, the voices fading into the distance. For a moment I felt safe, as if I had skirted the danger. Then I heard footsteps behind me. I picked up my pace and broke into a run. But a man caught up to me. A muscled arm wrapped around my neck and the man's voice ordered me to drop to the ground.

I jolted up in bed, the terror of the moment still fresh. I looked around my Brooklyn apartment. I could hear the distant rumble of the train and the faraway siren of a police car, but otherwise everything was quiet. Safe. Peaceful. Why did I want to leave?

Although I lived in an "up-and-coming" neighborhood in Brooklyn and had traveled to higher-crime cities in Haiti and Nicaragua, I never lived *alone* in these places. Especially alone in a rickety trailer with a questionable lock on the front door. Headlines like these graced major newspapers and websites and added to my uneasiness:

AN OIL TOWN WHERE MEN ARE MANY, AND WOMEN ARE HOUNDED

WEARING SKIRTS IS DANGEROUS IN INDIA AND NORTH DAKOTA

HUMAN TRAFFICKING A PROBLEM IN NORTH DAKOTA

My boyfriend hugged me tightly before I boarded the plane to San Francisco, where I'd start my journey to the Dakotas. "Be careful," he said, kissing my forehead. After arriving in California, my typically peaceful, turn-the-other-cheek dad gave me brass knuckles in the shape of an angry-looking pit bull to attach to my key ring as a parting gift.

I then drove over 1,500 miles to Williston, North Dakota, in my dad's tiny 1999 Chevy Metro hatchback. I started from my parents' house in Mount Shasta, California, and spent five days heading northeast, through Idaho, Wyoming, and Montana. My parents wanted to help me get there, partly out of goodwill but more likely out of fear for my safety, and they pulled their 2001 pop-up trailer behind their car as they followed me on the freeway. My cousin Bill was writing a book about national trails and tagged along as well. Over five days, we passed through wheat fields, cattle pastures, and ghost towns; swerved around tumbleweeds; descended into canyons; crossed slow-moving rivers; and slept in one-factory towns and flat, sprawling cities. During driving breaks at truck stops and $39-a-night motels, I'd occasionally mention my final destination to people. Most had never heard of Williston, but as I got closer, that changed. "You're going to the oil patch?" one man asked, sounding shocked. "I hope you're bringing a gun." Later, when I was traveling outside of Williston, the owner of a campground, a blond woman wearing a snug tank top and thick nail polish, told me to watch out for pimps there. "I heard they come through town and kidnap women," she whispered in my ear as I checked in.

The first sign I saw for Williston was near the Montana–North Dakota border. I began to see traces of the oil boom: A pumpjack on the left, bobbing hypnotically in the sun. A train pulling hundreds of shiny black tanks of oil rumbled by us as we waited at the stoplight. Finally I saw the North Dakota state welcome sign. A green rectangle with NORTH DAKOTA in large letters sweeping across it. Underneath the letters was a tiny black-and-white headshot of Teddy Roosevelt and "Welcome to the West Region." The sign was located in a grassy ditch with a muddy stream nearby. A semi hauling pipes rumbled by. Popcorn clouds lumbered above me. I took a photo of the sign and we continued on. Williston and my new home were 30 miles ahead.

7. CINDY MARCHELLO

One of the first people I met in North Dakota helped ease my worries about feeling outnumbered—her name was Cindy Marchello. An oil worker from Utah, Marchello had no problem standing out in a crowd of men. When she walked onto an all-male fracking site, if you didn't notice her, you'd likely hear her voice. "What are you looking at?" she'd yell at a male worker if he stared at her for longer than she liked. "I'm old enough to be your mom!" If that didn't work, she'd ask, "What's your wife's name?" while hacking up a wad of spit and projecting it toward him. If the man kept looking, she'd threaten to throw rocks.

Marchello is a 56-year-old grandmother with wispy blond and gray hair, pale skin with rosy cheeks, and a short, curvy figure. She once visited a dusty well site surrounded by cornfields and heard a man's voice hollering over the loudspeaker: "Woman on location, woman on location." Everyone noticed her that time.

As the only woman on her crew, Marchello lived at a "man camp" called Rough Rider Housing on the outskirts of the 250-person town of Trenton, North Dakota. Trenton had no grocery store or library. It used to have a rickety gas station and a convenience store, but the building burned down. A handful of women lived in town, but most stayed locked in their homes or trailers, waiting for their husbands to return. Marchello said she liked living in this man camp better than others because she had a small kitchen here. Her first man camp had shared eating quarters and a communal laundry room. Men flocked around her as she ate supper, and someone stole her underwear out of the washing machine. "It was the last time I did laundry there. I bought enough socks, underwear, everything, so I could go two weeks without doing laundry," she said. "I never owned so many bras in my entire life." She looked up at the fluorescent light in the small living room of her mobile trailer. "That man camp was really hard for me."

Most oil field workers in North Dakota lived in man camps— barracks for oil workers that look more like prisons or shipping container yards instead of employee housing. By 2013, an estimated 25,000 people in western North Dakota lived in such camps. Marchello's current camp housed about 200 men, but she avoided anyone who wasn't on her crew. "If you smile at them, they think you'll spread your legs," she said.

I had seen Marchello in a video called *Lady Roughnecks in North Dakota Man Camps* on CNN.com, one of the few national news organizations reporting on North Dakota's oil boom in 2012. In the video, she sat cross-legged on a twin bed. She wore jeans and her blond hair was down to her shoulders. She waved her hands around wildly as she explained her job and what it was like to live in a man camp. "What would I say to women? You can do it! You can do whatever you want," she said as the camera panned to heavy trucks pulling into a shop.

I emailed her Gmail address, "barefootbones," to introduce myself and she wrote back immediately. She said she'd happily meet me and couldn't wait to talk with another woman. She explained that she sometimes went weeks without spotting another female. She missed how clean they smell, she told me later. The previous summer, she went camping in Yellowstone and visited the women's bathroom. She didn't want to leave because it smelled like fruity shampoo and perfume. A woman tried to move out of her way, and Marchello stopped her and said: "I'm sorry, you just smell really good." The woman didn't seem to understand.

Though "home" for Marchello was the town of Ogden in northern Utah, for 90 percent of the year she lived and worked in North Dakota. Although the boom brought Marchello here, few other women had been hired to work on oil industry crews. Nationally, 85 percent of oil industry jobs are held by men, and most women in the field work as engineers, administrators, medical personnel, or on cleaning staffs. Oil companies tout this as gender diversity in their press releases, but women hold fewer than 2 percent of the jobs beyond those positions. The gender inequality in the field has made nearby Williston—the only population hub for over 100 miles—look like a seething all-male metropolis complete with strip clubs, greasy burger joints, Coors Light chugging contests, bar fights, and seatless Porta Potties on oil rig locations. The ratio of men to women was somewhere between 6 to 1 and 30 to 1, according to varying local estimates.

Many women in the area complained of feeling unsafe, and local statistics supported their fears. Cases of assault, harassment, domestic violence, and rape had risen dramatically since the once-sleepy region began attracting thousands of male workers. Women spoke of carrying concealed weapons when they shopped at the grocery store and avoiding the bar scene, teeming with lonely males looking for female company. Rumors were rampant about where the next attack might occur—I frequently overheard women chatting about which areas to avoid or where a friend of so-and-so was attacked while walking to her car.

I met Cindy Marchello one night at Rough Rider Housing in late July 2013. She worked as a pump operator for an oil service company called C&J Energy Services, which primarily did "coil tubing"—a process that requires running bendable pipe down oil wells after they're fracked to get the well to start producing oil. Her first job was at Halliburton, and she'd been working in North Dakota's oil field since the early days of the boom in 2010. I called her to set up an interview, and she told me she was on a well location and wouldn't be home until 9 p.m. She said to come to trailer number 40. I assumed I would meet her, chat with her for 20 minutes, and be on my way.

To get to the man camp from Williston, I drove 15 miles and turned onto a gravel road near a water disposal site. I saw 64 identical rectangular trailers, lined in two neat rows facing each other. Dozens of pickup trucks were parked outside the trailers. Across the street were train tracks, and trains hauling hundreds of barrels of crude oil rumbled by every few minutes.

I pulled into the camp and saw two men standing outside their trailer smoking cigarettes. Otherwise it was quiet. Each trailer looked exactly the same, except there was a small grill outside one and a rusty patio swing behind another. Weeds speckled the gravel road, and clusters of tall grass grew between the buildings. I parked my car next to two large pickup trucks, knocked on the glass screen door of her trailer, and Marchello answered excitedly, wearing an oversized T-shirt and sweats. The trailer was sparsely decorated but clean. It had particle-board cabinets and a small matching table next to the stove. On the refrigerator, a paper sign read NIGHT WORKER SLEEPING DO NOT DISTURB in large red letters. I sat down in a recliner and Marchello cozied up on the couch, crossed-legged. Then she started talking and didn't stop for two and a half hours.

"I went to work at six o'clock in the morning and I worked until midnight and I came home and I went back at five and I worked until nine o'clock the next morning," she said, talking as fast as an auctioneer. "In the last three days, I have worked 67 hours. I am beyond running on empty. I slept in the truck for only about two hours. I texted my boss, 'Unless God himself is ready to burn on the cross again you better not talk to me for two hours.'

"Up here, you get more deaths. We think it's because there are more wells and longer hours. There's so much work, you can't shut down in the winter. You have to work all night. So we work around the clock."

I tried to interject with a question, but she didn't seem to hear.

Marchello continued, jumping to another subject: "Drillers are a subspecies. Oil field trash—they call us that for a reason, but we each have our differences. Guys who are snubbers are just weird, guys who work on the derricks have no social skills. You'd do better in a prison.

"All men and no families live here. A few women that are the housekeepers do live here. I don't venture out. I don't make a lot of local friends. I don't especially like the cleaning ladies. A couple of them, like the ones from Montana, are quite the bar party girls. I'm not. I can't afford to be. Because what's she going to do? She's going to get up and vacuum in the morning. I'm going to go drive a 100,000-pound truck. I need more sleep than that."

She paused and I asked how she found herself here—living in a man camp on a remote North Dakota prairie.

She came to North Dakota in 2010 out of desperation, she said. She had recently gone through a difficult divorce with her husband of 28 years, lost her home to foreclosure along with thousands of other Americans, and declared bankruptcy. She lived in her car for nine months and slept on the couches of her adult children.

"I was on unemployment, applying for jobs, being super frugal with my money, and I am laying on the couch a lot. Then I met a guy who was a driller up here in Williston and he said, 'Number one, quit applying everywhere and go to Halliburton in North Dakota. You have no experience. It is going to take a boom to hire you.' I said, 'I'm not going to North Dakota, that's 1,000 miles away! I can't do it.'

"My second application to Williston, I was hired in frack. I was a gold mine for Halliburton because I was over 50 and a woman and I was on unemployment. They got all kinds of tax breaks for me. Most of my bosses are, like, my kids' age."

She paused and looked at me. "I want you to know, I've been trying really hard not to cuss around you. I wear rubber bands to remind me."

After two and a half hours, there was a knock at the door. Marchello unlocked it, and a large young man, clean shaven with a crew cut and baggy coveralls, stood in the doorway. I later learned his name was Scott Morgan. He stepped in but didn't sit down. He said he couldn't stay long. He had to be back on the well location in a few hours because they were going to "haul off bottom" at 3 a.m. I wasn't sure what that meant, but he sounded tired and worried.

Marchello and he discussed their new manager and the rumors about guys putting feces on a coworker's porch and the cops being called. Marchello told him one guy called her a cunt the other day but apologized later. They complained about one of the secretaries who worked in the office, a young woman in her 30s. Many guys on the crew flirted with her. "She's pretty, but she doesn't realize that she's gained weight since high school," said Marchello. "There's this on-going bet to see which button on her shirt will pop first." She giggled.

"Hold on, hold on," said Morgan. "How do you get she's pretty? I haven't seen my girlfriend in a long time, but I would need copious amounts of booze to do anything with that woman."

"I guess I'm just saying that because she's young and she displays her bosom, and she has very long hair," said Marchello.

"Oh, woopdy damn do. I'd rather have one a little bit older that I don't have to put all that effort into."

They seemed to notice me still sitting there. Morgan explained to me that his girlfriend was 25 and attended school in Wyoming. She wanted him to settle down.

Morgan opened the fridge and looked around. "If you don't have beer in here, I'm going back to location."

Marchello told him that unless one of the guys put some in there, it wasn't likely.

He headed out the door muttering that he needed a shower. He turned to me and said: "Nice meeting you. Welcome to fucked-up North Dakota."

8. PASTOR JAY REINKE

T his is where the big fire was," Pastor Jay Reinke said as he drove toward the east edge of Williston in his clunky blue '97 Lumina. "There were two big buildings here that burned down. The road was blocked off for a good week or so after the fire." He slowed down and I craned my neck to get a better look. We stared at the charred ground and steel skeleton of what was once the Red River Supply, an oil field supply store. The store exploded just after midnight one summer night in 2014. The hot blaze rose 500 feet into the night sky, and the popping and booming sounds of the explosion echoed through town. Oil drilling chemicals—calcium chloride, calcium bromide, and calcium nitrate—burned all through the night, creating a black plume of smoke that settled over the town the next morning. The pastor lived with his wife and three kids just north of the fire. There were no casualties, but the city had to call in a hazardous materials response team to clean up the damage, and nearby residents were told to stay indoors for 24 hours because of concerns about air quality.

We made a sharp left and headed toward one of the first man camps that opened in Williston. Called the Muddy River Lodge, it was owned by the most famous oil field company in town, Halliburton. The building stood three stories tall and looked like 20 giant shipping containers had been fused together. Out front was a red sign with the Halliburton logo. There was a thin layer of frozen snow on the ground, and a security guard sat behind a tall fence. I wondered if it was as hard to leave the complex as it looked like it was to enter it. "This was the first man camp," Reinke explained. "In the middle they have a gymnasium and a restaurant. A lot of people don't like man camps, but I think they're great. When the boom is done, they're going to get packed up and moved away."

There seemed to be two groups of residents living in Williston—those who thought the oil boom was a temporary burst of money and workers flowing into town, and those who believed the money and people were there to stay. Some residents never had the chance to find out—they had been priced out of the homes they rented and forced to leave. For the most part, Reinke, who came to Williston 20 years ago, was happy the boom was there, but he didn't believe it would last forever. His plan was to outlast the boom and not let it exile him, as it had done to hundreds of other longtime Williston residents. People who had grown up on the quiet streets of the town, married in its churches, and sent their children to its schools were either being forced out by landlords who raised their rents from $500 a month to $3,000 or left voluntarily after their home values quadrupled and they sold them to escape.

North Dakota had seen oil booms before, in the 1950s and 1980s, but if you look at the state's economic history, those booms were a blip on the chart. If you blinked, you might have missed them. Nothing had ever compared to what was happening now.

Before the current boom, North Dakota had lost residents almost every year since 1930. It was one of the last frontiers to be settled in the United States, and about 80 percent of the first homesteaders who relocated there left within 20 years. The state's teachers earned some of the lowest salaries in the nation, and jobs had never been easy to come by. It was also one of the least-visited states—whenever I told my friends where I was going, they'd say, "Oh yeah, I drove through North Dakota once." Then they'd pause. "Wait, I think that was South Dakota." In Fargo, the visitor center gave out T-shirts that said YOU SAVED THE BEST FOR LAST, as if the state was proud visitors avoided the state as much as possible. One thing the state had was churches—about one church for every 400 people, giving it the distinction of being the state with the most churches per capita in the United States.

The state was also overwhelmingly white—North Dakota was settled by Scandinavian immigrants and was about 90 percent Caucasian, with any racial diversity on the reservations or in cities, such as Fargo and Bismarck.

Jay Reinke had moved to North Dakota in 1993 from Pierre, South Dakota, when he was 37 years old. After serving as an assistant pastor at a Lutheran church in Pierre for four years, he was offered his first full-time pastor position at Concordia Lutheran Church in Williston, a town with a population of around 12,000 people at the time. He moved to town with his wife, Andrea, and their three-month-old daughter, Clara. They purchased a small home downtown for around $32,000. They liked Williston at first. It didn't have as many public parks as Pierre, but people were friendly and the town seemed stable. Few people moved in or out. He and Andrea enjoyed the quiet, small-town atmosphere. Reinke figured it'd be a great place to build a church community and raise his family. Andrea, who had been a high school teacher on an Indian reservation in South Dakota, became a stay-at-home mom, and they had three more children.

Reinke is tall with a slight hunch and walks quickly. He has ruddy cheeks and blond hair and is a fast, expressive talker. His body movements and hand gestures are grand and attention-grabbing. Everyone knows when Reinke walks into a room. When he's angry, the wrinkles on his forehead bulge and his eyebrows curve downward. When he's excited, his eyes open wide, and he throws his hands up and grins like a Cheshire Cat.

As the pastor at Concordia, Jay Reinke became well known in the church community. He began writing a column for the local paper and had a program on a local radio station where he discussed scripture. Publicly, he rarely held back his opinions and was a proponent of many right-wing sentiments. He frequently fought to ban abortion by marching in Washington and used the church's front lawn to hold demonstrations. He staked over 1,000 crosses in front of the church every year to represent the annual number of abortions in the state. He vehemently opposed gay marriage, spoke out against a bill that would protect the LGBT community from housing and job discrimination, and fought to allow guns in churches. Though his political beliefs weren't extreme for western North Dakota, other pastors weren't nearly as vocal or eccentric as Reinke, and his outspokenness was isolating at times. Beyond their church friends and acquaintances, he and Andrea didn't have many other friends in town.

In 2009, he noticed more traffic in downtown Williston and read about the growing number of oil wells in the surrounding county. He saw more strangers and oil workers around town. Businesses seemed busier than ever. Lines had never been common in Williston, and suddenly people had to wait everywhere—at intersections, at Walmart, at the bank. "We noticed people walking on Main Street pulling suitcases behind them or carrying bags," he recalled. "You saw people sitting in coffee shops with bags around them and knew they just got to town." At times the newcomers stood out because they were more diverse than Williston was accustomed to. It was now not uncommon to see Black, Hispanic, Native American, African, Asian, or Arab workers walking the streets or at local restaurants.

As housing filled up, word quickly spread that rents were rising and vacant hotel rooms were difficult to find. Homeowners heard that some landlords had doubled, tripled, or quadrupled their prices and began listing extra rooms in their homes for what the market demanded. They assumed many new arrivals worked for oil companies and made at least three to four times the typical wage in Williston. When $1,000 didn't deter anyone, landlords tripled the original rent. Soon it was difficult to find an apartment in Williston for less than $3,000. Companies that had empty mobile trailers, called skid shacks, rented them for $2,000 a month.

Most older residents still remembered the 1980s boom, which went bust after only four years, and they didn't like the sound of another wave of boom and bust tearing through their town. They hoped it would be short-lived and they could return to living in peace. Longtime renters were already being pushed out of their homes. Elderly residents living on fixed incomes had to move away. Gloria Cox, a 74-year-old Williston resident, saw the rent on her mobile home lot go from $350 to $850 a month. "It's greediness, greediness, greediness," she said. "So many of us are living on Social Security. The rents are not feasible. We don't work in the oil field." Cox was old enough to remember the previous bust. "We had an oil boom before and it left us high and dry," she said. "The sooner this boom goes bust, the better."

But others welcomed the influx of money and jobs. The local Chevrolet dealer, Murphy Motors, could hardly keep new trucks on the lot—many were paid for with cash. The average wage in Williston rose to about $80,000 a year, up from $32,000 in 2006. By 2012, more than half of Williston's residents worked in oil-related jobs. The number of taxpayers reporting a $1 million-plus income in North Dakota went from 261 in 2005 to 1,265 in 2012.

Meanwhile, the "financial refugee" camp at Walmart grew. At night, as the sun disappeared behind the prairie, the parking lot filled up with rows of campers, RVs, and trucks with license plates from across the country, as far as Alaska and Florida. Fluorescent streetlights flooded spotlights onto the campers and cast shadows between the trucks and RVs. Men slouched in camping chairs drinking or smoking as Walmart shoppers hesitantly walked by them with their carts. The FOOD CENTER sign blazed brightly in the background. Locals began calling the parking lot Pioneer Square.

Reinke tried to help. He rented out the extra bedrooms in his home to newcomer men for $300 a month, significantly below the going rate, and in his newspaper column, he urged longtime locals to do the same. He pleaded for Williston residents to welcome the new arrivals and chastised one local woman he knew for calling them "human debris."

"We are at the epicenter of profound change. A migration. Thousands of people. Changed landscapes. It's here and life will never be the same," wrote Reinke in *The Williston Herald* in December 2011. "I have had the privilege of speaking to many of these new arrivals. Many have lost much, some have lost everything. They have suffered. They are also sons, and brothers, and fathers."

9. WILLISTON

From its birth, the city of Williston was filled with people looking for a place to start over.

Like many new towns during America's westward expansion, Williston sprang to existence in 1887 because of the railroad. That year, work crews laid some 545 miles of track across the state and into Montana—a rate that broke records and became known as the 1887 push. After the tracks were built, Great Northern Railway, which owned many acres of land in North Dakota, needed settlers. The railroad was offering land for cheap—only 10 percent down and seven years to pay the balance. Settlers could also acquire free land under the 1862 Homestead Act—all they needed to do was inhabit and improve an 160-acre plot for five years.

But when one of the railroad's land commissioners traveled 60 miles west of Fargo, he knew the area would be a hard sell—even at such prices. He described what he saw as "burned-over country" with "hard, dry soil." A "barren desert." Finding settlers for the area seemed "a hopeless task," he wrote. "The name Dakota had a faraway sound." Nevertheless, the free or cheap land was advertised in hundreds of newspapers all over the United States and in England, Norway, Sweden, Denmark, Holland, Switzerland, and Germany. In

1888, an advertisement in *Harper's Monthly* magazine called the region "the richest well-watered and favorably-situated agricultural and grazing lands of the entire public domain." The advertisement claimed the area had "mild and short winters" and that "cattle and stock graze the year around." An advertisement in 1907 read "Go to Opportunity Land. Get away from the over-crowded East—go where opportunities exist for every man willing to work—where industry reaps generous rewards—where a man is judged by 'what he does' and not by 'what he's worth.' Go to the great, growing, thriving Northwest."

The positive advertising worked. Soon immigrants and settlers migrated to the region, hoping for a new life. From 1878 to 1890, the population of North Dakota went from 16,000 people to 191,000—an increase of more than 1,000 percent. Most pioneers lived in tents and canvas-covered shacks at first. Lumber was in short supply and, in many instances, had to be hauled from 50 miles away. The roads were poor—most consisted of wagon tracks—and few streams or rivers had bridges. A large number of pioneers came from Scandinavia, especially Norway. Some townships in Traill County north of Fargo were more than 90 percent Norwegian. The dominant religion in the Scandinavian communities was Lutheran, and by 1916, 76,000 Lutherans were living in North Dakota. As was common with westward expansion, vagrants, prostitutes, gambling, and saloons came with the homesteaders. Though early settlers faced some violence from the Sioux tribe, the three main tribes in the area—the Mandan, Hidatsa, and Arikara—were peaceful and reluctantly allowed the settlement.

The pioneers soon discovered that the reality of North Dakota was different from what the advertisements had promised. One year in March a trainload of immigrants arrived in Williston during a blizzard and had nowhere to stay. They searched for a guide to help them locate a desirable 160-acre homestead, but no one would take them out in the storm. Many camped out in Williston's courthouse until the weather cleared.

The plots of land they acquired typically were marked only by mounds of dirt with oak stakes at the corners, and many plots weren't close to a water source. Families had to sleep in tents, wagons, or under wagons while they built more permanent structures such as sod houses or one-room dugouts with logs blocking the entrance. During the winter, settlers sometimes shared the dugouts with horses or oxen to keep the animals from freezing to death.

The soil on North Dakota homesteads was hard, dry, and tough to plow. Farmers worked long hours, fighting against extreme temperatures, rain, and snow. Pioneers battled lice and bedbugs, dust storms and prairie fires. "Wind-blown flames could outrun a galloping horse and sometimes leaped over streams and firebreaks, sweeping over large areas of open country and destroying grain, haystacks, buildings, and stock," wrote Elwyn Robinson in *History of North Dakota*.

In winter, temperatures could drop to the minus 40s. A blizzard in 1887 lasted 72 hours. During the storm, "men rode out on the range never to return," wrote Valerie Sherer Mathes in her essay, "Theodore Roosevelt as a Naturalist and Bad Lands Rancher." "Children froze to death only yards from their homes, women committed suicide, cattle . . . blew over in the gale force winds and died where they fell." As the snow melted, dead cattle were seen drifting down the swollen Little Missouri River. The next year, another blizzard killed nearly 100 people. Others suffered from frostbite. In 1889, a severe drought struck the central United States and hit the Dakotas particularly hard. Spring often brought terrible floods. In 1897, one flood swept away property and bridges, forming a lake 30 miles wide in the Red River Valley. And a typhoid epidemic nearly wiped out 10 percent of the population of Grand Forks in 1894 after sewage leaked into the city's water system.

Many of the first pioneers to the region, especially the women, wrote about the isolation and loneliness they felt. After a hard day on the land, men frequented saloons where women weren't allowed. Women would be left at home for days or weeks at a time while their husbands were away. Pioneer women often came from well-to-do families back east or in their home countries, and adjusting to the prairie frontier was difficult. The unpredictable climate, long winters, and barren, wide-open land added to their loneliness.

Thousands of pioneers left soon after they arrived. Speculators who had no intention of living in the state purchased huge swaths of land, hoping they could turn it over for profit, but most abandoned the land soon after. Many farms and lots were deserted. By 1890, an estimated 4 million acres of land were held by speculators and sat empty. Some settlers came with the intention of staying only a few years, building their fortunes, and leaving. In the boomtown of Bismarck, an Army officer wrote to his wife in 1876: "I have not fallen in love with Bismarck. It is a bad specimen of a frontier town, nobody incidentally expecting to stay here permanently, but hoping to make some money to get away with." After the exodus, some towns died completely. It was difficult to predict which ones were destined to become population centers and which ones would recede into ghost towns or tiny trading posts. Bismarck didn't empty out completely, but the city struggled. Home prices plummeted, and many dwellings sat abandoned. "In the enthusiasm of the Great Dakota Boom, the pioneers had inevitably made what can be called 'the Too-Much Mistake,'" wrote Robinson. "Much of the boom was a speculative, over-rapid, unhealthy growth. North Dakota had too much of too many things too soon."

Among those who stayed, some struggled to avoid bankruptcy, but many eventually adjusted and began to love the new frontier. They liked the adventure and were proud they could survive in such harsh conditions. Hospitality became a way of life, and most would do anything for a neighbor in need. They worked hard, lived cheaply, and eventually saw benefits to their sacrifices. As ranchers raised cattle and the land produced wheat, the value of the land rose. One pioneer, Mary Dodge

Woodward, wrote: "Nothing can excel this endless, enchanting view." The Norwegian settlers brought customs and cuisine that are still around today, such as lefse, a flatbread made with potatoes and flour, and lutefisk. "North Dakotans still retain some of the pioneer virtues: courage, optimism, self-reliance, aggressiveness, loyalty, and an independent cast of mind and spirit," wrote Robinson.

Tales of bravery, resilience, and social mobility came out of the region. In the government-run *North Dakota Magazine*, one writer told the story of a young man from Virginia who had been discharged from the Navy. He traveled to Chicago but couldn't find work. He became homeless and wandered the streets broke and destitute, with a jackknife as his only possession. Finally, he decided to seek his fortune in North Dakota. He sold his jackknife for 10 cents, purchased bread and tobacco, and boarded a boxcar. When he reached the state, he found work in the harvest fields and as a ranch cowboy. He saved enough money to buy land and started a farm, eventually moving into a stately two-story home. North Dakota had provided him with the opportunities to work his way out of poverty and achieve a middle-class lifestyle.

Theodore Roosevelt, who spent much time in the state between 1883 and 1887, had a strong affinity for the region. He purchased two ranches, one called Maltese Cross, or Chimney Butte, in the Little Missouri Valley and the other called Elkhorn, north of Medora. "I have always said I would not have been President had it not been for my experience in North Dakota," he said. He called the region "a land of vast silent spaces, of lonely rivers, and of plains where wild game stared at the passing horseman." As Roosevelt gained political influence, he worked to protect and conserve the lands he'd fallen in love with, including North Dakota's Sully Hill near Devils Lake, which became a 1,674-acre national wildlife refuge, and thousands of other acres in the state. Today, North Dakota has the most wildlife refuges of any state in the country.

After the turn of the century, the state remained mostly rural farms and small towns, but a few cities developed. Bismarck went from a small town of 2,000 in 1890 to more than 7,000 people in 1920, while Fargo went from 5,000 to 22,000 over the same period. The population of urban areas in the state grew 39 percent between 1910 and 1920, but most other areas of the state remained stagnant or lost population. Although North Dakota added 70,000 people during the 1910s, the growth was still less than the natural rate of increase.

The state experienced more prosperous years in the 1920s and went through a building boom as the population grew, but during the Great Depression, North Dakota once again fell on hard times. Not only did the state suffer from a depressed economy like the rest of the nation, but one of the worst droughts in the state's history occurred, followed by severe dust storms. Between 1929 and 1940, nine years had less than average rainfall, and 1934 was the driest year on record with only 9.5 inches of rainfall. By 1936, things got even worse. The state experienced the hottest (121 degrees in Steele in July) and coldest (minus 60 degrees in Parshall in February) temperatures ever reported and, once again, broke records with only 8.8 inches of rainfall. No prairie grass grew outside the Red River Valley in the eastern part of the state; dust storms swept across the land, preventing airplane or auto travel; and ranchers struggled to keep their herds alive, feeding them whatever brush or old straw they could find. In addition, a grasshopper infestation ravaged the prairie in the early 1930s and added to the destruction. Between 1932 and 1937, the per capita income in North Dakota was less than half the national average.

During this time, about one-third of North Dakota's families lost their farms. Over 80,000 people fled the state, and nearly half of the population lived on government relief. The western part of the state surrounding Williston and Minot, known for its semiarid climate and already-difficult farming conditions, suffered the worst. Slope County, located 150 miles from Williston in the southwest corner of North

Dakota, lost 29 percent of its population. The state's reliance on agriculture, the value of which fluctuated with the market, exacerbated the forces of the depression. North Dakota grew more dependent on aid and direction from the federal government, a fact that was difficult for many proud and self-reliant North Dakotans to come to terms with.

After the Great Depression, the state struggled to recover. Its population peaked at 680,845 (fewer people than the current population of a midsize city like Charlotte, North Carolina) in 1930 and didn't reach that level again until the most recent boom. World War II wealth, above-average rainfall, and rising prices for wheat helped many farmers settle their debts and expand their farms, but the depression scarred those who had stuck it out. Those who survived became hardened, stoic individuals who were reluctant to change. They knew hard times could hit again. State leaders attempted to diversify the agriculture business and attract industrial development, but they had little success—few factories wanted the added transportation costs of operating in such a remote area. In North Dakota, more income came from agriculture and less from manufacturing than any other state. State legislators considered doing anything and everything to bring attention and economic growth—from lobbying to drop "North" from the state's name to make it sound warmer and more inviting to tourists, to turning the prairie into a giant dumping ground for the country's nuclear waste. During the 1940s and 1950s, the state had one of the highest numbers of nuclear warheads stored there in the country. At one point, researchers even proposed returning the land to buffalo grazing territory. North Dakotans hoped for something— anything—that might boost prosperity for their state.

"The Dakotas are a place people are *from*," wrote Kathleen Norris in *Dakota*, "a place that has suffered a steady outmigration for the better part of a hundred years. What does this do to those of us who remain?" Remnants of past lives and abandoned dreams are everywhere on the prairie. Old, dilapidated homes vacated long ago lean against the harsh plains winds, almost as if the buildings themselves are trying to escape. Pieces of siding occasionally rip off and whip across the fields. As Chuck Wilder, a 59-year-old local bookstore owner who grew up in the state, put it: "Our best export was our people."

10. IT TAKES A BOOM

Colloquially called roughnecks, oil field workers in the United States typically come from blue-collar and working-class families. Jobs in the field began to decline in the mid-1980s when traditional oil reserves mostly dried up. But in 2009, a new crop of oil field workers entered the industry. Unlike their predecessors, these oil field workers had come up in a world where they watched the Twin Towers collapse, witnessed or participated in ongoing battles in the Middle East over oil, and saw the Great Recession wipe out almost any financial security they believed their families had. Many were raised on video games, Christian-based faiths, and gun culture and were die-hard patriots, believing America ought to be defended and protected at all costs. Others saw their parents feel betrayed after staying loyal to a company or participating in a union, so they had little desire to do the same. If they had work experience before coming to the oil field, it was likely in farming, construction, manufacturing, or, in many cases, the military. The boom coincided with the withdrawal of tens of thousands of troops from Iraq. If soldiers weren't killed in the war, they figured they might as well risk their lives searching for oil in the homeland. One veteran called North Dakota's Bakken region "the next deployment."

Many oil companies implemented programs to recruit and hire ex-military. A program called Retrain America was established in 2009 to prepare veterans and blue-collar workers with high school diplomas for energy jobs, particularly in engineering and oil field management. And ShaleNet, a $20 million federally funded program, launched in 2010 to retrain workers to become pipeline operators or oil field technicians and encouraged veterans to apply.

Like those before them, few modern-day oil workers attended college. Only 12 percent of oil and gas workers in Williston had a bachelor's degree or higher. When the boom first began, companies transferred workers already employed in the energy industry from states such as Wyoming and Pennsylvania, where development had stalled from the drop in natural gas prices. This satisfied a tiny fraction of the workers they needed, however. It's estimated for every drilling rig, some 120 workers are needed, and a third of those jobs involve truck driving. In the beginning of the boom, with an average of 100 new wells drilled or fracked every month, companies needed to hire quickly, and they hired almost any able-bodied worker who walked through their door. A few oil field service companies went to local high schools in western North Dakota and eastern Montana to recruit potential dropouts for the work. In 2011, at Sidney High School in Montana, an hour away from Williston, a record one-third of its graduates immediately entered the workforce instead of heading to college or the military. Enrollment at a community college in Glendive, Montana, fell by nearly half as fewer students in the area chose college.

The average oil field worker earned $20 to $40 an hour, and many received per diem bonuses, ranging from $35 to $750 a day, just for showing up to a job. In a good year with nearly every rig drilling, overtime and bonuses pushed most workers' incomes into the six figures. By the end of 2012, the average wage for oil field workers in North

Dakota was $112,462. In the rest of America, a high school graduate could expect to earn an average of $27,607; a high school dropout, a measly $19,642. A college degree gave workers a significant boost in the market: $50,096 on average, but with student loans, many college grads were barely making ends meet. It was easy to see the financial appeal of oil field work.

Despite local recruitment, few of the men and women who came to work in the Bakken oil field were actually from North Dakota. The local population could not sustain hiring needs, so companies looked elsewhere. Craigslist advertisements called for workers with "no experience needed!" "Work 20 days on and 10 days off!" "$22 an hour to start!"

Word traveled quickly, and a flood of workers showed up at the oil industry's doorstep.

There's little, if any, training to break into the oil field industry during a boom. Most jobs ask for a commercial driver's license (CDL), which workers can complete in three to five weeks, a clean drug test, and the ability to lift 50 pounds. Once hired, they go through a safety training class certified by the Occupational Safety and Health Administration (OSHA) for a minimum of 10 hours to learn about potential job hazards and safety protocols, like the dangers of hydrogen sulfide (H_2S), a gas present on well locations. For many companies, the training stops there. The new hire is placed on a crew with a supervisor and expected to learn on the job. Larger companies, such as Halliburton ("Big Red") and Schlumberger ("Big Blue"), put new hires through slightly more rigorous training regimens, meaning a few weeks of "rig school," before they're tossed out onto a crew.

New hires are taught how the equipment functions and standard safety protocols, but in the oil and gas industry, the stakes are high. It's difficult to prepare workers for what to do in a situation when a $2 million piece of equipment breaks in the well or when a highly pressurized hose releases a razorlike stream of air through a pinhole leak, potentially cutting off the limbs of anyone who walks by; or when a tank full of flammable liquid explodes into a ball of flames; or when a tornado touches down a few miles from the well, as happened to one supervisor.

Those coming to North Dakota also were not trained to work in extreme temperatures and weather—blizzards, hail, minus 40 or 50 degrees—temperatures so low that, if you're not careful, your hard hat can freeze to your head. One worker said he was drinking a soda on site and set it down; 15 minutes later, he went back and saw it was slush. Fifteen minutes after that, it was frozen solid. Before I visited North Dakota in the winter, I asked a worker to describe what it was like. He looked at me, dumbfounded: "I'll tell you what it's like. Put your head in the freezer and punch yourself in the face." I took his word for it. Such temperatures can also turn dangerous. "When you're tired and cold, you're more likely to get hurt," said Cindy Marchello.

In addition, North Dakota crews often faced dust storms and 50-mile-an-hour-plus winds, both of which could create unforeseen hazards and difficult-to-detect wear and tear on equipment. In the summer, the fire-resistant coveralls workers wore trapped heat and made working during the day miserable. "You're always fighting the weather, whether it's too hot, too cold, or there are too many mosquitoes," said Marchello.

Most of Marchello's 12-person crew regularly clocked 120 hours a week—with some logging an occasional 140- or 160-hour week. That meant they worked, ate, and slept while on the well site, though sleep was never a priority. Most workers took catnaps in an 18-wheeler's sleeper cabin. "When you're out in the field, there's not much sleep," said Marchello. "You get used to it." The most intensive bursts of hard labor were when a crew arrived to a location to set up the equipment or when they disassembled everything and hauled it away.

With extreme conditions, tight living quarters, and long stretches away from their families, it is easy to see the comparison to the military.

"It's like a war out there sometimes," said one of Marchello's co-workers. "You look out for each other—you have to. It's like a battle-field. You think, can we actually pull this off?"

The long hours, sleep deprivation, lack of training, extreme weather, and dangerous work were a particularly lethal mix. In 2011, North Dakota became the most dangerous state to work in, with the fatality rate nearly doubling since 2007 to 12.4 deaths per 100,000 workers. By 2012, the state job fatality rate was 17.7 deaths per 100,000 workers, more than five times the national average and one of the highest rates ever reported for a U.S. state. The most dangerous sector was in mining and oil and gas extraction—with 104 deaths per 100,000 workers, more than six times the national rate. Burn injuries among workers in North Dakota rose to more than 3,100 in 2015, but the state has no burn centers, so victims were flown 600 miles to the Twin Cities for treatment.

Oil worker deaths during the boom included Brendan Wegner, 21, who was burned alive his first day on the job when an Oasis Petroleum oil well exploded in McKenzie County in 2011. His body was found under a pile of melted steel pipes, his charred hands still gripping a ladder by which he tried to escape. His coworker Ray Hardy, 28, suffered such severe burns that he died shortly after the explosion, and another coworker, Michael Twinn, eventually committed suicide after having his burned legs amputated and suffering from posttraumatic stress disorder. Twenty-one-year-old Dustin Bergsing died by inhaling toxic hydrocarbon vapor on a Marathon Oil well site near Mandaree; 20-year-old Kyle Winters died after power tongs collided into his chest when he worked for Heller Casing; Joseph Kronberg, 52, was electrocuted on site. Between 2006 and 2014, a total of 342 workers died on the job in North Dakota. At least 74 of those have been from an accident in the Bakken—that's approximately one death every six weeks.

Between 2011 and 2015, only five to eight OSHA field investigators were employed in western North Dakota—the investigators were responsible for overseeing not only oil and gas industry safety but complaints in other fields, such as construction, covering more than 148,000 square miles in North and South Dakota. With eight investigators, it would take OSHA 126 years to inspect each workplace in North Dakota once.

When an OSHA investigator did find a safety violation, penalties were low. In fiscal year 2013, for example, the median OSHA fine in cases involving a death in the United States was $5,600. And within the North Dakota and Montana energy industry, only one oil exploration company that leases or owns wells was fined for a worker death between 2010 and 2015—a $7,000 penalty after a contract worker died in an explosion.

Though workers' compensation claims have more than quadrupled among the state's oil and gas workers, many injured workers don't file claims. Companies often reward workers for low injury rates and offer incentives to not report every accident. If a worker or their family does file, workers' compensation does little to help with the aftereffects from a serious injury or death. In the early 1900s, workers' compensation legislation waived workers' right to sue in exchange for compensation—such as payment for their medical bills and lost wages—if they were injured on the job. But many states have slowly chipped away at the system by shrinking payments, fighting claims, controlling medical decisions, and stopping payments before workers fully recover. In 2014, employers in North Dakota paid the least among the states toward workers' compensation, averaging $0.88 for every $100 they paid in wages. By contrast, North Dakota averaged $2.39 for every $100 in 1988. After filing for workers' compensation, many workers report being ostracized by companies for having an accident on their record. "If you're hurt out here, it will go on your record," said one North Dakota worker. "If it happens enough times, the company will get rid of you."

"North Dakota has a really bad workers' comp law," said Tatum

O'Brien Lindbo, a personal injury lawyer in the state. "A lot of these people go out to an unsafe oil rig and they get hurt, maimed, or killed and there isn't a whole lot I can do for them. It's just a terrible system for a worker up here."

If a worker manages to avoid any immediate injuries, long-term damage can also come in the form of silica poisoning, or silicosis. The disease is difficult to detect and causes irreversible lung damage, which can lead to lung cancer or tuberculosis. Silica poisoning can happen when fine bits of silica from fracking sand enter a worker's lungs. Each well requires some 2,000 tons of sand, which is used to prop open fractured rock, and the National Institute for Occupational Safety and Health found higher-than-recommended levels of silica in 92 of 116 air samples they took from fracking sites in five states, including North Dakota.

Marchello and most of her crew had experienced or witnessed some sort of serious accident during their time in North Dakota's oil fields. One worker needed back surgery after he was in a car accident while driving to location. Two men almost died when a crane tipped over. One guy blew a hole through his hand after he opened a pressurized valve in freezing temperatures and a chunk of ice shot through his palm. He was out of work for four months.

When Marchello was at Halliburton, a hose came loose and sprayed hot hydraulic fluid all over her, dripping down her hard hat and drenching her coveralls. If she hadn't been wearing protective clothing, it would've burned through to her skin. As she stumbled over to get her coworker's attention, she tripped on a lunch box, crashing down on top of it, and felt an intense pain in her leg. A welt on her thigh was already swelling bigger than a football. She had bruised her right thigh down to the bone. She kept her sunglasses on so the guys wouldn't see her crying. At first, she didn't want to report the accident because it seemed minor. The general thinking among her coworkers was if you don't need to go to the emergency room, don't report it. She tried to tough it out and not to put weight on her leg for the remainder of her shift: another 12 hours.

When she returned to the bus after her shift, however, she was in even more pain. She finally decided to report the incident and was told to contact a nurse through an "independent" medical consulting firm that evaluates oil field workers after injuries. Independent medical consulting firms are typically on a list of providers approved by the oil company, and medical personnel often make decisions on injuries after only brief exams. In treatment disputes, doctors employed by independent medical consulting firms have ruled against injured workers most of the time, according to a report by *ProPublica*. Marchello was sent to Williston's hospital, where a nurse practitioner conducted a drug test and gave her a Breathalyzer test to make sure she didn't have alcohol in her system. Marchello said after the nurse poked her leg a few times and took an x-ray, the consulting firm claimed the injury wasn't severe and sent her back to work, suggesting she do "light duty" for six weeks, which involved picking up trash and working at the Halliburton warehouse. "If they can bandage you up, they'll send you back to work," said Marchello. "Time off is what they don't want to give you."

Oil workers historically have had difficulty organizing, and most states where fracking and oil drilling occur are "right to work" states, which have laws that strip unions of much of their bargaining power. The national union in the field is United Steelworkers, but it represents only those who work in oil refineries, petrochemical plants, pipeline operations, or terminals. Because most oil field workers are employed by smaller service companies and travel so often, it's difficult for them to organize strikes or improve their bargaining power. Most of the workers I interviewed weren't interested in union membership anyway. They blamed the downfall of American's manufacturing industry on unions. Nationwide, labor union membership had fallen by half over the last 30 years. In 2014, only about 11 percent of all wage and salary workers were in a union, down from 20 percent in 1983.

Many workers I met said they saw a limit to the number of years they could stay in the oil field. They witnessed what happened to those who stayed too long—divorce, estrangement from their children, health problems, debilitating injuries, or early death. People often said oil field years were like dog years—for every year you worked in oil, you aged about seven years. Marchello estimated that with her oil field years, she was 92. "Mine quadrupled because I was so old when I started," she said. But pulling herself away from the high paycheck and transitioning to a slower pace of life was easier said than done.

All of the guys on Marchello's crew spent most of the year away from their families, causing a strain on marriages and family life that was a frequent topic of conversation. When people would ask Marchello where she lived, she'd reply: "In a sleeper of a truck, on a muddy location, somewhere in North Dakota." Workers missed birthdays and holidays and struggled to stay connected to home. Crew members often bonded over the difficulties of their long-distance lives. They gave each other privacy to call home when they were in pockets of cell phone reception and discussed suspicions of their partners' infidelities.

"I've seen people leave because they needed to work on their marriage," said one of Marchello's coworkers. "The time away is hard. If you don't have a strong foundation at home, this will tear you apart."

11. TOM STAKES

I met Tom Stakes a few weeks after I arrived in Williston. A local worker told me about a homeless camp at Trenton Lake, and on a sweltering, dusty day in July, I drove the 10 miles outside of Williston to see what I could find. A few years ago, the campground was a summer vacation spot for families visiting the nearby historical site of Fort Buford. But during the summer of 2013, it was essentially a tent city, scattered with homeless people who had traveled from thousands of miles away to try to make it in an oil boomtown. Priced out of the local rental market, and with no homeless shelter in Williston, they turned to camping.

When I arrived at the campground, I parked and stepped out of the car. There were wooden picnic tables, a rusty swing set, and a dozen or so tents pitched on an overgrown grassy field—in many ways, it looked like any other campground I've stayed at across the United States. Patches of green grass grew next to a murky lake that lapped up against a narrow beach. After living around dust and gravel for weeks in Williston, it was a welcome change. I was beginning to forget what it was like to be around greenery. I approached two teenage boys standing near a gray canvas tent with a blue rain cover. They introduced themselves as brothers, Trevor and Kevin Andresen. Trevor was tan, with a goatee and moppy curls. He was 21, the older of the two.

His brother Kevin was 18 but was taller and heavier. They were both barefoot. They explained they were from Utah and had been living at the campground for nearly a month. They lived out of an old run-down van and the small tent with their parents, pregnant sister and her two small children—a toddler and an 11-month-old—and their dog, Lita, who was tied up to a tree nearby.

"How many?" I asked, wondering how they could all fit in one tent. Trevor explained it to me: Three adults usually slept in the tent, with the children in the middle to keep their small bodies warm, and Trevor and Kevin slept under a tarp connected to the tent—except for the other night, when torrential rain forced the whole family to huddle together in the van and wait out the storm. "There's some moody weather here," said Trevor. "It's like the state has constant PMS." I peeked into the van and saw piles of clothes on the floor, crumpled bags of Cheetos, cigarettes strewn about the passenger seat, and a sleeping baby in the back, swaddled in a blanket and dirt smeared on her cheeks. The family paid $10 a night for the campsite, but they could only stay 14 days at a time according to camp rules, so every two weeks they'd pack up and spend a night or two at a campground in Fort Buford, 12 miles down the highway, then return to Trenton for another two weeks.

"Where is everyone?" I asked, wondering where the rest of the family was.

"Over in town," said Trevor, gesturing toward the gravel road I'd driven in on and referring to Williston. He explained that their sister and mother were applying for cashier and waitressing jobs that day, and their father was currently at work. Their father had found a job as a welder, but so far the two of them hadn't had much luck finding employment. The only job they managed to land was a few days pulling weeds for a guy who paid them $15 an hour under the table. As I was chatting with them, I heard from around the corner: "Who's that cute lady you're talking to?"

A scrawny, bespectacled man with long white hair appeared and introduced himself as Tom Stakes. "How come nobody told me there was a pretty lady here?" he said in a Louisiana drawl and laughed, not waiting for an answer. Stakes stepped in front of Trevor and Kevin and asked how he could help me. When I told him I was reporting the stories of people out here, he replied, "You wanna tell *my* story? I'm gonna get a piece of paper and write down *your* story!" He let out a loud, bouncy laugh and put his hand on my shoulder. "Jus' kiddin', girl! What do ya wanna know?"

Stakes explained that he was having trouble finding work for more than $10 an hour. "Now I'm kinda stuck," he said. "It cost me $300 to drive up here, and it takes me about a week or more jus' to earn that to get back. But in the meantime, I gotta eat, I gotta drive, I'm burnin' gas, and everythin' is jus' so far away."

After Stakes slept in the parking lot across from Bakken Staffing for two weeks, he heard about Trenton Lake Campground from a friend and decided to check it out. He set up his tent about 50 feet away from the family, went over and introduced himself, and they'd been hanging out ever since. "In a tent, you can stretch out. It's a lot better," Stakes explained. "It's almost like callin' a place home. You don't want to call your truck your home. And plus they have hot showers and everythin' else. There are grills outside where you can cook on a grill and little picnic tables. So it's better than jus' sittin' in your truck." The problem was, the campground was 14 miles from his job site, so he now spent $20 a day on gas. He made about $50 a day at his construction job, which left $10 for his campsite and $20 to eat and drink. "I don't like the traffic, I don't like the big trucks. It's too busy for me. I don't like the busy life, but if you gotta go out and do somethin', you do it."

A week later, I returned to their campsite with a six-pack. I spotted Stakes sitting next to Trevor and Kevin at a picnic table and six other people: two men, two women, and two kids—a little boy and the baby

I saw sleeping in the van earlier. A cloud of smoke rose into the sky from a cement grill, and open cans of Bud Light and Natural Ice sat on the table. Stakes jumped up and yelled my name. "Hey, girl, how ya doin'?" he said as he approached me. He patted my back and introduced me to the rest of the crew: There was Trevor and Kevin's dad, Mike, a middle-aged man who looked like he was in a biker gang. He had a long braid down his back, tattoos snaking up both arms, a backward baseball cap, and a Hooters T-shirt. Heidi, his wife, was a short, stout woman with curly hair pulled back into a messy bun. She stood at the picnic table chopping potatoes. A young woman, Billy, was sitting on a blanket spread out by the picnic table, playing with her baby. She was Trevor and Kevin's sister. Billy's protruding pregnant belly was covered by a tight white tank top with smudged dirt stains, and she wore pink pajama pants. A little boy, about three years old, ran over to her. A large man with short gray hair, named Web, sat in a camping chair, quietly mumbling about government conspiracies. Stakes explained that Web wasn't related to the family. Stakes had met him at a bar and invited him to come stay at the campground—Stakes was now sharing a tent with him.

Heidi and Mike insisted I stay for a meal. I thanked them but declined, saying I'd recently eaten. But they kept insisting, and finally I agreed to a small plate. It was a thick stew of canned beans, potatoes, carrots, and ground beef—the ingredients purchased at the minimart down the road and warmed up on the campsite grill. "They make the best meals," Stakes said in between bites. "I usually eat canned spaghetti."

Soon, after more cans of beer had been emptied, all of them started talking at once to me, and the volume grew louder as they tried to speak over each other. The only two people sitting quietly were Trevor and Kevin. Kevin shoveled food into his mouth and stared down at the table. Trevor's eyes were bloodshot. He looked stoned.

Mike told the story of how they arrived in Williston as I scribbled furiously in my notebook. In late 2008, Mike lost his construction job and filed for bankruptcy, hoping they could keep their house in Utah. It was a simple home, but on a few acres with six horses—Lady, Diamond, Webber, Buddy, Buttercup, Sassy, and a baby horse they called "Horse" because they couldn't agree on a name. The bank said it would refinance the loan on the house, but after Mike missed one mortgage payment, the bank sent him a foreclosure notice. They lost their house during the winter of 2009 and moved into a trailer in the backwoods. "By February, we were living in the fucking mountains. I shit you not," Mike said. They survived out there for 18 months. Mike struggled to find decent-paying work in Utah, and this summer, they decided to try their luck in North Dakota. He used his last paycheck to fund the trip, barely making it to Williston after their van broke down multiple times during the journey. "We came up here on a wing and a fetching prayer," he said.

Stakes nodded and took another swig of beer. "These guys are what America is right here," he said, gesturing to the family. "It's a tough life. You do everythin' you can to make a dime. Nobody wants to hire a 58-year-old man," he said, referring to himself. "I got no Social Security. I got no disability. I'm jus' livin' on whatever I can make. Sometimes I don't eat, sometimes I do. But I do know one thing—of all the people who have helped me in my life, it's been people like these people," he said about the Andresen family. "It wasn't the people who had a lot of stuff. These people will give you the shirt off their back."

Stakes pointed to Trevor and Kevin. "You guys are still young and got your whole life ahead of ya. Don't mess it up."

"By the time my brothers get a job, we'll be okay," said Billy. Her baby started to cry, and she rocked the child in her arms, soothing her.

It began raining. Lightly at first, but then it poured. Everyone huddled around the picnic table under an open-air shelter. The rain pounded against the tin roof.

Mike began humming and yelled, "Ladies and gentleman, live from

Los Angeles, California . . . the Doors!" He air-played the guitar and hummed louder, then broke into song. "I took a look around for which way the wind blows!" he sang. Stakes chimed in. "Met a little girl in a Hollywood bungalow! We were rockin' the lady in the City of Lights!" they sang together.

"The City of Night!" yelled Stakes. "City of Night!"

They sang a few more verses together, with Stakes imitating the guitar parts.

Afterward Stakes asked, "What's that old saying, that song?" He began singing softly. "'Those were the days my friend, we thought they'd never end.'"

He added quietly, "But they did."

12. DONNY NELSON

The good times ended for Donny Nelson around 2007. That year, he heard rumors about renewed drilling activity to the northeast of his farm. There had been oil extraction in the area before, so he thought little of it. But then drilling moved south of him. Then west. The town closest to him, Watford City, quickly became a hub for the oil industry—its population rising from 1,200 to 8,700 in just three years. Soon drilling was next door to him. First one oil well blocked his view of the farm from his favorite lookout point, then two, then more than he could keep track of. Nelson discovered that by 2012, Hess had applied for about 150 new drilling permits in Nelson's township and another 150 in the township next to his—some 300 wells within a few square miles. "I've seen three oil boom/busts in my lifetime already. But I've never seen nothin' like this," he said.

Nelson had 25 new wells on his farmland, but they were a small fraction of the 8,500 wells that were drilled or fracked in North Dakota between 2007 and 2014. Drilling some 1,200 wells every year is an astonishing rate for the oil industry. Never before had the United States seen oil production increase this much and this quickly in such a small area. And the oil companies were just getting started. By 2013, after six years of frenzied drilling, only 244 million barrels of oil had been recovered, or 3 percent of what was potentially available. "It could be a disastrous situation," Nelson said. "We still have sites here from the '50s and '60s. And now we're getting 10 times, maybe 100 times the wells."

Nelson never wanted oil companies in his backyard. Though he owned 8,000 acres of land, he didn't own everything underneath. In Pennsylvania and many other states, most farmers have the power to tell the oil companies to get lost, but North Dakota is one of the few states where landowners can't say no.

That's because in most states, the surface land and the minerals underneath are sold together, but in North Dakota and states such as Texas and Oklahoma, where oil and gas development has occurred, the majority of the minerals have been severed. In North Dakota, most landowners sold off their mineral rights at some point because they didn't know what the rights were worth or they were desperate for cash. Historically, the average household income in North Dakota has been one of the lowest in the nation, and when someone knocked on a struggling family's door offering to pay them a handful of cash for mineral rights they didn't even know they had, the proposition was difficult to pass up. Today, only about one in five surface owners in North Dakota actually owns the minerals beneath them.

Under North Dakota law, mineral rights trump the land rights of surface owners, so essentially people who live out of state but have North Dakotan ancestors can receive a notice in the mail that they own 500 acres of minerals, making them overnight millionaires. In contrast, the people who bought the surface land without the mineral rights would receive a one-time payment of maybe $3,000 for "temporary land loss," and get none of the profits, despite dealing with drilling crews, truck traffic, dust, possible drinking water and soil contamination, air pollution, and loss of property value. And even those 25 percent of landowners who own mineral rights would have a difficult time keeping oil companies off their land—oil companies have many legal strategies to gain access, and state laws tend to favor the companies.

The state's mineral laws meant that much of the wealth being created by the energy boom was being unequally distributed. One farmer near Williston said he named the oil well on his land "the hamburger well," because it earned him enough money to buy one hamburger a month, whereas retired farmer and rancher Lenin Dibble received royalty checks of nearly $1 million a year for his share of mineral rights. Nelson's friends, the Jorgensons, had no idea they didn't own the mineral rights under the 40 acres around their house and were shocked to find out that 110 strangers owned them. When oil companies came to drill, all the Jorgensons could do was stand by and watch.

Nelson owned a handful of the mineral rights underneath his land—but not enough to stop the oil companies from barging in and setting up camp. Because his land had been divided up and sold so many times, his mineral rights were jumbled together with those of others. And if 51 percent of the mineral owners on a 1,280-acre plot allowed drilling, all of them had to do so. Nelson owned some minerals around his farmhouse, however, so he was able to negotiate how close to his home oil companies could place a well. The companies had to keep wells about a mile away from his house, though they could still technically drill under his house, once they were thousands of feet below. Nelson received a sizable check each month from his share of royalties from four different wells, though if the wells started producing less or stopped altogether, so would the checks. "I've had people tell me, 'Why are you complaining? You're getting money,' and I say, 'Money doesn't make stuff right.'"

Anyone who wanted to fight back faced extraordinary legal fees. Negotiating a lease was a long and cumbersome process. Oil companies knew they could almost always outspend farmers and drag out legal proceedings to an unaffordable point. Nelson originally took his lease to a lawyer, but only a few in the area dealt with minerals, and since thousands of farmers were in the same situation, most were completely overwhelmed. Nelson could tell immediately that the lawyer put little care into his lease negotiation. Landowners with enough mineral rights also had the option of "going down the hole" with the oil company and sharing the profits, but this option required landowners to pay for the initial drilling costs, which could run upward of $10 million. "A lot of people throw up their hands and take what they give you," said Nelson.

All Nelson wanted now was a break—a break from the noise, the trucks, the phone calls from oil companies that started at 9 a.m. nearly every day, and the dust that billowed up every time a semi truck passed. He wanted his old life back.

The biggest mistake I made when I met Donny Nelson at his farm was bringing wine.

I don't know what I was thinking.

Donny drinks Bud Light or whiskey, not wine. Rena Nelson, his wife, doesn't like wine either. Donny showed me the handle of Jack Daniel's sitting in his freezer.

Donny is about as American West as you can get. Behind a bushy handlebar mustache, prominent lines carve deep into his tan skin when he smiles—almost as if he collects them, with each one representing the passing of another season and harvest. On most summer days, when temperatures rarely exceeded 70 degrees, Donny wore a short-sleeve vintage Western shirt with pearled snap buttons, Wranglers, and a hat to protect him from the elements. His favorite seemed to be a dust-covered Feiring Cattle Company cap with faded fabric on the rim. With few trees in sight, the blazing sun seemed to reach every crevice of land, and the wind could pick up without notice.

He lived with his wife in a two-story log house that he built himself when he was still a bachelor. He bought the logs from a neighbor, dug the basement by himself in the summer of 1996 and, with the help of friends and family, spent a year and a half building the house. The deep pine logs flanked the interior of the house. The stairway and second-floor balcony were lined with railings made from smooth juniper cedar that Donny recycled from old fence posts. The farmhouse sat at the bottom of a hill, shielded by small hills on either side. When you left his driveway and reached the dirt road, you were met with a skyline cluttered with a half-dozen oil wells. Beyond them was one of Donny's favorite spots—a butte that was the tallest land formation for miles, named Thunder Butte by the Native Americans.

Donny's farm was once part of the nearby Fort Berthold Indian Reservation before it was opened for homesteading. Donny attended school on the reservation in New Town because it was the closest school to his house. About half the students in his class were Caucasian homesteaders and half were Native Americans. "I've always had a good relationship with most of them," he said. "We have a lot of the same ideals."

Like most North Dakotans, Donny liked to hunt. Pheasants were his favorite, but he didn't mind shooting the occasional coyote (he pronounces it "cay-oat") that wandered onto his property. An elk head peered down onto his dining room table, and he kept a .220 Swift rifle in his truck. In his workshop was a sign that read VEGETARIAN: THE INDIAN WORD FOR LOUSY HUNTER. When I asked how many guns he owned, he said, "Let's just say I have plenty." Maybe because they shared a last name, he listened to a lot of Willie Nelson.

Donny was a bachelor until five or six years ago when he met Rena, a woman who grew up nearby in the small town of Watford City and worked at the local police department. They met at the annual steak and lobster festival dance in town, and she gave him her number. "I intended to call her, but then I got busy," he said. Donny didn't see her again until almost a year later when they ran into each other at another dance. After that, he finally called her.

Donny didn't use a laptop, and his computer was at least a decade old. He used a landline or an old flip phone to make phone calls. Since there was no cell phone reception at the farmhouse, he drove to the top of a hill to talk. He laughed when I asked if he was on Facebook, and he only recently purchased a TV. "It's nice, but now I can't get nothin' done," he said as we flipped through channels one night. One of his farm vehicles was a 1978 pickup truck with no muffler and no seat belts. "This truck'd be illegal in California," his 25-year-old farmhand, Adam, told me.

Donny traveled around when he was younger. After graduating from college with a degree in agricultural economics, he went to Australia to work on a sheep and cattle farm for six months, but quickly realized his farm in North Dakota was where he wanted to be. "Even while I was in Australia, it was pretty cemented in my mind that farming here was what I wanted to do," he said. "Once you get away from home and see other places and compare it to where you're from, I thought, 'We live in a pretty good place.'" He also traveled to Los Angeles once with Rena to visit friends and immediately decided the city was not for him. "We felt like a buncha hicks," he said, laughing. "I can't believe we survived."

His "pretty good place," however, was known among U.S. farmers for its extremely harsh conditions, and other farmers might run back to their (literally) greener pastures. The land here was unforgiving; a place where few crops could flourish except for robust grains, such as barley and durum wheat. The average rainfall was only about 17 inches, half the amount Iowa and Kansas received, and only a few inches more than New Mexico. The weather could be extreme and unpredictable. For most of December, January, and February, it was cold enough to freeze your nostril hairs as soon as you stepped outside. Droughts were frequent, with many scientists predicting that the drought cycle would become more severe in the coming years. While I lived in North Dakota during the summer of 2013, I experienced hailstorms with bouncy-ball-size pellets raining down on me, 60-mile-an-hour winds, and tornado warnings—all of which could completely take out a farmer's crop for the year. "In the end we don't own the land," said Donny. "It owns us."

13. CINDY MARCHELLO

There are three main steps to the shale oil extraction process: drilling, fracking, and completion. Cindy Marchello and her crew worked during the completion stage. But a lot had to happen before they arrived.

Step one is drilling. A drilling crew builds a towering 120-foot derrick as the support structure for the drill. Crew members use a diamond drill bit, hard enough to break through rock layers that can be 50 feet thick, and attach it to the end of a 90-foot pipe and bore into the ground, feeding more pipe as they go. They use drilling mud, mixed with diesel fuel, synthetic oil, and other chemical additives (the mixture is unique to each company, but ethylene glycol, a highly toxic chemical used in antifreeze, is commonly used) to keep the drill bit cool in the hole. They drill through the water aquifer (typically no deeper than 2,000 feet in western North Dakota) and continue drilling about 10,000 feet (or about the distance of seven Empire State Buildings stacked on top of each other), until they reach the Bakken shale formation. Once they hit bottom, they drill the "bend," a 90-degree turn that allows them to drill horizontally another 5,000 to 10,000 feet. This giant L-shaped hole in the ground, about three feet wide, is the well. Afterward, workers encase the top portion of the well with cement, pouring it down the sides of the pipe to create a leakage barrier—though the process is not always successful. Documented cases of leaks have occurred in Pennsylvania, where underground gases have migrated up the sides of wells.

Drillers are able to tunnel into the ground with impressive accuracy, typically staying within 10 feet of the target path, and the time it takes to drill a well continues to decrease. It took about 40 to 60 days to drill a well in the early stages of the Bakken development, but by 2013, some wells were being drilled in as few as nine days. After drilling, the rig is packed up and moved to the next drill site before a wireline crew and a fracking crew arrives.

The wireline crew, colloquially known as gun hands, tosses explosives down the hole to blow small perforations in the pipe with shrapnel pieces, which allows gas and oil to seep through. Not surprisingly, this is one of the most dangerous jobs in the oil field. Crew members on site have to turn off all cell phones and electronic devices during the perforating process to avoid triggering the explosives. The horizontal section of a well is divided into 20 or 30 zones. Each zone is isolated by using rubber stoppers, or "plugs," and must be perforated and fracked separately. The wireline crew blows holes in the first zone, then stands by for the frack crew.

The frack crew brings an in army of trucks and heavy machinery. This step requires about 6 to 12 pumps, some 3 million to 5 million gallons of water (enough to sustain an American family for 34 years), and 2,000 truck trips from the water depot to transport it all. Often the crew builds a 1.8-million-gallon tank nearby to store some of the water, or brings in dozens of smaller tanks. About 1.5 million to 6 million pounds of sand also are needed, nearly enough to fill an Olympic-size swimming pool. The sand isn't the kind you find on a beach. Sometimes it's manufactured ceramic pellets shipped in from China; other times it comes from quartz-rich sandstone mines in Minnesota and Wisconsin.

The whole system of pipes, pumps, storage tanks, and trucks extends over an area about the size of two football fields. Fracking crews are made up of about 30 people and tend to have a lot of new arrivals. Since so many frack hands are needed, it's typically someone's first job in the oil field. Scott Morgan, Marchello's coworker, calls them "punk-ass kids." "If you can drive a truck and chew gum, and if you can say 'yes sir, no sir,' you can be an all-star fracker," he said.

The crew attaches a blow-out preventer to regulate the pressure at the well head, then it blasts sand mixed with "slick water" down the hole with some 9,000 pounds of pressure per square inch—enough to shatter the shale surrounding the pipe. The liquid is called slick water because the actual texture is slimy—it contains 98 percent water but is mixed with a long list of chemicals, some highly toxic, and the combination of which is proprietary. The pressure forces the sand and slick water through the perforations in the pipe to create fissures in the rock. Crews pump 840 to 1,680 gallons of sand per minute down a conveyor belt. The sand fills in where the rock was eaten away by chemicals and acts as a spacer for the oil to seep through.

Once the fissures have been created, a mixture of slick water, sand, oil, natural gas, and naturally occurring saltwater known as flowback begins flowing back out of the well. This flowback has to be separated and divided into barrels. The water and sand are sent to a disposal well; the gas is flared, piped, or trucked away; and the oil goes to a refinery. The wireline crew then returns to perforate the next zone. The entire process can take 20 hours to three days, depending on how many delays occur.

As soon as the fracking team finishes with the last zone in a well, the completion phase begins, and Marchello and her coil tubing crew clean out the plugs and excess sand to help the oil flow. A coil crew is also called if a well suddenly isn't producing as much oil as expected—its job is to figure out why, just as a plumber diagnoses a clogged sink. "We try to wake it back up," explained Marchello. The coil crew trucks in a spool of 24,500 feet of bendable steel pipe, which would stretch nearly to the top of Mount Everest if rolled out, to send down the well. It takes skill and caution to keep the pipe steady and level while feeding it down the hole. "It's like squeezing a wet noodle through a straw," said Morgan. The coil tubing method is more efficient than other methods involving disjointed pipe segments that have to be individually fed down the hole. Once the pipe is set, the crew pumps in slick water and nitrogen gas to help lift debris and plugs out of the well.

Coil tubing requires more technical skill than some of the other jobs, and the crew is smaller, usually only six workers on site at a time. If everything goes smoothly, the job takes about six hours to two days, depending on the well depth. But there are frequently delays and setbacks. After the crew is finished, another crew installs a pumpjack to keep oil pumping up to the surface.

I asked Cindy Marchello if I could go to a job site with her, but she shook her head. She'd have to get permission from upper management, and, in general, oil companies were secretive and didn't like journalists poking around. She could get fired if she snuck me onto a site and her manager found out, but she said she'd ask for me. She did, however, manage to procure one of her old hard hats and coveralls for me "just in case" I managed to get clearance. On location, workers had to wear fire-resistant coveralls and gloves, a hard hat, and steel-toed boots. The steel theoretically would protect my feet from being chopped off or crushed if anything were to fall on them, but the tiny piece of metal on the boot's toe was hardly reassuring.

As I worked on gaining access to a well site, Marchello was becoming my window into the male-dominated world of the oil field. A month after we met, Marchello invited me to her man camp to meet her crew. They were in between jobs and had a rare day off. My photographer, Brad, was staying with me that week and tagged along.

We met Marchello and a male coworker in her trailer. The man introduced himself as Curtis Kenney. Kenney was short with narrow eyes, scruffy facial hair, and a receding hairline. He and Marchello seemed friendly with each other, but they sat on opposite sides of the room.

Kenney was an ex-felon from a tiny town 40 miles south of the Canadian border in northern Washington that had "about 100 people in it when everybody has company over," he said. He previously worked in logging but came to the oil field in 2010 after he lost his job. He had a wife, Anna Marie, who lived in Washington and had Parkinson's disease, and three grown kids. At 48, Kenney was one of the oldest guys on the crew. Everyone else, besides Marchello, was in their 20s or 30s.

Kenney and Marchello met when they both worked for Halliburton. The boss at the time put Marchello on Kenney's crew to punish him, and Kenney supervised her. He spoke about the time fondly. "A lot of new guys under me would take four hours to find a hammer; I couldn't trust them to do anything. But I could ask her and she'd get it done," he said, looking over at her.

Marchello and Kenney discussed how their jobs worked. But with Marchello's speed talking, Kenney attempting to talk over her, and oil field jargon mixed in—terms like "snubbers," "goosenecks," "wet kits," and "duck ponds"—my notes looked like hieroglyphics afterward. I had to interrupt to ask what they meant every few minutes.

Kenney turned to Brad. "If I told you to go get a stripper, what would you do?"

Brad seemed stunned by the question. "Uh . . ."

Marchello laughed. "It's a tool."

Kenney looked pleased with himself for stumping Brad. "Everybody's wife says, what are you doing getting strippers?"

"One time someone asked me what I was doing," Marchello said. "'I'm driving the truck because our stripper died,' I said. They were, like, 'Whaaat?'"

Kenney explained that a stripper is a rubber disk surrounding the coil tubing to "strip" away mud as the tube came out of the hole.

At one point, Kenney puffed up his chest and claimed he'd been "the deepest anyone had ever been in the Bakken."

Marchello nodded her head. "It's a big brag."

I asked them to explain. Kenney said on one job, their equipment went more than 20,000 feet into the earth, whereas most wells stopped around 10,000 to 15,000 feet. He took out a photo of the computer reading and showed it to me. REAL DEPTH 20193.23 FT, the numbers read.

Kenney and Marchello discussed how much they hated living in Williston. "There's a certain amount of riffraff here," Kenney said. "I wouldn't want this to happen to my hometown. The locals aren't nice here anymore."

Marchello nodded in agreement. "People are so tired. There's too much driving, waiting in line."

When they were out on a well site, they were told not to talk to the farmers. That job was for a "landman," the person who negotiated mineral rights contracts with landowners. "It's their job to keep the farmers happy, though they're not always successful," said Kenney. So for the most part, he and Marchello kept their distance from the locals, many of whom resented their presence.

As Marchello talked, I watched her and thought that she didn't seem 56 years old. It wasn't that she didn't look her age, but her mannerisms made her seem like she was in her 20s. There was a youthful cuteness to her. The way she became excited when she talked. Her rosy cheeks. Her laugh. I suspected this made her a target for many men's affections. I made a note to ask her if any crew members had crushes on her when Kenney wasn't in the room.

I was glad I saved the question. Because her biggest admirer, I found out later, was Kenney himself.

Marchello said she wanted to introduce me to the rest of the crew, especially a man named Mana Kula who was a field supervisor at C&J Energy Services and the leader of their crew. Marchello had met Kula two years earlier when they worked together at a company called

Cudd. We walked down the dirt path to trailer number 33 and Marchello knocked on the door. A Polynesian man opened it and she asked if Mana was home. The man invited us in. The room appeared much smaller than Marchello's trailer due to the many large men who were crowded into it.

One man introduced himself as Mana Kula, and I immediately understood why he had influence over the group. He was one of the largest men I'd ever seen. He towered over me, and was almost as wide as he was tall. His head was the size of a beach ball, and he had tan Polynesian skin and thick, silky black hair that framed his face in curly ringlets. His hands looked like they could wrap around mine three times. When he laughed, the entire trailer shook.

I also met Tui, who was married to Kula's older sister. Tui came to the oil field after his flooring contract business in California went bankrupt during the recession. He had nine children back home to support. A man named Larry stood next to him—Larry had worked with Kula at a previous company and was from California as well.

Marchello explained that Kula had taught her how to play poker, specifically Texas Hold'em. Kula asked me if I knew how to play.

I nodded—though I wasn't sure if my experience betting with nickels and dimes during casual games qualified me to play poker with a bunch of oil workers.

They were playing the following night, they said. Would I like to come?

14. TIOGA

The first time companies drilled for oil in North Dakota was way back in the 1910s, a time when other areas of the country were experiencing oil booms. The United States had become the primary source of oil, producing more than half the world's oil—and it stayed that way for another 40 years. Geologists suspected that North Dakota could have large reserves, but its unique geology proved to be more difficult to explore than in Texas and Oklahoma. One company, Pioneer Oil & Gas, drilled in the Williston area in 1916, but after four years, it found nothing and abandoned the operation.

More companies explored the area in the early 1920s after a geologist published a press notice titled "Possible Oil & Gas in North Dakota," but they too had little success. Most oil was deeper than in the productive areas of Texas, and technology was not advanced enough to reach the reserves below. One well achieved the shocking depth of 10,281 feet (by comparison, early oil wells in Texas were closer to 1,000 feet) in 1938, but still no oil came up. What the company didn't realize at the time was that it *had* drilled deep enough—but it was a few thousand feet off. This company wasn't the only unlucky one in the state. For years, engineers and wildcatters struggled to extract oil and find a producing well in North Dakota, bankrupting companies and their investors, many of whom were swindled into believing they were investing in a "gusher" and would become overnight millionaires. Because of the many dry wells, North Dakota's oil and gas exploration lagged far behind the rest of the country.

In 1951, that all changed, and the region had a taste of what oil could do. The first successful well was located in Williams County near Tioga, and 50 miles away from the town of Williston. The well was called Clarence Iverson No. 1, after the farmer who owned the land, and the drilling was led by Dr. Wilson Morrow Laird, the state geologist, for Amerada Petroleum Corporation.

Drilling began on September 3, 1950, and after initial tests around 10,500 feet, one pint of oil bubbled up. Laird was thrilled, but he asked his workers to place the oil in a jar and hide it out of sight. Laird didn't want anyone to know he might be onto something. He continued drilling to the lowest possible depth, finally stopping around 11,700 feet, when the high pressure became too dangerous. Due to the harsh winter that year, the well tests took months longer than expected. But on April 4, 1951, on a clear, calm day, with melting drifts of snow surrounding the well site, the first economically producible oil gushed up the well. The crew collected more than 300 barrels in 17 hours. It was a historic moment for North Dakota. "We will not soon forget that hectic day of April 4, 1951," wrote Charles S. Agey, an assistant geologist on the site at the time, "and electrifying news that North Dakota was now an oil-producing state was spread to the corners of the earth."

As the oil began to flow, someone yelled, "Light the flare!" and a worker tossed up a flaming, oil-soaked rag into the air to ignite the gas flare. The well produced one of the largest gas flares anyone had ever seen—some 30 feet high and visible from miles away—it was certainly a unique spectacle for the region. A large crowd quickly gathered. "The glare in the sky had drawn several hundred interested spectators," wrote Bill Shemorry, the photographer for the *Williston Press Graphic*, who covered the event that night. "The drilling rig and surrounding area were lighted by a huge gas flare. It was almost as if it were daylight. . . . The silver derrick was illuminated by the light of the flare and stood out in stark detail against the black night sky." *Life* magazine, *U.S. News & World Report*, and many other national publications covered the news. Laird quickly rose to fame throughout the country for his discovery. Two years later, on the original site, a plaque was placed that read: THIS WILLISTON BASIN DISCOVERY CLARENCE IVERSON NO. 1 OPENED A NEW ERA FOR NORTH DAKOTA AND REAFFIRMED THE CONFIDENCE OF HER PEOPLE IN THE OPPORTUNITIES AND FUTURE OF THIS GREAT STATE. The location continued to produce oil for 28 years until the old casing collapsed beyond repair.

North Dakota had rarely been the subject of national news, and the pride was palpable throughout the state. Leon "Tude" Gordon, one of the workers on the site who analyzed the original pint of oil, later created popular oil field bumper stickers, including OIL FIELD TRASH AND PROUD OF IT! and STRIVING TO KEEP AMERICA RED, WHITE AND BLUE WITH GAS AND OIL.

The 1951 discovery sparked western North Dakota's first oil boom. Other areas of the state were explored, some with more success than others. The Bakken layers were discovered in 1953 and were named after farmer Henry Bakken, whose property in Tioga had one of the first wells. Some 150 oil operators and hundreds of laborers traveled to the region, living wherever they could—granaries, sheds, garages—and overcrowding the small towns. "The [newcomers] and their families jammed community services, crowded schools, wore out roads . . . gas flares lit up the night," wrote Elwyn Robinson in *History of North Dakota*. By the fall of 1953, 800 people were living in trailers in Williston. And the small town at the hub of the activity, Tioga, grew 250 percent in three years. Companies began leasing mineral rights from landowners as quickly as they could. Some landowners sold their rights for as little as 62 cents an acre, not knowing the worth of the earth below them. Other farmers were better informed, and a few tracts went for $2,000 an acre. By the end of 1952, nearly two-thirds of the state had been leased. Within 10 years, 2,806 wells were drilled, and North Dakota became the tenth-highest producing state in the United States.

Oil production continued to increase in the state until 1966. That year marked a steady drop in production when companies failed to discover new oil to replace the natural decline of their current wells. Due to the depth of the oil—many pools lay at 14,000 feet—wells were incredibly expensive to drill, and the state's remote location increased the cost of transporting the oil.

Production didn't pick up again until 1974, when the Organization of the Petroleum Exporting Countries (OPEC), the alliance of mostly Arab oil-producing countries, imposed an oil embargo and significantly increased the price of oil worldwide, making exploration once again profitable in many parts of the country, including North Dakota. The state went through another boom after two productive oil fields—the Charlson-Silurian Pool and the Little Knife Field—and a number of other smaller fields were discovered. In 1981, a new record of 834 wells were drilled, and production peaked three years later at 52.6 million barrels. But this boom was short-lived. Around 1983, overproduction caused a major price drop, with prices plummeting from about $40 a barrel in 1980 to $12 a barrel in 1986. Companies quickly downsized and reduced drilling operations; many went bankrupt or moved out of the state.

During the 1980s boom, Williston became an oil field hub. The town added thousands of people, and the city bought land and borrowed money to build infrastructure to keep up with the growth. When the bust came, Williston was stuck with a mountain of debt, which at one point consumed 40 percent of the city's budget. "That boom went bust overnight, and it was really hard on the city," said Chuck Wilder, who grew up in Williston. "A lot of people went bankrupt and houses were lost. It was kind of dark for a while." Walmart came to Williston in the early 1990s, and the town began to resemble many other small towns across America—a vacant downtown, few jobs, struggling small businesses, and a declining population.

After North Dakota's 1980s boom, most people gave up on the state. Despite promising beginnings and two booms, North Dakota wasn't an oil-producing region like Texas or Wyoming.

Meanwhile, a process called fracking, the drilling method using a combination of sand, water, and chemicals to break apart rock formations, began to garner attention.

The fracking process itself wasn't new. The practice of fracturing rock to extract oil was first tried back in the 1860s by a Pennsylvania driller, Colonel Edward A. L. Roberts, who dropped a torpedo down a well to break apart the rock formation. Not surprisingly, the work was highly dangerous, and workers could be blown to bits if anything went wrong.

The method had mixed results for extracting oil and gas, and few improvements were made until 1947, when Stanolind Oil and Halliburton, the rising oil field service company that specialized in cementing wells at the time, experimented with fracturing rock to tap into natural gas reserves. The companies used compressed nitrogen to pump chemical-infused foam down the well to break apart the shale rock.

The method was time-consuming and expensive, however, and was used infrequently until George P. Mitchell, a Texas billionaire, and his company Mitchell Energy & Development spent nearly two decades developing the fracking process to access the natural gas reserves in the North Texas Barnett Shale formation. Mitchell focused on gas because, at the time in the 1980s and 1990s, searching for oil seemed like a losing battle. The Barnett Shale area had been abandoned by large energy companies, such as ExxonMobil and Chevron, which were off looking for fossil fuels in Africa, Latin America, and Asia. They were searching for large pockets of oil or gas that they could easily, and relatively cheaply, extract with a vertical drill. But Mitchell persisted, betting everything he had on finding a way to extract natural gas from the tight shale rock for a profit.

Instead of using expensive foams and gels, Mitchell Energy used "slick water"—thousands of gallons of water mixed with friction-reducing chemicals—and combined it with thousands of pounds of manufactured silicate sand to force the rock to fracture. The method gained recognition in the late 1990s and quickly spread to large natural gas reserves, such as the Marcellus Shale formation in Pennsylvania. Today, some consider Mitchell's impact on American history similar to that of Henry Ford or Alexander Graham Bell.

Not far from Mitchell's operations, a company called Oryx Energy was experimenting with horizontal drilling in the Texas Austin Chalk area. The method was a variation on diagonal drilling—a drill bit is sent a few thousand feet down, then turns and drills hundreds of feet horizontally, unlocking huge reserves of oil. But when Oryx tried the technology in other, denser rock formations, the results were not nearly as impressive. Horizontal drilling was briefly tested in North Dakota's Bakken and seemed encouraging—the success rate for wells drilled in certain areas was between 97 and 100 percent. But despite the high chance of finding oil, the wells were expensive to drill, and the oil didn't flow as easily as other wells, so companies quickly abandoned their efforts. "We didn't have fracking capabilities," Oryx's geologist Kenneth Bowdon told author Gregory Zuckerman in *The Frackers*. "That was the magic ingredient missing for a technological breakthrough."

Many drillers, including Mitchell, determined it was too technically challenging to drill through the dense, deep rock, and gave up on North Dakota. In 1995, the U.S. Geological Survey (USGS) estimated there were only 151 million barrels of oil in the Bakken—or about eight days of oil consumption in the United States. In the late 1990s, however, a

Denver geochemist from the USGS studied the Bakken shale and came up with a wildly different number: He thought 413 billion barrels of oil sat in the layers below—nearly 3,000 times the USGS's estimate—but his research was never peer reviewed, and most people thought his number was completely overblown.

In 2001, North Dakota's state geologist, John P. Bluemle, saw potential as well. "A large volume of oil and gas remains trapped within the Bakken Formation across much of northwestern North Dakota," he wrote. "However, economic volumes of oil or gas cannot be produced using today's technology. . . . Perhaps some other new technology will be developed. . . . If this happens, many wells will be drilled for the oil and gas in the Bakken Formation."

Despite Bluemle's prediction, few people were up for this challenge. It wasn't until 2004, when Harold Hamm, a rising oil tycoon who came from a poor sharecropper family in rural Oklahoma, decided to test horizontal drilling and hydraulic fracking technologies on the largely forgotten formations in North Dakota, that it became clear the technology had the potential to revolutionize the U.S. oil industry.

Hamm had studied the Bakken area for years and convinced investors to take a chance on him. Hamm's company, Continental Resources, drilled its first well in North Dakota in March 2004 with a few feet of snow still on the ground. To cut costs, the company used a preexisting well in Divide County that had been abandoned in 1981; instead of drilling from the surface, they only had to extend the well, then drill horizontally before fracking it. The well produced oil, but other wells nearby generated mere trickles. Soon the company experimented with fracking wells in stages. Workers would seal off sections of the well and send the fracking fluid into a smaller, pressurized area. The technique was expensive—about $8 million per well versus $4 million for a well fracked all at once, but the results were promising and unlocked significantly more oil from the shale layers. In total, the first batch of wells produced just 7,000 barrels of oil a day for the company, less than 1 percent of what ExxonMobil produced daily, but it was enough to keep going. Hamm tried to keep his efforts quiet while his company leased cheap land. Nearly a decade later, Hamm became the twenty-fourth richest man in America, with a net worth of more than $18 billion, and owned more oil under U.S. soil than any other American.

Another company, EOG Resources, once a division of the infamous Enron, also had begun leasing land in North Dakota's Mountrail County and on the Fort Berthold Indian Reservation. EOG drilled its first well in April 2006, and it was a disappointment, producing less than 100 barrels of oil a day. But the next wells were huge successes, with some producing over 5,000 barrels a day. Each well seemed to be better than the last. Other drillers and industry insiders began to pay attention.

Though companies in the Bakken were extracting more and more oil, they remained quiet about how much oil they were discovering, and the rest of the country barely noticed.

As far as most Americans were concerned, oil production on U.S. soil had slowed to a trickle. Once a world powerhouse in oil production, by 2005, the United States produced about half what it once did in 1970 and imported a record 60 percent of its oil. The traditional pools of oil that produced so many gushers in the 1950s were drying up, and a large portion of U.S. oil production came from offshore fields along the Gulf Coast.

Americans had to look hard for any mention of U.S. oil development in the news. The only time "oil" and "U.S." seemed to appear in the same sentence was when discussing America's declining oil production or fear-inducing literature about "peak oil"—the idea that worldwide oil production would soon peak and decline rapidly, causing global populations to spiral into depressionlike conditions and starvation. Essentially the message was this: The world faced complete economic and societal collapse if we didn't find more oil reserves quickly or transition to alternative energy.

At the same time, public opinion of foreign oil was at an extreme low. Evidence was mounting that oil was a major factor in the U.S. invasion of Iraq. Before the invasion, Iraq's oil industry was nationalized and off limits to Western oil companies. But a few months before President George W. Bush made his "mission accomplished" speech in 2003, Vice President Dick Cheney, the former chief operating officer of Halliburton, organized a meeting with representatives from Exxon-Mobil, Chevron, ConocoPhillips, and Halliburton, among others, to discuss opening Iraq's oil industry to outsiders. A decade later, the industry was largely dominated by foreign firms. During a roundtable discussion in late 2007, General John Abizaid, the former commander for all U.S. forces in the Middle East, said: "Of course it's about oil, we can't really deny that."

After more than 3,500 U.S. soldiers lost their lives in Iraq and U.S. efforts to stabilize the area spiraled out of control, Americans were angry about the war, foreign oil, and U.S. dependence on the Middle East. But U.S. consumption of fossil fuels was as voracious as ever. In 2007, the United States consumed nearly 21 million barrels of oil a day, nearly three times the amount of any other country. With high demand and tightening supply, the price of oil climbed quickly. By May 2007, U.S. gasoline prices reached a record high of over $3 a gallon.

A number of energy executives had turned to alternative energy sources such as natural gas. Advancements in fracking had opened up large natural gas reserves in Pennsylvania, Wyoming, Utah, and Texas, and many experts touted natural gas as America's energy future. But as a glut of natural gas on the market caused prices to fall, oil became the crown jewel. At over $90 a barrel at the end of 2007 and rising quickly, more wildcatters and energy executives lusted for black gold.

Then in 2008, the secret was out. The USGS released a new survey updating its earlier estimate of 151 million barrels in the Bakken

Formation, which lies under western North Dakota and extends into Montana and Canada, to a potential 4.3 billion barrels of recoverable oil—more than in any other formation in the lower 48 states. Those who had doubted North Dakota's potential were shocked, and America finally started to pay attention to the state.

In addition to North Dakota, fracking unlocked oil fields in Texas, California, Louisiana, Oklahoma, Colorado, and many other states, opening reserves beyond the wildest dreams of energy experts. In less than a decade, the United States cut its oil imports in half and became the world's largest crude oil producer, surpassing Russia and Saudi Arabia. Today, 9 out of 10 oil and gas wells in the United States use hydraulic fracturing, and more than 15 million Americans live within a mile of a well that has been fracked. China, Argentina, Brazil, and other countries—all with large shale formations—began studying the technology, looking for their own oil and gas bonanzas. Even as oil prices fell in 2015, Harold Hamm remained confident as ever: "For the next 50 years, we can expect to reap the benefits of the shale revolution. It's the biggest thing that ever happened to America."

And western North Dakota lay in the center of it all.

North Dakota's Bakken region, about the size of Delaware, accounted for 40 percent of the growth in U.S. oil production. Some oil executives, like Hamm, believed that government estimates were too low, and there were closer to 900 billion barrels of oil buried deep in the state—more than in Saudi Arabia. Between 2007 and 2014, oil production skyrocketed 900 percent, and if you lined up the 8,500 wells that were drilled or fracked in the state, they'd stretch all the way around the earth. North Dakota became the number-two oil producing state in the nation, just behind Texas, and North Dakota alone produced more oil than OPEC member Ecuador. The pristine prairie transformed almost overnight into a maze of heavy industry and oil wells, with thousands of workers relocating to the state. The drilling was so frenzied and chaotic that David Petraeus, the former CIA director and U.S. Army general, referred to the region as a "war zone" during his visit in 2013.

A major boom—harking back to California's 1849 Gold Rush—was under way. But the fracking process itself was also falling under intense criticism. The word became infamous after the 2010 film *Gasland* showed residents from Pennsylvania to Wyoming lighting methane-contaminated tap water on fire due to nearby natural gas drilling. The public began to question the method as energy companies ramped up activity. What, they asked, was actually happening to the land as companies cashed in on their states?

15. DONNY NELSON

For farmers like Donny Nelson, the drilling activity began slowly. The surveyors came in with their tripods and maps to poke around on their land. Then the bulldozers came to clear away crops or vegetation. Then the trucks and crews arrived to install tanks and pipelines to prep the site for drilling. Usually once one company drilled a well or installed a pipeline, others came knocking. It was only later, after the drilling had already begun, that farmers realized just how disruptive the process was.

For one, there was the flaring. Nearly every well had a gas flare—most rose at least 10 feet into the sky and burned off millions of cubic feet of toxic natural gas into the atmosphere every day. Although companies in other states produced and sold their natural gas, oil companies in North Dakota burned away about one-fifth to one-third of the natural gas they were extracting, or some $100 million of it every month, emitting about as much carbon dioxide a year as a million cars on the road.

More than 60 types of pollutants have been identified downwind from flaring operations, including benzene, methane, propylene, and butane—many of which have been associated with cancer, birth defects, and organ damage. "We know that they're giving off volatile compounds into the air," said Nelson. "And if you don't flare the gas, it'll kill you."

Aerial images of North Dakota at night showed the entire state lit up from flares, as if the state were on fire. And in 2014, a researcher at the University of Michigan noticed a troubling increase in the global levels of ethane in the atmosphere, a natural gas that increases the ozone layer at the earth's surface and causes dangerous levels of air pollution. He decided to look into the Bakken region as a possible source of the rise. Researchers measured that the small region was emitting 250,000 tons of ethane every year—or about 2 percent of total global ethane levels.

There was another danger around the wells—the presence of hydrogen sulfide (H_2S), a highly toxic gas that can kill humans instantly in large doses. H_2S is produced when organic matter breaks down. The gas is colorless, and in low levels, it smells like rotten eggs; in high doses, it paralyzes your sense of smell—essentially giving no warning that you're minutes away from losing consciousness. One well by Nelson's house vented off H_2S gas every day. At first the company didn't tell Nelson about it, and he was furious when he found out. Workers began texting him when it was happening so he knew to avoid the area and not move his cattle there. "The guys working told me, 'Oh, we won't do it if the wind is blowing in your direction.' Well, what if the wind changes?" he asked me as we drove through his farm one day, knowing I couldn't give him an answer.

In a 1993 Environmental Protection Agency (EPA) report, researchers found significantly higher levels of H_2S at oil and gas wells in North Dakota than in other states. Levels at a few wells near Theodore Roosevelt National Park were 125 times higher than averages in oil-producing areas of Louisiana. More recently, multiple trains carrying oil from the North Dakota Bakken region have exploded, one of which killed 47 people. Explosions of traditional crude oil containers are extremely rare, and many hazardous materials experts speculated that H_2S was to blame, given the force of the explosions and how difficult the fires were to extinguish. Pipeline company Enbridge Energy Partners threatened to shut down one of its North Dakota rail facilities because there was too much H_2S in the crude oil being loaded there.

There was also concern about water contamination. Nelson continued to drink the water that came out of his faucet, which was piped in from Lake Sakakawea. It was a prospect that might horrify anti-fracking activists. Back in 2005, when fracking for natural gas was growing rapidly, the Bush-Cheney administration passed a bill that exempted fracking operations from the Safe Drinking Water Act. Companies were not required to disclose the exact chemicals they used, as such disclosures could reveal trade secrets. Even the pioneer of fracking, George P. Mitchell himself, advocated for more regulation before he passed away in 2013. He wrote that there were "legitimate concerns" about the rapid expansion of fracking and its "impact on water, air and climate—concerns that industry has attempted to gloss over."

Brenda Jorgenson, who lived 50 miles north of Nelson, was cleaning jars one day when dirty water gushed out of her faucet. Crews had fracked an oil well on her land a few months before. She had no way of proving there was a connection, but the incident scared her—her well was her only source of drinking water. She saved a jar of the tainted water in her refrigerator and tried to get it tested, but most places she called were unaffordable (one company quoted her $1,500), didn't know what to test the water for, or needed the sample sent to the lab within hours of the incident. Though the water from her faucet eventually cleared up, she now buys bottled water for her grandkids and pregnant daughter. She and her husband, however, continue to drink tap water.

Lynn Helms, the director for the North Dakota Department of Mineral Resources, claimed in 2011 that the Health Department had received multiple complaints from landowners about health concerns, but he couldn't disclose any of that information to the public. "I believe six or seven individuals have brought concerns about health effects to our attention," he said that year. But it was "personal information which falls under HIPAA [Health Insurance Portability and Accountability Act of 1996] regulations. Once an individual is alleging health problems as a result of oil and gas operations and once the Health Department responds and begins to work with them on blood tests and that sort of thing, that's highly confidential information. I'm not sure it will ever be made public."

The EPA has documented cases of groundwater contamination from fracking since the early 1980s. A nationwide 2015 study found evidence that all stages of fracking can lead to water contamination, including when fracking fluids are injected into the well, and during procedures to store or dispose of wastewater. Groundwater can also be contaminated from surface spills or pipeline leaks—the study concluded that the most common cause of fracking fluid spills was from equipment failure, such as valves and blowout preventers. Researchers found that public drinking water systems for more than 8.6 million people in the United States were located within a mile of at least one fracked well.

Contamination can also occur from leaks in the cement casing of a well, causing liquids or methane gas to rise up around the casing walls and migrate into underground water wells or aquifers. According to Cornell University professor Anthony Ingraffea, who has studied fracking's effect on cement casings in Pennsylvania, shale gas wells were six times more likely to leak methane than conventional wells, and he estimated that 40 percent of wells in heavily drilled parts of northeast Pennsylvania would eventually leak. Pennsylvania receives hundreds of complaints every year from locals about water contamination, and nearly 300 cases of pollution had been confirmed by 2017. The state's Department of Environmental Protection has issued numerous fines to local gas companies for methane migration. However, oil and gas industry leaders continue to assert that there is no evidence for groundwater contamination, and they fund studies to try to disprove the research. Few water wells are tested for methane or fracking chemicals before drilling begins, they argue, and without this data, there is no proof that the companies are responsible.

The oil and gas industry has spent millions attacking Josh Fox and his film *Gasland*, which was nominated for an Oscar in 2011. When you search for "fracking" on Google, some of the first articles that come up are pro-fracking pieces and trailers for films that claim to debunk *Gasland*. The oil and gas industry bumps up these search results by paying for Google keywords. (BP admitted to using similar tactics during the Gulf oil spill to combat negative publicity.) The oil and gas industry has also attacked journalists at *The New York Times* and *Rolling Stone* who published critical reports on fracking.

Of course, North Dakota has a different geological makeup from Pennsylvania. Oil companies and state researchers claim that North Dakota isn't at the same risk for water contamination from fracking. A common argument I heard is that wells in North Dakota are drilled much deeper and thus, in theory, are less likely to affect water aquifers that sit 200 to 1,000 feet below the surface. However, even "shallow" wells in Pennsylvania are drilled at least 5,000 feet deep, way below aquifers. Another argument is that the levels of methane gas in the wells in North Dakota are lower. Since most companies in the Bakken are drilling for oil, there shouldn't be the same problems as those that occur in the Marcellus Shale formation where gas is being drilled. While it's true that the Marcellus formation holds much higher levels of natural gas (149 trillion cubic feet of recoverable gas versus 12 trillion cubic feet in North Dakota's Bakken), even low levels of leakage can contaminate aquifers.

What few people realize is that new fracking technology has been happening for only a few years within North Dakota's unique geologic structure, and there has been little research on the local environmental effects. "The more we experiment with underground drilling, the more we discover that 'impermeable' layers can be surprisingly permeable and fractures in the rock can be interlinked in unexpected ways," wrote *National Geographic* journalist Edwin Dobb. Injecting fracking wastewater deep into the earth had even set off earthquakes in other parts of the country. Donny Nelson feared the environmental issues in North Dakota's oil patch wouldn't be much different from those in other states. "My biggest fear is water. We don't know what they're going to do to our water yet," he said. "They're drilling through every single one of our aquifers, and if you have any failure, man or machine, it's going to contaminate that aquifer. They'll sit and argue all they want that there's so much rock between it that it's never going to happen. But it's going to happen—it has across the U.S. before, so why should we believe that it's not going to here?"

Nelson and other farmers wanted to limit the damage as much as possible. In 2006, Nelson and his neighbors fought with legislators to move wells farther away from homes—from 350 feet away to 500 feet away. The legislation passed, but 500 feet was still uncomfortably close—and oil storage tanks or generators could be even closer.

Consider the case of Nelson's neighbors, Frank and Wanda Leppell. I visited them on a rainy Monday afternoon at their modest one-story farmhouse. They lived at the end of a long dirt road, with two dogs and three cats and seven horses in the backyard. ("Don't go in the bathroom," Wanda told me when I came in the house. "The cat took a dump.") Rusted farm equipment was scattered across their front yard. They poured me a cup of coffee, and we gazed out their front window from the dining room table at an oil well that sat a quarter mile from their house. Above the hypnotic bobbing of the oil wellhead, a vertical flame spewed into the sky. "It sounds like a blowtorch," said Wanda. "When you go to bed tonight, put a blowtorch in your bedroom, crank it up, and see how well you sleep."

She said the flare was tiny compared to what it once was. "It looked like the field was on fire," she said. The Leppells owned 30 acres and leased about 4,000 acres of cropland and pasture, but they didn't own what was underground. Twice Wanda had woken up to the house filled with gas. She and Frank often felt vibrations from drilling and some-times had to leave just to take a break from the smell. "There's a chemical, something in the drilling mud that smells like rotten egg," Wanda said. "I don't know if it's bad for your health."

The Leppells likely wouldn't be getting a good night's rest anytime soon. As we talked, another company was already clearing dirt to build a well 730 feet from their house. "I can't imagine what *that's* going to sound like," said Wanda. The edge of the pad, a large clearing for the wells, sat up against their chicken coop. The Leppells had been push-ing state legislators to set wells at least 1,000 feet from homes, but so far they had had little success. "There is no reason they have to put these so close to people's homes," Frank told state senators at a hear-ing in early 2013 when farmers tried to pass a setback bill. A lobbyist from Petro-Hunt, an oil and gas extraction company headquartered in Texas, spoke in opposition to the bill, and it never passed. Theodora Bird Bear, a tribal member from Fort Berthold Indian Reservation, also spoke in support of the setback bill at the hearing: "I support my neigh-bors' efforts to protect the health and public safety of western North Dakota residents," she said. "Right now, well blow-outs, explosions, or fires from well sites can potentially occur 500 feet from the door of any resident. As legislators, do you support this?" The answer, it seemed, was yes.

16. TOM STAKES

In addition to sleeping on Atlanta's streets, Tom Stakes was homeless another time before arriving in Williston. He once lived in a cave near Red River, New Mexico. At night temperatures could drop below zero, and he lived in constant fear of mountain lions and bears that roamed nearby. "Bears would come and piss all around the front of the cave. I'd throw rocks at 'em," he said. So according to him, being homeless in North Dakota wasn't so bad.

But others might disagree. At the campground, some nights it would rain—piercing, sideways raindrops as big as gumballs that would smack into you as you were walking—and Stakes's tent would fill up with so much water that all his bedding would be soaked. One storm brought 60-mile-per-hour winds and tornado warnings across the region. It knocked down trees and branches all over the campground. One camper's tent was crushed by a tree, but luckily no one was sleeping in it at the time. That night, Stakes and his friend Web held onto the walls of their tent for two hours to keep the flimsy canvas from blowing away. Web had woken up first and shaken Stakes awake. "Tom! We'll never make it!" he yelled over the howling wind.

"Just hold that tent!" screamed Stakes as they grabbed each corner. Neither of them slept much that night.

Stakes's favorite nights were when he and the Andresen family scraped together enough to buy a case of beer and cook a feast on the campsite grill.

Three days after I met him, Stakes was summoned to appear in court for a DUI charge. Earlier that month, he was speeding down Highway 2 in Williston at 1:30 a.m. after drinking at the bars, going 53 mph in a 40-mph zone. He was pulled over and had no license or proof of insurance with him. When the officer asked Stakes to count backward, he said "4, 2, 3, 1." When he was asked to walk in a line, he stumbled twice. When the officer asked Stakes to stand on one leg, he complied, but swayed and almost lost his balance. A Breathalyzer test showed that his blood alcohol level was 0.179, more than twice the legal limit. The officer strapped handcuffs on Stakes and put him in the back of the patrol car.

At the Williston jail, Stakes was issued a faded, black-and-white striped uniform, which made him look like a caricature in an old Wild West film, and orange Crocs, and he spent the night there. He couldn't afford the $500 bail, but the jail was at capacity, and officers needed beds for the growing number of criminals they arrested daily. In the county, DUI arrests had increased by over 1,000 percent since 2008. Police released Stakes after he agreed to certain conditions under a program called 24/7 Sobriety: He could not possess or use alcohol for two weeks and had to return to the jail twice a day for Breathalyzer testing—once between 7 a.m. and 8 a.m. and again between 7 p.m. and 8 p.m. On the second day, just after 7 a.m., Stakes failed the test. He'd been drinking the previous night and had a blood alcohol level of .065. He was arrested and spent the next two weeks in jail.

After his release, Stakes and the Andresen family were running out of time to find alternate housing. The park's closure date was September 1, and other campgrounds were closing soon for the winter as well. By mid-August, no one had figured out where they would live. Stakes seemed the most worried about it, as he didn't want to go back to sleeping in his truck and hiding from the police. "It's limited what we can do," he explained. "The cops give ya trouble. Maybe I'll move to California where it's warmer in the winter." The camp's supervisor, a plump, husky woman, knew most of her campers were homeless. Since she was retiring at the end of the summer, she threw a party for everyone on the last day.

I arrived at the party in late afternoon. Stakes approached me and gave me a long hug, squeezing me tight. I could smell the alcohol on his breath. About 30 people sat around on picnic tables under a large wooden pavilion. One table was full of food—potato salad, hamburgers, hot dogs, baked beans. Stakes pulled me over to the group and yelled, "Everybody! This is Blaire, my future wife."

I laughed uncomfortably and shook my head, trying to indicate to the crowd he was joking. "Nope, not true," I said. No one seemed to be paying attention. Stakes was drinking a can of Budweiser and handed me a Straw-Ber-Rita in a can—a new sugary alcohol product from Budweiser. As soon as I opened it, bees swarmed the can and one fell in, drowning in the sticky red liquid. We sat on top of a picnic table facing the group. I saw the Andresen family across the pavilion and I waved to Heidi. Billy and her kids were outside closer to the lake. I talked to a couple who had recently arrived to the campground from a small town outside of Chicago. The guy bragged that he stole his tent from Walmart. "They're just a corporate face," he said flippantly. "They won't even notice it's gone." Then he asked if we knew where to get marijuana.

Stakes laughed. "No, but we can get you some crystal," he said, changing his tone to a serious one. He paused, then laughed and told them he was joking. The couple looked disappointed.

Outside the pavilion, Heidi caught a frog and held it in her hand to show to her grandson, Damian, who had ketchup smeared on his cheek. A group of children who wanted to touch the frog surrounded her. Mike sat on top of a picnic table taking long draws from a cigarette and stared out at the lake. The sun was still high in the sky and there was a light breeze. The air was already crisper than just a few weeks ago. Summer was coming to an end.

The next morning, the campers folded up their tents, packed up their belongings, and left, leaving only small imprints of flat grass where they'd once lived.

17. WILLISTON

The first day I pulled into Williston, I had no idea what to expect. I entered through the west end of town, driving past a man camp and through a little town called Trenton. I didn't know it at the time, but it was the same man camp where Cindy Marchello and her crew lived. WILLISTON 7 MILES, the sign said. Nearby an abandoned bulldozer sat lonely on the prairie. As I reached the outskirts of town, an oil tanker truck flew past me, going about 70 miles per hour in a 55-mile-per-hour zone, rattling my little car like a glass of water during plane turbulence. Flat, boxy industrial buildings came into view as I drove over a hill, and I saw my first gas flare. Located on a dirt clearing surrounded by prairie grass, the flame roared out of a tall pipe, burning 20 feet into the blue sky.

As I neared the center of town, I passed a diner called Gramma Sharon's and a small makeshift trailer park. I had called this particular trailer park the previous week and discovered there was a long waiting list to live there. There was a newly remodeled hospital on my right and billboards advertising Carhartt work clothing and the local hardware store. At the intersection was a welcome sign that said WILLISTON: LET'S WORK TOGETHER! The left-hand turn signal at the intersection had gone out, so drivers waved and gestured to people when it was their time to go or just gunned their engines and hoped for the best.

All over town were billboards of the 10 Commandments—one was even prominently displayed next door to the local strip clubs. On the local radio, ads played about beer, car dealerships, employment-search sites, or Mitchell's Oil Field Service for "all your trucking, roustabout and crane needs." One ad wanted to convince lonely newcomers to attend church. "It's hard not knowing too many others here," a woman's voice said. "Perhaps you're staying home with young kids. I found some folks who welcomed me and my family. It was at my local United Methodist Church."

Businesses in town had tried to capitalize on the oil boom, building a man camp called Black Gold Williston Lodge, a restaurant called Wildcat Pizzeria, or a coffee stand called Boomtown Babes, with scantily clad women serving espresso. There were Williston tourism T-shirts with slogans like OIL FIELD TRASH; WHAT HAPPENS IN THE OIL FIELD . . . STAYS IN THE OIL FIELD; or PLEASE GOD, GIVE ME ONE MORE OIL BOOM. THIS TIME I PROMISE NOT TO PISS IT AWAY.

I camped at Lewis and Clark State Park 20 miles outside of Williston on my first night and waited until the next day to visit the trailer park, called Williston Village RV Resort, where I'd found an open space. It had recently opened and, as far as I could tell, it was the only place in town with availability.

The trailer park "resort" was 10 miles north of town and down an unpaved road. Approximately 200 campers lived on a swath of land the size of about two city blocks. The foundation had been laid for a laundry and shower building, but completion wasn't expected for another year. At night, semi truck drivers lined up along the park's perimeter to sleep, and the park was surrounded by oil wells. The flames from gas flares flickered along the horizon. There were no trees or landscaping of any kind, which kept the soil hard and cracked. It was just dust—more dust than I ever thought possible. Dry, gritty particles seeped into my eyes, my mouth, my hair. My laptop's keyboard was always covered with a film of dust that transferred onto my fingers when I typed. I washed my hands as often as I could, but it was never enough. The dust was always there, except when it rained. Then everything turned to mud.

I lived on lot number 305, which sat on the edge of a dirt embankment with a line of trailers below. I paid $795 a month, plus a $300 security deposit, to park my camper there. I had a view of the Love's gas station and a construction site. Next door, in lot 304, lived a family from Idaho. Their sparkling new Sandpiper trailer was about three times the size of mine and went for about $46,000 brand new. The woman who lived there looked close to my age. She had manicured nails, wore leggings and colorful tank tops, and drove a white Jeep Cherokee. She looked like a regular suburban young mom. When I saw her, which wasn't often, she was usually coming back from somewhere in the late afternoon. She'd carry her one-year-old daughter on her hip and walk quickly from her car into the trailer and close the blinds. I tried to talk to her a few times, but she always looked uncomfortable when I approached. Her husband was almost never home. Across from my trailer was a Hispanic family with two little kids, and on the other side of my lot was a middle-age couple. One night I watched them through their window, which was a few feet away from my trailer. They were sitting down at the table, facing each other, having an argument. The dim lighting and partly closed blinds blurred their facial expressions, but at one point the man threw up his hands and stormed out of the room. I watched the woman sit and stare at the papers on the table for what felt like a long time until she reached up and closed the blinds. Were they having financial troubles? I wondered. Or was this simply tension that builds between couples living in tiny quarters?

One evening after a long day of conducting interviews, I attempted to sit outside my trailer with a glass of wine to watch the sunset. There was no shade for miles, so I squeezed into a narrow sliver of shade the trailer made on the gravel. I heard a bird chirp and couldn't remember the last time I'd heard a bird call. I looked over in the direction the sound came from and saw a bird standing on the trailer's electricity meter, looking lost. The sun began to set. I watched tumbleweeds blow past my lot and down a ravine. Wisps of clouds blanketed the sky and turned bright red. A soft orange light settled over the Love's gas station in the distance. It wasn't quite like the prairie sunsets I imagined. As I sipped my wine, I wondered if the prairie life I'd read about would now be known for oil rigs and infrastructure and dust. A truck barreled by and blew a cloud of dirt into my plastic wine cup. Mosquitoes buzzed around my neck. I sighed, went back inside the trailer, and closed the window.

A few nights after I moved in, I experienced my first North Dakota storm. Thunder barreled through the prairie. Fierce winds, lightning, and rain were close behind. My trailer shook and the floor vibrated with each gust of wind. I huddled inside and imagined the trailer with myself and all of my belongings sliding down the hill and into the mud.

Williston's growing pains were apparent. The original "downtown Williston," where many retail buildings sat empty, seemed hidden. I often set up my office at a local diner downtown, and some days I saw only five other customers, many of whom were elderly. Surrounding the small downtown were two-lane highways, gas stations, and a few chain stores. They enveloped the mini downtown, almost swallowing it whole.

There was construction everywhere—a building frenzy had taken over the town. On average, nearly five new housing units went up every day in Williston. The city approved $353 million worth of building permits for new construction in 2013. And 9,000 man camp units speckled the city's outskirts.

Most people hung out north of downtown, at restaurants and chains like Walmart, McDonald's, Subway, and Taco John's. Almost every business had HELP WANTED signs. Applebee's was the most popular restaurant in town, with customers waiting hours for a table on Friday night. Walmart was more of a hub than Williston's downtown. It was always busy, with long lines at every cash register. On Sunday, which was a common day off in the oil field, crowds of people stood outside waiting for the store to open at noon. When the glass doors slid open, people rushed in with their shopping carts, swarming the aisles and collecting groceries and supplies. There were women with too-tight polyester tops and children running around their legs and groups of men still dressed in work coveralls and mud-splattered caps, looking tired and perplexed as they roamed the aisles alone. Shelves were often emptied within hours, and the overwhelmed employees stood back, exhausted, as customers tore through the displays they'd finished moments ago.

To the west of downtown was the public library and, next to it, the oil company–funded playground with the oil-pump teeter-totter, its shiny black metal frame bobbing up and down. The slide was funded by Enbridge Pipelines and the bridge by Halliburton. The jungle gym was named "Williston Basin Refinery."

Inside the library was a bulletin board with the sign LOCAL HIGH RISK SEX OFFENDERS and the mug shots of nine men staring back, plus a colorful explanatory poster of an oil rig and its components and a blown-up map of drilling activity in the Bakken. A few men slept in chairs behind rows of bookshelves or scrolled through websites on library computers.

Then there were the trucks. I'd never seen so many trucks in my life—Super Duty Ford 250s with turbo engines, Chevy Colorados with mud splattered on the tailgate, RAMs, GMCs, Chryslers, trucks with bumper sticker slogans like NORTH DAKOTA: GOIN' DEEP AND PUMPIN' HARD and clouds of diesel exhaust spewing out of rear pipes. Some vehicles were entirely caked with layers of dust and mud, with only a small patch of windshield cleared for the driver to see the road. Eighteen-wheeled monstrosities seemed to be around every corner and at every stoplight. My first week in town, I pulled up next to a semi truck at one of the town's main intersections and saw two burly men sitting in the front seat. The man in the passenger seat sat with his arm out the window and his T-shirt sleeve rolled up, revealing heavily inked skin, faded blue-and-black shapes that I couldn't make out. He noticed me and grinned, one side of his lip rising higher than the other. He poked his friend and pointed at me. "How's it goin' there?" he yelled out the window, grinning wider. The light changed, and I sped off as quickly as I could.

It was noticeable how outnumbered I was. Men roamed the aisles of the grocery store by themselves, filling their carts with chips, Coors Light, and frozen burger patties. They clustered in groups at the local diner, their baritone laughter rising above the clanking dishes and restaurant chatter.

I was relieved to see a few other women around. Although everyone in line with me was male, the checker at the grocery store was a middle-aged woman who smiled as she bagged my zucchini. A waitress at the local diner took my order and hurried off to the kitchen. The cheerful gas station clerk, with adorable dimples and perfectly straight teeth, looked about 19 years old. I felt relieved. These women are surviving here, I thought. Maybe I can too.

18. ROUGH RIDER MAN CAMP

For the poker game, we were told to arrive at 7 p.m. and bring beer to trailer number 33. My photographer, Brad, and I picked up a six-pack of Shiner Bock. I figured it was a safe choice. Not too fancy but not too cheap.

We walked into the trailer and saw five guys and Cindy Marchello sitting around a round laminate table. Two guys sat on camping chairs, and another one had pulled up a leather recliner to the table. Mana Kula sat next to Marchello, his size making his chair look like it was meant for children. Curtis Kenney, whom I met the other day at Marchello's trailer, sat across from them, wearing a shirt that said AS AMERICAN AS IT GETS.

Tui, whom I also met the other day, sat next to another Tongan guy named Sam. Sam was from Utah and was married to Kula's cousin. Kula's iPhone rested on the table playing pop music. We presented our six-pack and they laughed. "You got the fancy kind," said Kula. Everyone else was drinking Bud Light or Corona. Kula pulled out a Corona bottle, ripped off the cap with this teeth, and passed it to me. I stared at it dumbfounded and mumbled a thank you.

We were playing Texas Hold'em, tournament style. Each player bought in with $5, a surprisingly low amount given how much money most of them made. I handed Kula my money and Kenney pulled up a camping chair for me. Kula chewed tobacco, spitting the remnants into an empty water bottle, and divvied out red, white, and blue plastic poker chips to everyone. Texas Hold'em follows the regular rules of poker, but unlike traditional five-card or seven-card draw, each player starts with two cards facedown, five cards are displayed faceup on the table, and you make the best five-card hand you can out of the seven.

Kula dealt the first two cards. I had two low cards, but since no one was betting high and I was curious, I stayed in. The first three cards, or "the flop," came down, and there was a king of diamonds, a four of diamonds, and a five of clubs. The hand could go many ways from there as there's a possibility for a flush, a chance for a straight, and no pairs showing. But I didn't have diamonds or high cards, so I folded. Marchello pouted and folded as well. Kula threw in a couple of chips and Kenney and the guys stayed in. After another round of betting, the fifth card came down, and it was a jack of diamonds, giving everyone a higher chance for a flush. Kula went all in, and the others folded. Players don't have to show their cards in this situation, but Kula did. He had a pair of jacks and therefore had almost nothing until the last card was dealt. From what I could tell, he was the one to beat.

I found out more about the guys as we played. Mana Kula was an ex–college football player and a former coach for Southern Utah University. He only made $22,000 a year as a coach, and left after he and his wife needed to relocate to care for her sick father. He briefly worked as a telemarketer for a get-rich-quick scheme called John Beck Free & Clear Real Estate System but quit when he discovered just how much the company was scamming customers. (The Federal Trade Commission eventually sued the company for $450 million.) Then Kula started working in the natural gas fields in Utah and Wyoming as a field hand, retrieving tools or doing grunt work for higher-up guys. He worked his way up and now made over $200,000 a year as a supervisor. He was divorced but supported his seven children back in Salt Lake City.

Kula and most of his crew were from Tonga or another Polynesian island. They came to North Dakota from Salt Lake City, Utah; Spokane, Washington; and Monterey, California. Many had grown up together or had a connection to Kula's family. First it was just a couple of them, but then someone's brother or cousin or nephew was laid off and wanted a job in the oil field, so Kula found an opening and the crew grew.

Around camp, they were called "the Nation." Kula and the Nation had built up a reputation as being one of the best coil crews in the state. People sometimes called them "the ghost crew" because they were incredibly efficient and worked so hard that no one ever saw them at the equipment yard. They were always out on a job. Kula didn't trust a lot of people in the oil field. He told me how a good friend had betrayed him a few years ago in an attempt to take over his job, so Kula chose the people he worked with carefully. At C&J, only a few non-Polynesian workers had become friendly with the Nation. One was Scott Morgan, the young man I had met the first time I met Marchello—though he typically worked alone. He was in a different department and didn't have the same schedule or supervisor as the rest of them. Then there was Matthew Anderson, Marchello's son-in-law. Like Marchello, Anderson was a devout Mormon who didn't drink—a strange concept to most of their coworkers. Anderson was married to Marchello's youngest daughter, who lived back in Ogden, Utah, with their four young children. Anderson applied to the oil field around the same time Marchello did. They shared a trailer at the man camp, but he was back in Utah this week. "We can share living facilities together because his wife doesn't care he's living with another woman," joked Marchello. There was also Curtis Kenney, and I realized quickly that he was not popular with the group, but Kula liked him. And since Kula called the shots, he stayed. Then of course there was Marchello, the only woman. Since most other crews in the oil field were young, white, and male, they were like a crew of misfits.

As the night progressed, more players fell out. Kula knocked out both Kenney and Tui with a full house. I took Marchello out with a flush. Then it was down to me, Kula, and Sam. I stared at my dangerously low stack of chips and figured this was the last hand I could play. My first two cards were a jack of diamonds and a five of diamonds. Not great, but it could be worse. I pushed all my chips to the center of the table. Kula, whose stack of chips was much higher than mine, matched me. A 10 of hearts, a 3 of clubs, and a 7 of diamonds came down first. Didn't help me much. Then a three of hearts. Still nothing for me. Finally a queen of spades came down, and Kula and I flipped over our cards. He had a pair of fives. Also not much, but it beat mine. I was out of the game. Kula beat Sam a few hands later.

Marchello announced that it was her bedtime and said good night to us. The guys wanted to play another round. My photographer and I glanced at each other and he nodded, so we both scooted closer to the table. Kenney gnawed on the end of a baguette, and more beers came out. Without Marchello there, the guys became rowdier. Kula asked if we wanted to see a trick. He gripped a Bud Light can in his palm like it was a kid's toy, put it up to his mouth, and made one swift jerk with his head. The top of the can ripped open. A perfect cut. My jaw dropped. The top dangled on the side of the can, held on by an inch of aluminum. Kula saw my look of shock and threw his head back and laughed, shaking the trailer.

Suddenly there was a loud *snap*, and everyone looked at Kenney. He had fallen to the floor. He stood up and dusted off his jeans. "My chair broke," he announced. The guys hooted and slapped their knees, collapsing into fits of laughter. Kenney fixed the chair as best he could and sat back down, but he was now three inches shorter than before. His chin barely cleared the table.

Kula asked which football team I rooted for. I said I didn't watch football often but if I had to pick, it'd be the 49ers. As another round of cards hit the table, he said, "Hey, Blaire, you remember losing to those two fives?" referring to the hand we played earlier. "I do. It was just like watching the 49ers play the Super Bowl. They didn't quite make it." He laughed again.

One of the Tongan guys prepared more drinks, mixing whiskey and Mountain Dew. He couldn't find enough cups so people handed him their empty Bud Light cans. Kula had already ripped the lids off most of them.

Kenney asked me why I wasn't drinking one of the whiskey–Mountain Dew concoctions. I told him I was driving. "If you want to stay here, we have an open trailer. I'm in 37 and there's nobody in the trailer next to me," he said.

I thanked him but declined his offer.

Suddenly his tone changed. "Only Cindy can get away with this 'whiny and tired' shit. You think I'm being a jerk? When you're having fun, you just stay and have fun."

The room fell silent, and everyone looked at Kenney.

Kula butted in. "No women are allowed at any of these man camps anyway."

I smiled politely and thanked Kenney again for the offer but told him we needed to head back to our trailer tonight.

But Kenney continued, slurring his words a little. "I'd volunteer to let them share my room."

I wasn't sure if he was talking about me and my photographer or women employed by C&J. Either way, my skin crawled at the thought, and I tried to change the subject. I asked the group if they ever missed having more women around. Kenney said no, and explained that having women on the crew was inconvenient if one had a wife. "We're all married, and when Cindy come to the crew, it really put a damper on things."

"Inconvenient for Curtis," joked Kula. "Speak for yourself, buddy. We don't have a girlfriend here at work." The guys laughed.

"They're just plain, flat jealous," said Kenney.

"Because if we were to say anything to Cindy, Curtis would be pissed. He wouldn't let us look over at her," joked Kula.

I was quickly catching on that Kenney and Marchello had known each other for a while. I couldn't tell if anything had happened between them. An affair? Harmless flirting? A crush? I later learned Kenney's relationship with his wife, Anna Marie, was complicated—she had Parkinson's disease, and one reason Kenney stayed in the oil field was to pay her expensive medical bills. But there were also rumors Kenney had cheated on her, though he later denied them. When I later asked him why his wife didn't move out to North Dakota, he replied: "Housing is too expensive, and she wouldn't see me anyway," referring to how many hours he was away from the man camp. "And girls by themselves aren't safe here," he added.

The song changed. Fergie's voice played out of the iPhone speakers, "You got me trippin', stumblin', flippin', fumblin', clumsy 'cause I'm fallin' in love," and Kula dealt another hand. Finally around midnight, my photographer and I announced it was time for us to go. Kenney made another offer for us to stay there, but again we told him we had to leave. Kula had won most of the money, but I came away with $20. I told Kula next time I'd take his money. He threw his head back and laughed.

19. CINDY MARCHELLO

Cindy Marchello was a lot of things before becoming an oil field worker. She had been a cab driver, a paralegal, an acupuncturist, a farmer, a cheese factory worker, a nylon factory worker, a cook for a hunting camp, a waitress, a wagon train reenactor, a Tupperware salesperson, a healer at Native American powwows, and a long-distance hiker on the Pacific Crest Trail. But for much of her life, she was a stay-at-home mom, raising a houseful of children and married to a man named Richard for 28 years.

Cindy was born in 1957 on a farm in Twin Falls County, Idaho, to Earl and May Marchello, and she could skin a pheasant by the time she reached first grade. The farm was 10 miles from the nearest town, with fields of alfalfa, sugar beets, and grains. Every morning, she, her sister, and two brothers woke up at dawn to start chores. Cindy took care of pigs, cows, and chickens and, when she was eight, drove the tractor. She hated wearing dresses and from an early age she was treated more like a lesser son than a daughter. "My older sister is quite girly, so she did chores in the house but she didn't do outside stuff," said Cindy. "Then my brothers were rather spoiled. They didn't help with dishes or take out the trash. So, I did. I got up in the morning to milk cows before I went to school, and I milked cows when I came home from school."

They lived in a rickety farmhouse with no foundation or insulation, and the structure was often infested with moles. They had no telephone, and only one channel in black and white came in on the TV. The entire family would sit around the TV and watch whatever was on— Christian evangelist Billy Graham, soap operas, the Western series *Bonanza*. Cindy loved *The Wizard of Oz* when it aired, and she walked on the top of the fences around her farm just like Dorothy did in the movie. Her family made their own bread, soap, and clothes and canned vegetables from the garden. "We were always gardening, always pickin' somethin', weedin' somethin', cannin' somethin'," she said. They used a ringer washer to do laundry and hung their clothes outside, even in the winter.

Their water came from a cistern on the farm, and the pipes froze frequently. To keep the pipes warm, her father placed a ditch burner, or a propane bottle with an open flame, near the pipes under the bathroom floor. "It would catch the floor on fire all the time," said Cindy, "and over the years there was no bathroom floor because my dad had burned it out with this stupid torch thing. I was in my 20s before I realized that everybody didn't have their pipes freeze all the time."

Money was always a struggle for them. "We were poor farmers and we always knew we were poor," she said. When Cindy was seven, her parents had to file for bankruptcy after her older sister, Vicky, became ill and had her tonsils removed. They had no insurance and the out-of-pocket medical bills drained all their savings.

Her parents were devout Mormons, and they took Cindy and her siblings to the Jesus Christ of Latter-Day Saints church every Sunday and to smaller church gatherings during the week. Her father, a large man at six foot three and weighing about 300 pounds, was always hard on her. At age 10, Cindy helped him stack hay bales in the truck. He threw six bales up to her at a time, three in each hand, and expected her to do the same. "He'd be mad at me the whole time because I couldn't keep up," she said. "Most men cannot pick up a bale in each hand, let alone three bales in each hand, and for him to be mad at me because I couldn't do it? So because of that, to this day I think I'm lazy."

She attended a school 20 minutes away that had only 16 kids in a class. In fourth grade, she learned about the oil field for the first time during a class lesson and saw a photo of an oil derrick. It looked exciting. She remembered thinking, *I want to go up in an oil rig.*

But by 16, her career dreams fizzled. She started dating that year, and knew she needed to find a husband soon. Almost every girl she knew married around that age—she'd been attending the weddings of her peers ever since freshman year. "If you weren't engaged by the time you graduated from high school, there was something wrong with you," she said. College was out of the question. She was told women could do one of four things: get married, become a teacher, become a nurse, or become a secretary—and the jobs were usually for the less-attractive girls. She chose marriage. One night, she was invited on a double date. One of her girlfriends had a crush on a boy named Don, and Don brought along his friend, Steve. Cindy and Steve dated after that. One year later, just after Cindy's seventeenth birthday, they were married.

The wedding was in August at her parents' house, and her mother made her dress. About 30 people attended, and for Cindy, the day was a blur. "The one thing I remember about the wedding was a guy had his pants unzipped in all the pictures. Why didn't the person holding the camera lean over and say, 'Zip up your pants?!'"

Soon she was pregnant. She entered her senior year of high school in 1974 five months' pregnant, and her principal told her she wouldn't be able to walk at graduation with her class. She explained that she wouldn't be pregnant by graduation—the baby was due in January—but he said it didn't matter. Being pregnant at any point disqualified her. She was angry and quit early. "I finished everything except the final test," she said. "People say, 'Do you have a high school diploma?' Yes, I did everything that I was supposed to do except for that jackass."

When the child was born, she named her Earline, but she could tell something was wrong with the baby from the beginning. Her skin was yellow, and she didn't eat or sleep. She cried for hours on end. Cindy had cared for many neighbors' babies and knew this much crying was out of the ordinary. She took Earline back to the hospital. "She had no gallbladder and no glands in her liver, and she had big holes in her heart," Cindy said. Five months later, after spending much of her life in the hospital, Earline died. Cindy was heartbroken. "When my baby died, I couldn't speak. And my mother went ballistic because she'd try to talk to me and I couldn't answer her. But my baby had just died."

Losing the baby was difficult on her relationship with Steve, which had always been tumultuous but now got worse. "We'd get in big ol' knock-down, drag-out fights," she remembered. He didn't attend Earline's funeral, and Cindy was furious with him. They worked on the relationship for another year, moving to Missouri and Iowa and back to Idaho in attempts to find work, but eventually she had enough. She found out she was pregnant again and wanted a better life for her unborn child, whom she desperately hoped would live. One weekend, when she and Steve were living in Idaho, her parents stopped by her house on their way to relocate to the Seattle area. She stole away in the moving truck without telling Steve. It would be the last time she ever saw him.

She and Steve stayed married on paper for five more years before she applied for a divorce. They had lived together for a total of eight months during their marriage.

Cindy was now 19, single, pregnant, and living with her parents in Stanwood, Washington. She gave birth in July 1977 to a healthy boy and named him Ricky. At first she was sick with worry that something might happen to him as well, but after a few weeks, she relaxed. She adored being someone's mom. Being a single mother in the Mormon community was difficult, however. Very few women in her community ever got divorced—if they were single, they were usually widows. Her hope was to find another husband quickly. "If I didn't have any options at 16, why would I have any options as a 19-year-old single mom? I had no skills, no knowledge, no resources. I had to just figure it out."

In Stanwood, she was hired at a local cannery and befriended an attractive coworker, also named Steve. They dated briefly, and he left her pregnant again. She gave birth to a baby boy named Matthew in October 1978 when she was 21 years old. Cindy didn't have much contact with the second Steve when she was pregnant. She moved with her parents to Price, Utah, a tiny coal mining town in Carbon County where her parents were from. Steve stayed in Washington. When Matthew was about a year old, she traveled up to Washington with both her sons to stay with her sister and reconnected with Steve. She wanted Matthew to know his father. One rainy night, after she, Steve, and the kids went to the movies, he drove them back to her sister's house. He told Cindy to unlock the front door and he'd be right behind her with Matthew. Cindy took three-year-old Ricky, but as soon as she got to the door, she heard Steve rev the engine and leave with Matthew still in the car. She called the police, but what she didn't know was that Steve had already filed custody papers and hired a lawyer. She tried to take Steve to court, but to win back custody, she'd have to prove that Steve was unfit to be a parent. The judge decided in his favor—Cindy lost the case and custody of Matthew.

Devastated, Cindy returned to Utah to live with her parents. She worked as a cook at a 24-hour diner called Bob's. One day, a large man with lush dark hair and a cream-colored polyester jacket walked in. Compared to the rough-looking coal miners and railroad workers who frequented the diner, he looked like a movie star. He was about six feet tall, muscular, clean shaven, and, according to Cindy, he resembled country music star Glen Campbell. For the next two weeks, he came in often and sat at the counter to watch Cindy cook. Finally he asked her out to lunch. She said yes.

His name was Richard. A Vietnam vet who had worked as an Army combat engineer, Richard came to Utah's coal mines after working on pipelines in Alaska. Richard already had three children, ages seven, five, and three, from a previous marriage, and Cindy began caring for them. To her, he seemed like a great catch. He was smart, well traveled, and had a stable job. He was divorced as well, so he understood her situation. He was gregarious—everyone she introduced him to fell for him. She was proud to be seen around town with him, but even as she fell deeply in love with him, another side of Richard appeared behind closed doors. He had wild mood swings—one second they were talking and laughing, and the next instant there was a flash of anger. "There were huge red flags, but I didn't pay attention," she said later. "I couldn't see them."

Soon enough they were married. On their wedding night, instead of having a romantic evening, she watched the kids while Richard watched TV, and she fell asleep alone on the couch. Later he would tell their daughter Jennie that he married Cindy because "she was cute and I didn't want to pay a babysitter."

If Richard and Cindy's marriage was off to a shaky start, it would only get worse. Financial troubles plagued them. Richard was laid off from the mine. They moved back to Stanwood, Washington, for Richard to find work, and Cindy hoped to reconnect with her son Matthew. But Richard struggled to hold down a job there as well. The country had slid into a deep recession. The national unemployment rate reached 10.8 percent in 1982 and 12.2 percent in Washington, the highest in the state since the Great Depression. A lot of families were out of work. Richard and Cindy mostly lived off his small disability checks from his time in the Army. They moved into an old camper with parts of the floor missing to save money and avoid paying rent. It was located on a friend's property in a remote area about 60 miles away from

Stanwood. Cindy was soon pregnant and gave birth to a daughter, Elizabeth, in April 1982, and two years later, to Jennie. She was now taking care of six children and, on occasion, Matthew as well. Cindy legally had visitation rights to see her son, but she said that Steve sometimes wouldn't let her see him.

There's a photo of Cindy and Richard and the seven kids, taken at one of those department store photo studios, where they're smiling like a happy family. Cindy has a perm, her cheeks are painted with blush, and her long blond hair is dyed dark auburn, a red bow clipped to one side. Richard's neck is hidden by a thick beard that's neatly trimmed. His upper lip is completely shaved, making him look Amish. The kids circle them, with the three girls lined up neatly on the left and the boys, including Matthew, on the right, with Richard's eldest daughter in the center. Jennie is five years old with long braids and thick, blunt bangs. She gives the camera a goofy smile. They look like a typical 1980s middle-class family.

Behind the smiles, however, life was much more chaotic. As Cindy describes it, Richard was hardly around, and when he was, he would instigate fights. Cindy suspected he was seeing other women, but when she confronted him about it, he told her she was crazy and hallucinating things. Eventually, she started to believe him. "Things were never stable with Richard. He was never there, we never knew where he was or what he was doing," she said. As their youngest daughter, Jennie, explained their relationship: "When they were together, it was gasoline on the fire, always."

Richard constantly tried to invent new schemes to make money. He was arrested when they lived in Lake Stevens, Washington, for writing bad checks. The second time he was arrested, he'd been hired to burn down a friend's trailer to collect the insurance money. Instead of showing up for court, he packed up the family and moved to a remote location where he hoped the police wouldn't find him. For a while, they lived in a bus parked in the woods.

In 1989, Richard's ex-wife didn't like what she was hearing about their lifestyle from her daughters and called Child Protective Services. The police came to the girls' school to take them away. After the police questioned the daughters, they arrested Richard and accused him of sexually abusing them. Richard posted bail after his arrest and waited for trial. Cindy didn't believe that the charges could be true. Richard convinced her that he was innocent, and although she believed him, from that moment on, she didn't allow Richard to be alone with her two daughters. Cindy was also terrified CPS would take her children as well, and hid them away at friends' houses. Every couple of days, Cindy moved them to another location in the middle of the night. Cindy taught her kids to not talk to the cops. She'd say, "If somebody starts asking questions about your mommy and daddy, you tell them 'It's none of your damn business.' You close your lips and you say nothing else." A few months later, Richard's eldest, Eric, left to live with his mother. They quickly went from seven kids to three.

Before the trial, Richard ran from the law to avoid possible jail time and moved his family into the woods again. They lived in tents often. They boiled snow for water. The checks they lived off of were in Richard's name, so Cindy had to ask him every time she needed money for groceries, clothes, or household items. Many times, he spent nearly every last penny before giving any to her or the kids. When he did give Cindy money for groceries or supplies, she said that he berated her if she spent too much on what he considered frivolous items. She recalled that once when he saw her put baby carrots instead of the cheaper, regular ones in the cart, he picked up the bag and threw it at her. Whenever Cindy had extra money left over after buying groceries, she hid it away for later. But with no income, no car, and no driver's license, her options were limited. She felt trapped.

"She was in a very stressful situation," remembered Jennie. "She didn't have even the basic necessities for her children. But she couldn't see that it would have been better for her to go get a little apartment in town, to take her remaining children and get a job."

The family moved around often, parking the camper on people's properties until they overstayed their welcome. Anything to keep Richard hidden from the police. "We just went from place to place to place," said Cindy's oldest daughter, Elizabeth. Sometimes they piled into the car and just drove, living out of the car or camping all summer long. "We moved about every six months, from one funky situation to another," Elizabeth recalled. A lot of times they moved because Richard became suspicious of the neighbors.

Richard and Cindy would fight often—their fights were loud and angry and, a few times, they became physical. At her lowest moments, Cindy took out her frustrations with Richard by hitting Elizabeth and Jennie. Jennie remembered Cindy forcefully pinching her until she screamed. Cindy would say, "Scream if someone is hurting you. It's the only way you can defend yourself."

Today, Cindy has made amends with her daughters. "I tell the kids, 'I will spend the next 20 years apologizing to you and trying to make up for the mistakes in the first 20 years.' In the moment I knew it was bad and I couldn't fix it. I didn't know how to fix it. I didn't have the resources, especially with Richard. When I hear them talk about stuff, I'm like, 'If you never spoke to me again, I would absolutely understand.' "

Happier memories were when they traveled on wagon train reenactments together. In 1989, they trekked across Washington State as a family in full wagon train–era costumes, hand-sewed by Cindy. "My mom never asked if I had homework or anything, it was just like, 'Let's do this craft project' or 'Let's go on this hike,' " said Elizabeth.

Sometimes Cindy told the kids, "I don't know where I'm going, I'm not sure when I'm coming back, but you have a half hour to get ready." They'd drive to the Four Corners, Colorado, Utah, the Grand Canyon.

The first time they went to the Grand Canyon, Cindy wrote in the family photo album: "We were so broke we couldn't even afford the 25 cents to go up in the tower. Spent pennies to get enough gas to drive to Phoenix." Once Cindy announced they were leaving for a trip when Elizabeth had a friend over and the friend went too, but Cindy never told the friend's mother. They were gone for eight days. "Sometimes we wouldn't get too far," said Elizabeth. "She would take her money, split it in half, and we would go until half her money ran out, and then we'd go home." They constantly had car trouble—the car would overheat, the muffler would fall off, or they'd run out of gas and have to walk to the nearest station. "These were occurrences we talked about like other people talked about birthday parties," Elizabeth said.

When the kids were sick, Cindy began to use home remedies. They had no health insurance, and she mistrusted hospitals and traditional doctors. Soon neighbors heard about her medical talents and brought their kids over whenever they had minor ailments, like pink eye or warts. But when the ailments started getting more serious, Cindy decided she needed professional training. She applied to a three-year acupuncture program in Denver, and to her surprise, she was accepted.

Richard, however, wasn't happy about it. He begrudgingly said she could go but insisted they live in a run-down building four hours away from her school. The thought of driving four hours each way to school to live in another dump enraged her. For the first time, she threatened to leave him and take the kids. She remembered telling him: "I will figure out a way to do this. You can take every penny you want, but you are not taking this away from me." But two days before Cindy was set to leave with the kids, he apologized and announced he was coming with them. They rented a house in Brush, Colorado, an hour and a half from her school, but something had shifted in their marriage. "It was the beginning of the end," said Cindy. At 35, she now had a goal—she knew practicing acupuncture could give her a way to make money and provide for herself. "Acupuncture was a huge shift in who

I was and in how much backbone I had," she explained. "I realized there was a world beyond. How I grew up, you get married and there's your husband and your kids—there is no you."

In Colorado, for the first time that Jennie and Elizabeth could remember, they had consistent electricity and running water. They attended school regularly. All three of the kids had their own bedrooms, which was strange at first. The girls snuck into Ricky's bedroom at night because they were scared to sleep alone. Richard was still running from the law and wasn't around much. For three months, he lived in a tent in the woods and Cindy delivered food to him once a week. Ricky, now 15, babysat the girls while Cindy was at school. One day, in 1993, Richard's past caught up to him. He was arrested and sent back to Washington. "I was in school and they arrested him in front of our little kids and hauled him off," Cindy recalled.

In Washington, the child abuse charges were dropped, but Richard was convicted of "bail jumping," a felony, and two counts of "communication with a minor for immoral purposes," which were misdemeanors, and sentenced to six months in jail.

Despite her newfound independence, Cindy didn't seriously consider divorcing Richard. She was terrified that Richard would take her children and run away where she couldn't find them. It took another 11 years for them to split up.

20. FORT BERTHOLD

About 70 miles away from where I lived in Williston sat the sprawling Fort Berthold Indian Reservation, home to the Mandan, Hidatsa, and Arikara tribes, or the Three Affiliated Tribes.

Before the boom, about 6,000 tribal members lived on nearly 1 million acres of land—an area larger than the state of Rhode Island. For the most part, they lived peacefully but in poverty. About 40 percent of the tribe's workforce was unemployed, and many people lived in small homes crammed with three or more families. As on other reservations throughout the United States, alcoholism permeated the lives of many Native families. Life expectancy on the reservation was 57 years, compared with 79 for the state of North Dakota.

So when reservation leaders realized so much oil lay under tribal lands, they were ecstatic. They had been skipped over by small oil booms in the past and wanted in this time. The tribe's chairman, Tex Hall, believed that capitalizing on the boom could be their ticket out of poverty and reliance on government assistance. Hall wanted the reservation to be appealing to oil companies and did everything he could to streamline the permit process. He testified in Congress against new fracking regulations. "When the white man said, 'This will be your reservation,' little did they know those Badlands would have oil and gas," Hall said in an energy company video. His motto became "sovereignty by the barrel."

Hall's tactics worked—oil companies came in droves to set up on tribal land. By 2011, one-fifth of North Dakota's oil came from the reservation. But as oil companies lined up to drill, Hall decided to line his own pockets. He launched his own oil company on the reservation, a direct conflict of interest with his political responsibilities—a conflict the tribe's council ignored. Rumors spread about Hall using his political power to drum up more business for his own company and undermine competitors.

"[Tex Hall] was very pro oil and had everything going for him—very charming and charismatic," said Marilyn Hudson, a 78-year-old tribal elder and historian from the Mandan and Hidatsa tribes on the reservation. "He had the attention of senators and Indian people throughout the nation. He was always in favor of big oil and to lessen restrictions."

At the same time, the tribe's budget wasn't subject to the same disclosure and auditing requirements as other U.S. governing bodies, and the council was managing millions of dollars with little oversight. For example, the tribal government set aside $421 million in the budget for a "special projects" fund but didn't disclose what those special projects were or how the money would be spent. A few purchases became controversial and symbols of mismanagement within the government: one was a 96-foot, $2.5 million yacht, supposedly to bring in more revenue for the casino located next to the man-made Lake Sakakawea. But it sat unused on dry land. "I don't know why they bought it," said Hudson. "Money is being spent hand over fist, but it's being spent without any long-range planning or thought."

Fewer than half of the tribal members owned mineral rights—the rest belonged to the tribe as a whole or to outside buyers—so while they received oil royalty checks (some upward of tens of thousands of dollars a month), many tribal members weren't seeing a dime and continued to live below the poverty line—only now they had to stand by and watch their neighbors become rich. "We still feel like we're in a ghetto," said Lisa DeVille, a 41-year-old tribal member living in the small reservation community of Mandaree. "The tribe is collecting millions of dollars a month, but yet Mandaree's still sitting there with a school that was built in the 1950s. It has an old boiler room with black mold in it. We are in great need of housing—70 percent of our community is living in overcrowded conditions."

Oil companies began buying up property to house workers and evicted longtime Native residents. In late 2011, a new owner bought Prairie Winds Trailer Park in New Town to house his employees. He told the 180 residents, many of them families with young children, that they had a few months to relocate. Protesters marched down Main Street, angry that Natives were being removed from their homes to make room for workers and out-of-towners.

More and more tribal members began to question Hall's unbridled embrace of oil development on the reservation. As time went on, the downsides became increasingly apparent. Hundreds of semi trucks roared through New Town every day, causing a rapid spike of traffic accidents and deaths. Residents began calling Route 23, which runs east to west through North Dakota and cuts through the center of town, "suicide road." In the early days of the boom, Marilyn Hudson's granddaughter was hit by a semi on the road and died immediately. She was only 23 years old. The boom brought an increase of crime, drug use, and damage to sacred tribal lands. Industry trucks dumped toxic fluid into ditches by the road or unloaded radioactive waste, a byproduct of fracking, into garbage bins and backyards. A large number of deer disappeared off the reservation in 2012, and many suspected the oil activity was to blame.

In a strange twist of events, Hall was called to testify in a trial of two murders that occurred on the reservation in 2012 and 2013.

The main murder suspects were both newcomers—James Henrikson from Oregon and Timothy Suckow from Spokane, Washington. Henrikson was accused of hiring Suckow to murder 29-year-old Kristopher Clarke and 63-year-old Doug Carlile because of a business deal gone wrong. But Tex Hall had a connection to the suspects. After Henrikson launched a business on the reservation, Hall became friends with him. And one victim, Clarke, was last seen leaving Hall's property before he vanished. Investigators never found evidence to charge Hall with a crime, and Hall denied any wrongdoing, but he testified at the trial about his business dealings with Henrikson, who was sentenced to life in prison. "He let himself be taken in by crooks," said Marilyn Hudson. "That's what puzzles everybody—how could he be so dumb? Two men were murdered. There were so many elements of it that were unbelievable." Finally, in 2014, Hall lost his run for reelection. People began calling Hall's time in office the "reign of terror." After stepping down, Hall launched a business to produce and sell marijuana, which had recently become legal on the reservation.

The murders not only shocked tribal members but accentuated their feelings of mistrust toward the non-Indian newcomers and oil workers. The population of the reservation had more than doubled by 2013, and crime was rising. In 2012, the tribal police department reported the most murders, sexual assaults, domestic disputes, drug busts, gun threats, and human trafficking cases in reservation history. The next year, police ran "Operation Winter's End" and made a 22-person drug bust, involving heroin and methamphetamine, on the reservation. Police later arrested at least 40 more people connected to the original bust. In the past, the Justice Department had never seen heroin on the reservation—the first case was in 2012. Though the number of addicts was rising quickly, the tribe had one substance-abuse treatment center, which could house only nine patients at a time.

A number of rape cases involving non-Indian men and Native women also fueled fears. In the spring of 2012, three oil workers offered a female tribal member a ride home from a bar in New Town; instead, they drove her down a dark road, raped her several times, and left her there. There also was evidence of sex trafficking on the reservation. Native girls as young as 12 and 13 would disappear from their homes, then resurface a week or two later with matching red flag tattoos. Investigators suspected pimps had branded them.

When it came to making arrests or prosecuting crimes, the reservation was a jurisdictional nightmare. According to the 1978 U.S. Supreme Court case *Oliphant v. Suquamish*, tribal officers are forbidden to arrest and prosecute non-Indians who commit crimes on Indian land. Thus, if a perpetrator was non-Indian, an officer outside the reservation had to make the arrest. There was frequent confusion over who should respond to a call, and getting the right deputy to the scene could take hours, given the reservation's enormous square mileage. Plus, each deputy already had an overwhelming workload. The tribal police force employed only about 20 officers to cover the entire reservation. The bureaucratic mess added to the lawless, Wild-West feeling of the area. As one white mechanic on the reservation told a reporter from *The Atlantic*: "Basically you can do anything short of killing somebody."

For Marilyn Hudson, the feeling that outsiders were disrespecting Indian lands was all too familiar.

Hudson was born on the reservation and is the great-great-granddaughter of a man named Cherry Necklace, a warrior in the Hidatsa tribe who adopted a young girl who would later become the legendary Sacagawea (known as Sakakawea in North Dakota, though no one knows the true spelling of her name). Marilyn's Hidatsa and Mandan ancestors had farmed in a fertile valley near North Dakota's Heart River for centuries, an area that at one time was home to more than 14,000 Native Americans. In 1804, two explorers, Meriwether Lewis and William Clark, visited their villages. It was there they hired the 14-year-old Sakakawea to help them make the journey to the Rockies.

But the arrival of Lewis and Clark was the beginning of a long history of heartbreak for Marilyn's ancestors. A smallpox outbreak tore through the area in 1837, taking half a million Indian lives. Many of the victims died within hours of their first symptoms. The heaps of bodies—which had turned black from the disease and swelled in the sun—grew higher every day.

In 1851, with the Treaty of Horse Creek, the federal government allotted 12 million acres to the three tribes, but over the next 20 years, the government proceeded to chip away at that acreage, many times justifying the breaking up of Indian lands as an attempt to "civilize" the Native population. By the time the official reservation borders were drawn in 1870, a few years before the first homesteaders arrived in the Williston area, the land had been reduced by nearly half.

The federal government's takeover didn't stop there. Congress passed the General Allotment Act of 1887 in order to take away communal land from tribes and create individual landowners. On the Fort Berthold Indian Reservation, heads of families were given 160 acres each, unmarried men and women were given 80 acres each, and children received 40 acres. This shift to individual ownership made it easier for white settlers to purchase Indian lands, and 1.6 million acres of reservation land opened to white settlers during this time. By the early 1910s, fewer than 3 million acres of the reservation were owned by Native Americans.

Within that acreage was a town called Elbowoods, located in a valley about 40 miles from New Town, and where Hudson and her siblings grew up in the 1930s and 1940s. Her upbringing was in many ways similar to that of her ancestors. She and her family hunted, gathered wild foods, rode horses, and farmed the productive valley. There were nine villages along the Missouri River, and Elbowoods was a social hub. People from the outlying communities would come to the town's main square once a month to gather, pass tobacco pipes, and tell stories. Tribal members knew everyone by their first name, which clan they belonged to, and who their ancestors were. They lived peacefully and sustainably. When Hudson was a young child in the mid-1940s, fewer than 3 percent of those living on the reservation received federal assistance.

Hundreds of miles downstream from Hudson's family, however, in Nebraska and Iowa, non-Native farmers along the lower Missouri River were fed up. Those who had survived the Great Depression and dust bowl of the 1930s were now battling unpredictable floodwaters that were destroying valuable crops. Floods in the spring of 1943 had caused millions of dollars of damage. The farmers' losses and complaints would result in the Army Corps of Engineers and the Bureau of Reclamation proposing the Pick-Sloan Plan, flood-control legislation that would construct 110 dams—the first, largest, and most ambitious located about 60 miles from Elbowoods near a small town called Garrison.

Once built, the Garrison Dam would flood some 800 square miles of rich farmland. The Army Corps of Engineers claimed the new dam would bring "immeasurable wealth to North Dakota"—but somehow the plan would disproportionately flood Native American lands and avoid white communities like Williston. Less than 10 percent of farmland to be covered by floodwaters was owned by white farmers. Hudson's father, Martin Cross, the tribal chairman of the Three Affiliated Tribes and the vice president of the National Congress of American Indians, fought with everything he had to stop the plan. He testified before the U.S. Senate, wrote letters, and argued with lawmakers over the plan's legality. But in the end, his efforts failed. The plan was approved, and some 155,000 acres of land and 436 properties owned by the Mandan, Hidatsa, and Arikara tribes were set to disappear underwater forever.

The tribes received only $12.5 million in compensation for the loss of land, their homes, and their livelihood, a gross undervaluation (private appraisers had estimated the land's value to be $21 million). The package was also intended to cover the relocation and reconstruction costs for homes, schools, hospitals, roads, cemeteries, and more. The final draft of the bill forbade the tribe to use the money to hire lawyers or agents to represent them to appeal the plan. When the tribe's then chairman, George Gillette, added his signature to the bill in Congress, he wept openly in front of the crowd and media photographers.

One of the few items the compensation package did protect, however, was the tribe's subsurface mineral rights—which at the time were thought to be worthless. Most of the mineral rights from the "taken" land would be transferred to the Bureau of Indian Affairs, and displaced landowners were given plots of land with the mineral rights intact above the valley.

When it was time to start moving homes, many residents didn't receive notice of the date their house would be relocated. Some were in the middle of eating dinner when they heard rattling and felt their home move beneath them. Others, like 21-year-old Louise Holding Eagle, came home from the grocery store to find her home, along with her husband and two children, gone—all that was left was an empty field and the home's foundation. The Corps had stopped by while she was out, loaded her house onto a flatbed truck, and driven it away. She didn't even know which plot above the valley they took her home to.

A few elders said they'd rather die than move. One local businessman committed suicide instead of packing up his dry-goods store and the home he shared with his wife and daughter. The dam was completed in 1953, and in late summer of 1954, water lapped onto the streets of Elbowoods. Some residents stubbornly waited until the last minute to make preparations and were too late—they watched their beloved homes swallowed up by the floodwaters and scrambled to evacuate. Many sacred religious sites washed away. As the water level rose, a group of former high school basketball players realized no one had packed up the trophies in the trophy case at the high school; they maneuvered rowboats down the school's hallways to retrieve them.

Hudson graduated from high school a few months before the flood and was part of the last graduating class of Elbowoods High School. She left to attend college in Minot, and her family moved to a shack in Parshall while they waited for their home to be moved to its new foundation near Main Street. The toll of fighting the dam and the loss of his community broke her father's heart. He and her mother split in 1954, even though divorce was practically nonexistent in the Elbowoods community before the area was flooded. Martin Cross moved to a ranch 20 miles south of Parshall with no neighbors for miles and attempted ranching, with little success.

The transition to life on higher ground was difficult for the displaced tribal members. Most were now scattered across some 1,500 square miles of land, and close-knit clans were now separated by the vast, 178-mile-long Lake Sakakawea. On the high ground, people were exposed to forceful prairie winds and had little protection from weather extremes. There was little water for farm irrigation or to grow small gardens, the soil was arid and unproductive, and the wild game population for hunting was thin. "All of a sudden you've got all these people living out here and their livelihood has been taken away," said Hudson. Few jobs were available in Parshall and the newly formed New Town, and most that existed paid minimum wage or less. In Parshall, a mostly white town established in 1914 by Scandinavian homesteaders, racial tensions worsened as hundreds of Native Americans moved in. A study by the Bureau of Indian Affairs in 1964, 10 years after the move, concluded that relocation had "created a situation in which actual starvation for many of these people is a real possibility."

Hudson's siblings relocated to northern California, Seattle, and Denver, and hundreds of tribal members did the same. For those who stayed, by the 1990s, members relied heavily on government assistance and more than a third lived below the poverty line. "The Mandan,

Hidatsa, and Arikara people went from being the only self-sufficient tribal enclave in the U.S. to being one that was almost wholly dependent on outside help for day-to-day survival," wrote Paul VanDevelder in *Coyote Warrior*.

So when oil companies came, it was easy to see why many tribal members signed away mineral rights and cashed in. With those funds, some were able to live free of government assistance for the first time in their lives. After the boom began, unemployment on the reservation fell to the single digits. But this time, the money was coming from a new type of outsider—one with deep pockets, slick salesmanship, and, like those who came before, a desire for Native lands.

21. CHELSEA NIEHAUS

When Chelsea Niehaus arrived in North Dakota, she had no idea tensions were rising between tribal members and newcomers. Or that newcomers like her and Jacob Klipsch living on the reservation had become a symbol of the pain and suffering tribal members were experiencing. All Chelsea knew was that she needed to clean the camper, unpack, and figure out dinner before the sun went down.

Right away, she got to cleaning. There were no whiskey bottles or dirty laundry strewn about, as she'd worried, but a layer of dust had coated the cushions and the carpet, and grime had built up in the crevices of the fiberglass walls. There was no water and no working toilets so they drove to the Cenex gas station about a mile up the road when someone had to use the restroom. The nearby truck-stop showers that Jacob used were notorious for being unsanitary and filled with grimy men recently back from their long shifts in the oil fields. Chelsea decided she and Will could go at least a few days without bathing.

The first evening in the camper, Chelsea watched a thunderstorm roll in—the lightning burst through the open sky and crept closer. She and her family settled in for the night to wait out the storm. As the thunder crashed and echoed, Chelsea lay awake listening to the wind howl outside while Jacob slept next to her. Dust blew in through the crevices of the camper walls. The master bedroom was only a crawl space. She could barely sit up, let alone stand. Will slept on a camping mat in the narrow space between the bed and the wall, and Thor curled up on the other side of the bed. Eventually Chelsea drifted off to sleep.

After three days in the trailer park without water, Jacob received approval to move into a different RV park. He had been hired at a new company, called DuCon, an oil field services and supply company, and his boss wanted him to live closer to his coworkers. The new park was located 20 miles away in Parshall, North Dakota, but still on the reservation. It was situated on a large plot of scoria gravel, surrounded by tall prairie grass scattered with oil rigs and aging grain storage bins in the distance. There wasn't a patch of green lawn in sight, but this park had running water, plumbing hookups, a shower house, laundry facilities, and Wi-Fi. It felt luxurious compared to the previous lot. At $800 a month to park there, it was double the price, but DuCon paid half the rent. They hooked up to the water source, turned on the hot water heater, and Chelsea took a hot shower for the first time since they arrived. Soon after, however, the rain came.

When it rains in North Dakota, it rains hard, fast, and with purpose. It's not the quick sheets of downpour like in the East or the slow constant drizzle in the Pacific Northwest. Rainstorms on the prairie are not for the weak. You can see a storm coming from miles away, the dark clouds marching through the expansive sky like determined soldiers, with angry winds accelerating their encroachment. Then the sky darkens—the sun's rays have no chance to peek through. The thunder booms, shaking you to the core, and lightning bolts announce the storm's arrival. All you can do is hunker down to hide, wait it out, and hope it clears before dawn.

At the new Parshall trailer park, it rained and rained and rained. The rain would let up for a moment but then thunder down on top of the trailer's thin rubber roof with even more force. Chelsea worried they could be washed away. Jacob's company halted work because of the rain—the unpaved roads leading to the oil rigs morphed into thick, muddy, impassible channels (though plenty of companies operated in such conditions). Most of the time, forceful winds accompanied the downpours. "It felt like the trailer was going to blow over because the wind just blew and blew and blew," Chelsea said. If she had to leave the trailer for any reason, she'd immediately sink into mud like quicksand. The doormat and steps to the trailer's entrance became permanently cemented over with a thick sludge.

With Jacob unable to work, the three of them holed up in the camper together for days on end. Their patience with each other withered. A testy remark or small squabble turned into a screaming match within seconds. "Woo . . . there was some tension there," Chelsea recalled. "We were all piled on top of each other, and we couldn't go anywhere and it was raining and the wind was blowing . . . it was painful to watch." Jacob drank more. He paced back and forth in the camper or puttered around outside. Most days, the windows inside the camper fogged up and they couldn't see out. Will ran around screaming as Chelsea tried to do craft projects or read books with him. When it stormed outside, she thought about the stories Jacob's mother had told her before they'd left Kentucky about women living on the plains 100 years ago, who went crazy from the sound of the wind. "I felt like the walls were closing in," she said later. She began to truly understand how women could lose their minds here.

In early June, after Chelsea and Will had been there two and a half weeks, Jacob broke down one night. He had too much to drink at his boss's camper. When he came home around 2 a.m., he was belligerent. He threw dishes and tossed some of their belongings out of the camper. He didn't hit Chelsea, but at one point he forcefully grabbed her waist. "He just lost his mind," Chelsea said. "He was drunk and acting fucking crazy." He screamed at them, telling Chelsea she was a horrible person, and eventually the police knocked on their trailer's door. Chelsea never found out who made the call. The police officer asked four-year-old Will if Jacob had hit him or his mother. Will shook his head and said no. Jacob seemed calmer and Chelsea promised the officer they were fine, but Chelsea was furious at Jacob. "I'd never dealt with anything like that before. I was just horrified," she said.

The next morning, she packed their bags, and she, Will, and Thor left. They stayed at a hotel in Minneapolis that night and she drove to Jacob's parents' house in Vincennes, Indiana, the next day. She left Will with his grandparents and drove to Louisville. The Walnut Cottage house still hadn't sold, and Chelsea almost cried when she saw her old home. She was so happy to have a place to return to, even if most of the furniture was gone. Two days later, she turned 33, and spent her birthday alone. It was one of the worst birthdays of her life.

She and Will stayed in Kentucky for six weeks. Jacob apologized profusely for the incident, and, eventually, Chelsea's anger softened. She also knew she couldn't stay at the house forever. Financially, they were struggling again. Without Chelsea's full-time job and with Jacob not working, she couldn't continue the mortgage payments much longer. Chelsea heard that a friend and her partner were looking for an affordable rental, so her friends moved into the Walnut Cottage home and Chelsea packed up and returned to North Dakota with Will and Thor. The sun was shining when they arrived, and Jacob was back to working full time. Chelsea was determined to last in North Dakota for the rest of the summer.

Chelsea met Jacob in German class in their sophomore year of high school. She was the new kid at school—a transfer from a small Catholic school in Vincennes, Indiana. Lincoln High School was more than four times the size of her old school. Jacob was a former football player who then joined the marching band. He had made a reputation for himself the year before at a school assembly, after the administration announced it would start drug testing. Jacob stood up at the assembly and said the testing violated everyone's rights, then dropped the microphone and walked out. Kids at school were still talking about it when Chelsea enrolled.

In German glass, Jacob sat near Chelsea and tried to get her attention by yelling random things like "I have a snake!" "He was goofy and different," said Chelsea. She saw him perform in the marching band, and it inspired her to try out for the color guard. They went to band camp together, talked on the phone often, and hung out at each other's houses. "We obviously liked each other," she said. At age 15, their parents went to a party and left them alone together in the house. They kissed for the first time. "We basically grew up together," Chelsea said. "Even if we couldn't make it together, we'd still be friends. We've been through so much together. Sometimes I don't like him—especially when he's drinking. Jacob when he's drinking is a total nightmare. But we have a kid to raise—we're going to have to get along."

I drove out to meet Chelsea and Will one Sunday afternoon in late July 2013 while Jacob was away at work. Thor was tied up outside and barked when I pulled in next to Chelsea's Mitsubishi. Chelsea had placed a few potted plants outside, growing tomatoes, basil, and mint. An Oriental rug covered the dusty ground in front of the camper's doorway. The carpet was held down by large rocks to keep it from blowing away. Next to the doorway was a mini-fridge draped with a blue tarp. There were two men working on the trailer next door, maneuvering some PVC pipe that lay on the ground. A four-wheeler was parked behind them. Grasshoppers leapt onto my jeans as I exited my car.

Will watched from the window as I approached but hid when I reached the foldaway steps leading into the camper. Chelsea was behind a rickety screen door in the kitchen and gestured for me to come in. The door banged shut behind me. Chelsea was wearing a long flowing skirt with a tank top and greeted me with a big smile. Her straight brown hair cascaded down her back and framed her round face. She had soft features, and light brown freckles speckled her pale cheeks. She apologized about Will; he was shy, and it took him a few minutes to warm up to new people. She was busy making pulled pork in a Crockpot—the sweet, pungent smell saturated the small space.

The trailer was tidy. Will's crayon drawings were posted on the walls. A cut-out paper butterfly was taped to the window, framed by handmade curtains. Egg cartons and children's books were tucked into an alcove above the couch. Next to the window behind the couch was Chelsea's sewing machine. I slid into the kitchen table bench, padded with a faded leaf-print cushion. The foldaway table was held up by one leg and wobbled as I leaned against it. A few flies buzzed around the room. Chelsea opened the refrigerator, and it was filled with pantry items and canned goods. The fridge didn't work, she said, so they used it for storage. They kept a small refrigerator outside for cold items.

Chelsea explained that she and her family had slowly been adjusting to living in a small space together. At their house in Kentucky—where they had multiple rooms and a huge backyard—it was easy to find an empty room, close the door, and not speak to anyone. Here that was more difficult. "Not having alone time is something that's really hard for me because I'm very much an introvert," she said. "There's nowhere to kinda hide and regroup. There are times Jacob comes home and he's exhausted and I'm like, 'You have to sit here and watch this child for a minute. I have to go into the bedroom and just be alone.'"

Jacob was trying to stay sober, and avoided hanging out with his coworkers because most of them drank heavily. His coworkers were also recent transplants to North Dakota, and many were first-generation immigrants from Mexico. "It's safer that way," Chelsea said. "We just kind of stick to ourselves and do family stuff." But since his coworkers lived in the same trailer park, it was difficult to avoid them completely.

Chelsea hadn't made any friends yet, but she hoped to find other women she could connect with. On her trips to nearby New Town, the largest town on the reservation, she'd chat with two older ladies who worked at the post office, and she followed the Williston chapter of a group called Oil Field Wives on Facebook. She also began blogging—for her personal website and for a national site called Real Oilfield Wives. She wanted to share her experience because there was limited information online about what it was like to live in an oil field camper with a family. She hoped she could show other moms it was possible to raise a well-adjusted kid in such conditions.

In her first post for Real Oilfield Wives, "Our Camper Life: An Introduction," she told the story of their journey to North Dakota. Her writing was breezy and positive. "Jacob has been working in North Dakota as a roustabout for about eight months now, so we are fairly new to the oil field lifestyle," she wrote. "He really seems to have found his niche and I'm so very proud of him! I am so grateful for the freedom our oil field lifestyle has afforded me so that I can work on my own projects and home school my son. . . . I hope you will join me as I chronicle our family's adventures with camper living, home school, and life in the North Dakota oil patch. It may be an unconventional lifestyle, but it works for us and I hope you will enjoy reading all about it!"

Subsequent posts included recipes and camper-living tips. There was also a post on the "not so fabulous things about living in an oil field camper," like dealing with dust, small spaces, and camper repairs. It was one of the few negative posts, though toward the end she included a positive note. She wrote that she "wouldn't trade [camper life] for the world," if it meant being with her family.

On Fridays she posted a photo called "This Moment," inspired by another blogger, to capture a single moment that she wanted to remember from the week. A "moment" from the summer of 2013 was a photo of Will. He stood in a gravel lot with wind-blown prairie grass behind him. In his tiny hand, he held a string. On the other end was a plastic bag, suspended in the air and puffed up from a breeze. Will had made himself a kite.

On the blog, Chelsea didn't delve too deeply into her personal life or the politics of being connected to the oil industry. "I just don't quite feel comfortable getting into the politics of it yet," she said. "It is such a touchy subject. I think the truth is somewhere in the middle." Her personal politics leaned toward liberal, and she tried to be environmentally conscious in her everyday life. She believed you could be both while staying affiliated with the oil field—although being an environmentally conscious liberal was quite unconventional in the area, especially for an oil field family. She argued that Jacob and his coworkers tried their best to avoid spills and protect the environment. Sure, there were a few bad apples, but for the most part, she believed people followed the rules.

Chelsea also refrained from blogging about the trailer park drama she experienced on almost a daily basis. The culture at their park was proving difficult to adjust to. They'd recently had trouble with their neighbors, who worked in the oil field as well. A rule at the trailer park was owners had to keep dogs tied up, which Chelsea followed diligently with Thor. But other residents disobeyed the rule. Dogs would approach Thor and Thor would lunge at them. Her neighbors berated her for Thor's behavior. "They really didn't like us," she said later. "But they were the idiots that should've obeyed the rules."

She ranted about the situation in a Facebook post:

In the past 48 hours I've been gossiped about so loud I could hear it . . . had my dog threatened with a knife and otherwise been made into the bad guy because people let their dogs off leash and they run at my dog who, of course, fights back. Yet still I go out this morning and there are dogs running all over the damn lot with no leash. Kiss my lily white Kentucky ass, folks. I am NOT the bad guy because you can't follow the rules! Next time I won't break up the fight your dog picks and I'll just let my dog eat yours. OVER IT!

In addition to dog-related squabbles, her next-door neighbors were often rowdy and drank late into the night. Chelsea called them "drunken preschool children." They'd sometimes circle their trucks together, drink beer, and listen to loud music. There was also drug use in the park. Jacob once found a meth pipe in the bathroom of a man he worked with; the man sometimes holed up in his trailer for days without emerging. Chelsea didn't like leaving the camper after dark. "There are murderers out there, there are people that disappear, there are Mexican drug cartels," she said. She kept her .38 revolver in the trailer and was glad to have a big dog like Thor.

Despite her reservations, during our visit Chelsea was positive and hopeful, with a we-can-do-this! attitude. She missed home, but Jacob was making good money. Their rent was affordable and their camper was paid off, which wasn't the case for many of her neighbors. She considered their camper to be in the mid- to lower range. "We got a hell of a deal," Chelsea said. "I try to remind myself that when I see some of the behemoths with dishwashers and laundry facilities that I sometimes lust after."

She explained there was a Fuzion camper in the park, a luxury RV that starts at around $85,000 new and could easily go up to $110,000 with all of the upgrades and features, such as a surround sound stereo system and a gas-burning fireplace. It cost more than their home in Kentucky. She walked by the RV when the blinds were open and saw a big-screen TV in the living room and little flat-screen TVs in other rooms. "I'm, like, we don't even have a TV!" She chuckled. "What's so weird out here is the appearance of wealth. Where we're from, if you're making that kind of money, you're driving a Mercedes, a BMW, a Porsche. Out here, it's not that flashy. People drive a huge truck, get a boat, or get a camper that's twice the size of ours. . . . But then you get these people who take out a loan to buy a trailer and get in over their heads. They can't make ends meet and they have to go home because they didn't play it smart."

With many local residents receiving $50,000 to $100,000 a month in oil royalties and plenty of oil field workers making over $100,000 a year, some people didn't think twice before plunking down $100,000 in cash for a luxury camper. Pockets of wealth were being created all over the region. By 2010, the average income in the county where Chelsea lived had doubled to $52,027 per person, ranking it among the richest 100 U.S. counties per capita—counties that included New York City and Marin, California. In 2012, about five millionaires were made every day in North Dakota, or some 2,000 a year, according to one researcher's calculations.

Back at Chelsea's trailer, Will approached me to show off his stuffed elephant. "See the twunk?" he said, holding it up. "Elephants pick food up with their twunks and put them in their mouth." He squished the elephant's body in half as he pushed on its trunk, then ran back to his mom.

Chelsea stepped outside to smoke a cigarette; the screen door slammed shut behind her from a gust of wind. Will watched her leave. As soon as she was out of sight, he went up to the wall and licked it, then giggled and ran back through the trailer to his room. Chelsea heard the commotion and came inside to check on him. "Ya-hoo!" he yelled, running past her.

She shook her head. "He does this many times a day." Will mostly played indoors, but sometimes he rode his bike and played in the dirt outside. Once he built a fort using camper chairs and a blue tarp. But Chelsea made sure he stayed close and she could watch him from the window.

Chelsea was glad to be able to home school Will. Staying in the camper with him all day was tough sometimes, but she didn't see any other options. "I don't want to send him to any of the reservation schools . . . I've not heard good things about oil field workers' children going to reservation schools, so I'm a little leery of that." The reservation schools weren't ranked high, and she didn't want him to be singled out as a newcomer oil field kid.

She felt that many people on the reservation didn't want her or her family there. We looked out her camper window at the row of trailers and prairie grass beyond. "I get it," she said. "These people came into your town—they've invaded your space. But you know, let's grant each other a little grace."

22. PASTOR JAY REINKE

One day, in May 2011, as Pastor Jay Reinke was holding his office hours at the church, a man walked in and asked to speak to him. The man told Reinke he'd been sleeping in his car. "I just can't do it anymore," the man said. His name was Stuart Bondurant and he had come to Williston from Rawlins, Wyoming. By the time he arrived in town, he had only $20 left to his name. He'd applied to jobs for three days, but despite having a commercial driver's license, no one seemed interested. He'd spent his remaining funds on gas and had a few dollars left for a slice of pizza at Pizza Hut. When he looked up from eating his meal, he saw Concordia Lutheran Church in the distance. He knew churches sometimes helped people out. If nothing else, maybe someone there could tell him about a homeless shelter or give him a free meal.

When Bondurant walked in around 1 p.m., Reinke told him to sit down, and they chatted. Bondurant said he was considering giving up and going home to Rawlins, but he didn't know what he'd do there either—plus he didn't have money to make the trip. Reinke felt for the man. He remembered saying "You know what? I probably shouldn't do this, but we've got floor space here. Why don't you just sleep on the floor tonight? Then you can keep looking for a job tomorrow." Bondurant agreed. He rolled out blankets in the TV lounge down the hall from Reinke's office. That night, alone in the church, he went into the dark sanctuary room, sat in the pews, and prayed. He prayed that the Lord would watch over him and keep him safe. He prayed for guidance. Was coming to Williston the right decision? So far, the locals seemed angry at him for being there. He'd received dirty looks at restaurants and grocery stores. When he went to wash his clothes at the laundromat called Bubba's Bubbles, the attendant muttered: "We don't want your kind here. You're dirtying up the machines." He wondered if he should've stayed back in Rawlins.

The next day, after Bondurant put away his blankets and left the church, he went across the street to apply for a job at the Airport International Inn. To his surprise, he was hired as a maintenance worker at $16 an hour, significantly more than he was making back in Wyoming. The job, however, didn't offer housing, so Bondurant returned to the church. Reinke agreed Bondurant could sleep at the church for a couple weeks until he saved up enough money to afford his own place.

About a week later, word got out that Pastor Reinke had someone sleeping at the church. A friend called Reinke and said he knew of another man who needed a place to sleep. "Would he be able to stay [at the church]?" his friend asked. Reinke agreed. What harm could come of it? he thought. It seemed like the Christian thing to do. He had no idea of the floodgates he'd opened.

In early 2012, Walmart had had enough. Managers worried they were scaring away customers. They had stopped allowing overnight parking but had difficulty enforcing the rule. They'd tried giving stern warnings, they'd tried calling the police to hand out tickets, but the people kept coming. Every night, there'd be a new set of pioneers who had recently arrived in town. Evidence grew of prostitution, drug use, and theft in the parking lot. In February, Walmart hired a security guard to patrol the lot at night and, in cooperation with the city, announced every car would be towed if it remained there past closing hours. The next morning, for the first time in nearly two years, the parking lot was empty.

Meanwhile, Pastor Reinke agreed to allow more and more men in his church. Nearly every day another man knocked on his door. "People just started gravitating to the church," said Reinke. He had a soft spot for the men—he lent them money when they needed it, and he gave a few men he trusted, like Bondurant, keys to the church and asked them to keep an eye on things when he wasn't there. He even invited some men to sleep at his house with his children, two of them teenage girls.

A few members of the congregation began to feel frustrated with the men sleeping in their church. There was sand on the pews during Sunday's worship service, and the men's restroom smelled. Men talked on cell phones outside. Some families who had attended the church for years stopped coming, and the church's neighbors started to complain.

"One night we saw a cop handcuff someone out here, and I just don't feel secure anymore," a neighbor, Donna Sieg, told the local paper. "I'm forever locking my doors and carrying my pepper spray with me, and I just don't feel comfortable in my own little neighborhood anymore."

"You got this cold-hearted response from everybody when they knew you weren't from the Williston area," said Bondurant. "It was not a very nice congregation. They didn't want nobody there and made you feel so unwelcome. You'd leave church feelin' like you were trash."

Reinke overheard locals complain about the influx of new people— if newcomers weren't planning to move their families to Williston and settle there, they said, they shouldn't come at all. Reinke was angry when he heard this: "I thought, 'We should be grateful they're here to work. Let's build whatever community we can while they're here. They've got families. They've got a home they're trying to save. What are people supposed to do? They've got to survive.'"

Many locals were simply angry their town was being taken over. Crime was increasing. Statewide, homicides were at the highest level in nearly 20 years. Rapes were at the highest level ever, according to data going back to 1990. And there were 2,872 drug-related arrests in the state, up 64 percent since 2002. In 2012, the NorthWest Narcotics Task Force, which covered the oil patch area, confiscated more than $85,000 in methamphetamine. And alcohol was a factor in more than half of the deadly traffic accidents in the state that year. Headlines on the front page of the *Williston Herald* in 2012 included "Man Robbed at Gunpoint," "4 Arrested on Kidnapping Charges," "Man Shot in Williston," "Two Arrested on Burglary, Drug Charges," "Man Jailed for Indecent Exposure."

Then there was Sherry Arnold, a 43-year-old math teacher and mother of two from Sidney, Montana, who was out jogging west of Williston early in the morning of January 7, 2012, when she was abducted and murdered by two men from Colorado. The men had traveled to the area to look for work in the oil industry and were using crack cocaine during the attack. Her body was found in a shallow grave near Williston two months later.

The gruesome crime shook the area and received national attention. Locals began to fear any single man with a mysterious background arriving in their town. Women talked about feeling afraid to go out at night. Licenses to carry concealed weapons in the county increased. "It's because of the oil boom and all the money the people have," Andy Anderson, owner of Scenic Sports & Liquor in Williston, told the Associated Press. "People, even some little old ladies, are buying a lot of handguns and piles of Mace and stun guns because of the crime."

Soon after the incident, the *Williston Herald* editorial staff decided to print a full list of registered sex offenders living in the county—their number had doubled in the past 16 months. "Williston and Williams County is not the same community it used to be. We all know that," the article stated.

Evidence of sex trafficking and prostitution in the area added to the uneasiness. Ads for female escorts in Williston filled Backpage.com, like "Riley," 22 and from Hawaii, who "always aimed to please." And "21-year-old Megan," who claimed to be "fetish friendly." Rumors spread about prostitutes targeting man camps and truck disposal lines, where truckers would sit and wait for hours to unload oil field waste, to find new customers. Williston resident Gloria Cox stopped letting her 13-year-old grandson walk anywhere alone because of the child trafficking rumors she heard.

Police departments in the area felt overwhelmed and understaffed. The Williston Police Department went from receiving 6,089 calls for police services in 2009 to over 17,000 calls in 2012. Before the boom, Williston's local jail, built in the 1950s, could house only 37 people and rarely filled up. A $14.5 million expansion in 2008 increased its capacity to 112 beds. The facility was expected to last five decades, but as soon as it opened in 2009, the jail was already full. Many inmates were there awaiting sentencing from the backlogged courts. The region lacked mental health services and alcohol and drug treatment programs. There were no psychiatrists in Williston. Scott Busching, the county sheriff, told the *Williston Herald*: "We simply let people out of jail that probably should be here."

In March 2012, a man on YouTube under the screen name "Lasvegas collapse" posted a video telling potential newcomers that Concordia Lutheran Church was a place where people could sleep. In the video, he drives by the church with his camera, revealing the exact location. "Parking lot fills up, so you got to get here early. As you can see it's not very big. There's probably about 30 spots," he says in the video. The video received over 30,000 views, and Reinke soon saw an uptick in men arriving at his doorstep saying they had heard about it through the video.

Men would show up to the church in tears, saying that coming to

Williston was their last hope. "It became kind of a beacon for people," said Reinke. One man told the pastor his beloved wife had recently died of cancer. He'd been laid off from his job after she passed away. He struggled daily with grief and mounting debt from her medical bills and his unpaid mortgage. He believed coming to Williston was his last chance to turn his life around.

Reinke began calling the men who slept at the church "the Overnighters." In the evenings, men played cards or Skyped with family members back home. Occasionally someone dropped off a home-cooked meal or buckets of fried chicken from KFC. Some men stayed a few nights, found a job that provided housing, and were on their way—grateful for Reinke's help. But other times, the number of people asking for help was overwhelming. "I remember one time it was bitterly cold, and we had like 50 or 60 people in the building. It was way too many. We had them everywhere," said Reinke. "Then three guys showed up late at night. I said, 'We cannot have this. You've got to find another place.'"

At least once a week, Reinke had to turn a man away—sometimes because the church was at capacity and other times because he simply didn't want the person to stay. It often took one look for Reinke to decide. If the man looked unkempt or like a vagrant, Reinke would tell him to move along. If the man said, "I hitchhiked to get here," Reinke took it as a sign the man was transitory and not planning to build a life in Williston. He'd let the man stay the night but would ask him to leave in the morning. "There were people who shouldn't have come to Williston," said Reinke. "I remember one guy had long straggly hair and looked like a beat-up guy. We all go through adversity, but he's not going to survive in Williston. So let's get real here—it's time to go home. It wasn't always peaches and cream."

Other men overstayed their welcome. Initially, Reinke gave each Overnighter a two-week deadline to find employment and another place to stay. But two weeks simply wasn't long enough. He extended the deadline to a month and sometimes longer, depending on the situation. "Unless they got a job with housing, it just didn't happen that quickly," said Reinke. But he wanted to be clear the church was a short-term solution, not anyone's permanent residence. He had to nudge some men out the door. One man stayed for nearly six months because of health problems that made it harder for him to survive in Williston, but it was rare for men to stay longer than two or three months. "When there are no options, you can't just kick them out," said Reinke. "It's harder than that."

The last thing Reinke wanted was for people to think he had started a homeless shelter. One eccentric middle-age black man who stayed at the church often carried his personal belongings in plastic Walmart bags. Reinke told him he needed to knock it off. He looked homeless, and he wasn't going to find a job by looking homeless. He'd tell other men to cut their hair, improve their personal hygiene, and stay away from the local parks where the homeless tended to gather. "I was sometimes merciless," said Reinke.

Reinke soon established rules for the Overnighters—no alcohol consumption, no showing up to the church intoxicated, no tobacco use in the building or parking lot, no weapons, no fighting, no profanity, no interpersonal loans, no long-distance phone calls from the church phone, no food preparation in the kitchen except the microwave, no work shoes worn inside the church, shirts must be worn at all times, photo ID is required, occupants must sign in and out, no one is allowed in the building between 7 a.m. and 9 p.m., devotions after 9 p.m. are mandatory for those in the building, and the doors are locked at 11 p.m.—there were 23 rules total. He asked each Overnighter to sign an "Occupancy Agreement" with the rules listed. The first line of the agreement was: "By the grace of our Lord and Savior Jesus Christ, Concordia Lutheran Church would like to welcome you."

In addition, Reinke implemented background checks for the men sleeping in his church—mostly to placate the growing complaints from members of his congregation, the city, and his neighbors. Reinke used his own discretion on whether he would allow an Overnighter with a criminal record to stay at the church, and it was rare he turned someone away on their record alone. He "welcomed sinners," he said. He still let men with felonies sleep in his church and, at times, his home. Two registered sex offenders stayed at Concordia. One was Keith Graves, a 36-year-old man from Los Angeles who had a 1999 conviction for a lewd act with a minor under 14. A reporter at the *Williston Herald* received a tip that Graves was staying at the church and questioned Reinke about it. Though the reporter never published a piece on the topic, Reinke worried Graves might jeopardize the Overnighters program and moved Graves into an extra bedroom in his home with his wife and children. A few years later, Graves was arrested for organizing a sex trafficking operation in Williston—some of which likely occurred while he was staying with Reinke—and sentenced to 33 years in prison.

Despite Reinke's efforts, some men had little intention of turning their lives around. They were simply running away from their past. Williston became a place where men with dark pasts could easily hide; a destination for people to run from the law, or disappear—literally, in some cases.

Disappearance cases increased, and the police department had few resources to solve them. "We have a very transient population," said Detective Caleb Fry. "Guys will go missing and they just stop calling their wives or families completely." Most of the time, they eventually showed up, but not always. There was Kristopher Clarke, 29, who came to North Dakota to work in the oil fields, but went missing in 2012 and was never found. For two years, his family searched for answers, only to discover that Clarke was likely murdered by James Henrikson and Timothy Suckow. Or Jack Sjol, 58, who was reported missing from his rural ranch in April 2013. Three weeks later, his body was found in a private dump site east of Williston.

Then there was the case of Joe Lee. Lee came to Williston in 2012 from Arizona and stayed at Reinke's church off and on in 2013 as an Overnighter. "He was just a wonderful, wonderful, wonderful guy, and almost brilliant," said Reinke. "He became one of the primary leaders at the church." Lee eventually moved out of the church—he found a job at a burger joint in Williston called Big Willy's and another place to live. Reinke knew Lee had struggled with drugs in the past but hoped he had found a fresh start in Williston. "He seemed like a real survivor, almost like a cat—always landing on his feet," said Reinke.

But on June 1, 2013, Joe Lee borrowed a friend's truck and never returned. A few days later, the truck was discovered abandoned by a shallow creek north of Williston, and Lee's boots and socks were found 200 yards away. The police never found a body. "It was an odd case," said Detective Fry. "He was a loner. He didn't do much with anyone else. He moved from place to place, and there was meth use involved."

Reinke speculated drugs had something to do with his disappearance. He talked to Lee on the phone the day before he went missing, and Lee wasn't making sense. "I thought, something's wrong, something's wrong. He's doing something," said Reinke. "He was talking fast and very rapid."

Detective Fry claimed that the police department did an extensive search and used a search-and-rescue robot to scan the stream's bed, but many of Lee's family and friends believe that after the initial search, police moved on too quickly. "I feel that the investigation went nowhere because they chose to not do anything about it," said Blake Hall, one of Lee's closest friends in Phoenix. "'Cause he wasn't important. And that's not really fair."

A local woman named Stephanie Nelson, who volunteered to search for missing persons in the region and helped search for Lee, agreed that the police department didn't do all it could at the time of his disappearance. "He got lost in the shuffle because people were so busy," she said. "We had a lot of people missing at that time."

Blake Hall believed Lee was either murdered by drug lords or staged his disappearance to escape but had little evidence to support his theories. And being 1,500 miles away, he was unlikely to find out more about what Lee was doing the day he disappeared. "I miss my friend Joe. Whatever happened to him, he deserves better than this. It's sad no one's probably ever gonna look into what happened to him."

Lee's family is still hoping for answers.

23. TOM STAKES

Tom Stakes's life wasn't always this way. Years ago, Stakes was a pastor in the small town of Kenbridge, Virginia. He had a stable job, a wife, two sons, a three-bedroom house in a brand-new subdivision. In many ways, he had accomplished the American Dream. Growing up as a poor orphan in the South, he graduated from college and achieved a level of success others from his childhood could only dream of.

In 1955, Tom was born out of wedlock in Tampa, Florida, to a woman named Joanie Johnson. At birth, his name was James Thomas Johnson, but he's gone by many different versions over the years—James, Tommy, Thomas, Jim, Jimmy, and today, Tom. In Georgia, he's Jim. In Louisiana, he's Tommy. "People can call me whatever they feel comfortable with callin' me," he said. "I mean, they could call me asshole—jus' don't call me late for supper!" Today, when people ask him his name, he says, "Tom. Just Tom. That's all there is."

The memories of his time with his mother are hazy, but he remembers being left alone often. No one seemed to care if he came home from school or not, and there were no rules at home. "I could leave after school and never go home. And when I showed up, they didn't care." Eventually, Child Protective Services intervened, and six-year-old

Tom and his little brother, Dennis, who was four, were placed in foster care. For two years, they were shuffled through eight different foster homes. It was a confusing time for Tom—he didn't understand why he was taken away or who his parents were supposed to be. "As a child, you get passed around from one family to another, tossed around like a rag doll. You get kinda weirded out, with who to trust. It messes ya up."

When Tom was eight years old, he and his brother were adopted by Henry David Stakes and Mayonie Stakes, and he became James Thomas Stakes. His adoptive mother was a schoolteacher and his father was a Baptist minister, and that same year they moved to the small farming town of Transylvania in northeast Louisiana for his father to preach at the only church in town. Located about a mile away from the Mississippi, the town had only 600 people, one convenience store, one gas station, and a cotton mill. It was surrounded by soybean and cotton fields. Tom and his brother liked to play behind a levee next to the Mississippi. They borrowed neighbors' horses and rode bareback through the fields. Tom loved animals and soon after they moved to town, he caught a wild baby rabbit in a field and took care of it. He cared for abandoned baby squirrels until they were old enough to fend for themselves. He raised beavers, deer, possums, armadillos, birds, stray cats—any orphan animal he came across, he took it in. "Oh, bless their hearts," he said. "I've rescued so many little animals in my life. They were jus' beautiful because they jus' loved you unconditionally."

Mayonie and Henry were strict parents who expected their children to follow the rules. If rules were broken, there were harsh consequences. Pastor Henry had a temper, and would beat the boys until they bled while Mayonie stood by and watched. "They'd whoop them kids for nothin,'" said David Kirby, Tom's childhood friend. "His daddy was hard on him and his mom was mean as hell. I don't know the reason they adopted those boys. I don't think they ever did love 'em." Tom wore a towel under two pairs of pants to help cushion the blows. His father couldn't tell Tom was wearing the extra clothing, but the boy still gave a dramatic performance to convince his father the beating was excruciating. "He was pretty conniving," said Kirby. "He's street smart. You could turn him loose anywhere and he'd survive."

Mayonie and Henry had another adopted son, John Alton, who went by Al and was two years older than Tom. For the most part, Al followed the rules, but Tom and Dennis were troublemakers. "I gave 'em hell," said Tom. "I rebelled against everythin.' Nobody was gonna tell me what to do, 'cause I had already learned to raise myself by that time. I didn't trust anybody." He shoplifted, burglarized stores, smoked marijuana, skipped school, started fights. He showed an affinity for substance abuse at an early age, and would sniff gas just to feel a buzz.

His parents tried to instill Christian values and a belief in God in him, but he went to church and agreed to be baptized only to appease them. When he became a teenager, he questioned the existence of a higher power. One day, to test his beliefs, he stole $5 from his mother. Tom felt guilty about it and said, "God, if you want me to give it back, then let it rain tomorrow." He knew the forecast was sunny and clear. The next day, sure enough, it poured down rain. He still resisted, not wanting to return the money, and while riding in a tractor with a friend, his favorite wallet made out of elephant ear—an expensive gift from his aunt—slipped out of his pocket with the $5 bill tucked inside. By the time he noticed it was gone, it was too late. He never found it. In his mind, the message from God was clear. "God said, 'I'm gonna get it from you one way or another!'" Tom said.

At 16, his parents sent him to a reform school called the Louisiana Training Institute. It didn't do much good. Tom only felt more abandoned and rebelled just as much. (It was later discovered that institute staff members were abusing the children.) When he turned 18, he joined the Army in an effort to impress a girl and hoped it would "make a man out of him." It was 1973, the year the United States withdrew troops from Vietnam and the draft ended. Tom survived basic training and was stationed for over a year at a base in Fort Campbell, Kentucky. In addition to combat training and marksmanship, he learned how to parachute from airplanes, navigate his way across a mountain range, and survive in the wilderness. "They trained me to be a killer," he said. His family thought he was finally becoming a responsible young man. Then suddenly Tom went AWOL.

Tom had fallen in love. Her name was Linda. She attended North Georgia College and they met while he was stationed at the nearby Ranger camp. When he returned to Kentucky, they dated long distance. One weekend, the sergeant gave Tom a pass to visit her but warned there would be consequences if he didn't show for Monday morning drills at 8 a.m. Tom intended to be there, but on the way back late Sunday night, he pulled over to rest, fell asleep, and didn't awake until late morning. He missed the drills. He knew he was already in trouble, so he turned around, headed back to Georgia, and married Linda the next month. When he finally returned to base, his sergeant gave him two options: undesirable discharge, which was a few levels above a dishonorable discharge but would disqualify him from any veteran's benefits, or stay and be tried in military court. Tom wanted out. He took the undesirable discharge.

Tom and Linda stayed married for three years. Married life was much different from their whirlwind courtship period, and their initial infatuation quickly fizzled. "I don't know what went on in her life. I mean . . . she didn't want to have sex. I couldn't deal with it," he said. Tom left her for another woman.

Tom met his second wife, Patti, a few years later while he was living in Gainesville, Georgia. They had two children together, James David Stakes and Daniel Josiah Stakes, and Tom was amazed at the power of fatherhood. "My happiest times was seein' both of my sons born. When I saw them come into the world, that made my world 'cause I didn't think I was capable of doing somethin' that beautiful."

Patti's father was also a preacher, and she attended church regularly.

Tom tagged along grudgingly at first but then found himself enjoying it. "I started believin' some of the doctrine they had," he said. "I felt like God was leadin' me to the ministry." He decided he wanted to become a minister like his father and enrolled in Atlanta Christian College in East Point, Georgia. He didn't excel in school, but he passed, receiving mostly Bs and Cs. He and Patti lived in campus housing and on weekends went fishing and swimming in nearby lakes. After four years, he graduated with a bachelor of science degree in Christian ministry, and the couple moved to Kenbridge, Virginia, for Tom to preach at the local church.

Tom loved preaching—he felt like he was making a difference in people's lives. "I can read people. I know who needs help and who doesn't need it, just on their mannerisms and their voice, how they speak. There's things you learn," he said. He was also good at it—church filled up every Sunday. But at times, having so many people who needed his help was difficult. "I love people," he said, "but sometimes you feel their feelins' and their pain, their hurt. And sometimes it's more than I can handle." He claimed he didn't drink while he was a pastor, but he still smoked marijuana in secret. After a few years, Patti's parents fell ill and they moved back to Gainesville, Georgia, to care for them. Tom couldn't find work there as a pastor, so he became a supervisor at a poultry plant. Patti worked at a bank, and they bought their first home together.

On the outside, everything looked great for their family—they were well on their way to a stable, middle-class life. But on the inside, life was hard. He and Patti fought constantly, and he was working long hours. Day-to-day parenting was difficult for both of them. Tom would come home exhausted from work, and Patti would list the boys' bad behaviors that day. She'd tell Tom to punish them. Tom would whip his boys just as his father did to him. "I whooped 'em hard and I hate myself for that," he said. "That hurt me so much. They were a part of me, and I loved 'em with all my heart."

Soon Tom started to lose it. At the poultry plant, he fell madly in love with a Hispanic woman who was married and wouldn't be with him. To calm his frustrations, he bought a motorcycle, a boat, and a new truck. He grew out his hair and beard. Finally, he quit his steady job at the plant. "My life was changin'. I started thinkin,' is this all there is? I like to have fun, I wanna go out and have some fun." He joined a motorcycle crew and met a woman named Diane who had recently divorced her second husband. They started having an affair, and Tom told Patti he was leaving her.

During this time, he job-hopped. He sold vacuum cleaners, worked at a printing company, did construction, built cabinets. "There wasn't a lot of stability in my life," said Tom. "I went from job to job. If I could get a raise from another guy, I went with that job. If it didn't work out for me, I'd get another job with somebody else." He and Diane launched a construction cleaning business together in Oakwood, Georgia, called J & D Cleaning (J stood for Jim, the name he went by at that time). But after a few months, it all fell apart—his relationship with Diane, the business, his family. The patterns of his childhood were resurfacing. He took off to Atlanta to get away and sort out what was happening to him. Patti was angry and told him his sons wanted nothing to do with him, even though his son Jay later said the opposite was true; they asked about their father constantly. Soon he moved to a double-wide trailer in the woods near Dahlonega, Georgia, with a friend he knew from his military days. He wanted to escape.

Tom didn't hear from his family again for some time until his 15-year-old son, Jay, called him unexpectedly. It wasn't good news— his adoptive mother, Mayonie, had passed away. "My son called me and said 'Dad, are you sittin' down?' I said, 'Well, hang on, let me sit down.' That's when he said, 'Your uncle Billy called and—your mom just died.' They found her dead. She was gettin' ready to go to church that Sunday mornin'. She was by herself, in her slip, slumped over in the bed. The doctor said that she didn't feel a thing, it just happened.

And so I was tore up. I didn't really care anymore, I just—that was a tough time for me." Although they had a difficult relationship, his mother showed more affection for Tom as she aged. His father had died 10 years earlier from a heart attack. Tom felt completely alone in the world.

Tom had always been a substance user, mostly alcohol, cigarettes, and marijuana, but he'd always felt in control. He'd never been interested in hard drugs. But something had changed. He used whatever substance he could get his hands on, including crack. He had inherited significant wealth from his mother—about $160,000, 15 acres of land with an oil well on it, and a couple of houses. But within a year of his first hit of crack, it was all gone. He and his roommate spent about $1,000 a night. Every last penny of his inheritance went to his addiction. "After I started, it was over. It was done," said Tom. "I didn't think I was gonna make it out of that. I didn't care. It grabs you and you don't care about anythin' but that high. You're not thinkin' straight. Within a year, I'd done spent everythin'." Patti, his brothers, and his remaining friends stopped talking to him. Patti told him never to contact her or his sons again.

After the money was gone, Tom went to Atlanta to try to find work again. He worked odd jobs but spent whatever he made on drugs or booze. It was there that Tom became homeless for the first time. With no money to pay rent, he slept under a big oak tree behind a bar. He had no blankets, only a jacket. "I huddled up against the tree to get away from the wind," he said. "There was a lotta homeless people down there. You'd see 'em, pushin' grocery carts with whatever cans they could find, sleepin' over hot air vents in the sidewalks." Tom never thought he'd be one of them. He had hit bottom.

24. "ON A MUDDY LOCATION, SOMEWHERE IN NORTH DAKOTA"

For months, I tried and tried to get permission to visit an active well—a few companies laughed in my face. After pulling some strings, a friend was able to get me onto a drilling operation across the border in Montana, but not on a location with Cindy Marchello's crew. One night, however, after I had known Marchello and Mana Kula for over a year, Kula said he could sneak me in. "But you can't get out of the car," he said. If anyone asked, I was to tell people I was an engineer. It was more likely for a woman on site to be an engineer.

I nodded and tried to hide my excitement.

The night we left, I met Kula at the man camp. Marchello was at the trailer, and she wished me luck. She advised me to use the restroom before I left—she had endless stories about the difficulties of being a woman on location and needing to go. There was supposed to be an outhouse on every location, but sometimes it wasn't there, or it hadn't been cleaned in months. "If it's dark, I crawl under the truck," she said.

Kula never slept well the nights his crew worked on location. Even though a man named E, a trusted childhood friend of Kula's, was supervising the crew that night, Kula still worried something might go wrong. His worst fear was an accident occurring on site that he could have prevented. Kula needed to pick up a flash drive on the site tonight, but he also wanted to check on his crew and make sure everyone was safe.

We left camp a little after 7 p.m. and stepped into Kula's heavy-duty pickup. We planned to drive two and a half hours to the well site, which was located somewhere in the Killdeer Mountains. Kula was also giving a ground hand, Chris, a ride out there. Chris was from Arkansas and had worked at C&J for almost a year. He'd recently returned from working in Saudi Arabia's oil fields. He wore a white bandana around his head and called me "ma'am." Kula and Chris sat up front and I squeezed into the narrow backseat next to a case of water bottles, a lunch pail, and a hard hat. A Polynesian lei hung from Kula's rearview mirror.

Chris chewed tobacco while we drove, spitting into an empty water bottle, and Kula talked about the constant driving they did in the field. Though his crew mostly worked in North Dakota, C&J had offices all over the country. Departments were sometimes short-staffed and needed help from crew members in other states. Recently, Kula and Sam drove from Texas to Oklahoma, then back to North Dakota, then to Pennsylvania. Then Kula headed back to Utah for his days off. After one day in Utah, C&J called and needed him back in North Dakota. Kula drove to Williston, looked at the problems, decided he couldn't fix them, and turned around and drove back to Utah. The entire ordeal added up to nearly 6,000 miles—some 85 hours on the road within a few days.

We drove past Theodore Roosevelt National Park as an orange sun slid below the horizon.

"Did you miss this?" Kula asked Chris with a mischievous smile.

Chris laughed. "Yeah, well, it's better than Saudi. It was a lot of false promises. It sounded good on paper, until you got over there." Recently Saudi Arabia had been recruiting more U.S. oil and gas companies and their workers in hopes of using fracking technology to exploit its own shale reserves.

Kula had written directions on a tiny scrap of paper. He pulled it out of his pocket to check that we were headed in the right direction. We sped along a dirt road at about 40 miles an hour, leaving billows of dust behind us. We passed hay bales, grazing cows, and a farm tractor. Soon we turned onto an unmarked dirt road. I had no idea where we were.

After another 45 minutes, Kula said we were nearing the well location. He slowed down in the middle of the road and pulled the truck into park. "I gotta take a leak," he said, opening the door and leaving it ajar. He stood in front of the door and faced northwest, looking over an open field of prairie grass, to relieve himself.

Chris exited the passenger-side door and faced northeast. He relieved himself as well.

I stayed in the backseat. I had used the restroom at a gas station over an hour ago and needed to go again. But there was no way I was joining them.

We continued on to the well location. Large halogen floodlights cast a harsh white light onto the dirt clearing. About a dozen metal trailers lined the site, and two dozen oil storage tanks and heavy trucks surrounded the well. Nearby was a giant spool the size of a small house that held tightly wrapped coil piping. It was connected to a reel house, a small metal box where the operator sat, with a CAUTION HIGH PRESSURE sign in front. A crane towered nearby. The well was owned by Petro-Hunt LLC, a company from Dallas, Texas.

Kula pulled up to a group of men standing by an outhouse and rolled down the passenger window, amplifying the roar of heavy equipment. A pungent smell of rotten egg, from H_2S gas present at a well nearby, wafted into the car. Sam, who had been at poker night, stuck his head in the window: "You guys bring something for us to eat?"

Kula apologized. The crew hadn't eaten anything since that morning, and he had forgotten to pick up food. Chris exited the truck and walked over to the outhouse to smoke a cigarette. The smoking area was only about 150 feet away from the active well. Kula invited me into the front seat, as long as I kept my head down and didn't tell anyone that I was a journalist.

Sam watched Chris walk away. "Dude, look at those shiny boots," he said to Kula. "Damn, he *is* a greenhorn!"

A man named Nick approached the truck to say hello. He seemed surprised to see a woman in Kula's truck and introduced himself. Kula told Nick I was a friend. I stayed quiet, not wanting to lie about what I was doing there. Nick nodded, but I wasn't sure if he bought it. He didn't ask any more questions, though.

After Nick walked away, Kula said to me, "Man, I hate for Nick to see you. He's a good kid and a smart kid, but he's trying to move up. He's got a big mouth. If I hear anything tomorrow, then I'll know who it was."

Kula drove around the site and explained what was happening: The crew was currently pressure testing the well before they "went down the hole" with pipe. If there was too much or too little pressure as the pipe made its descent, the well could explode and kill everyone on site. Crews were always dealing with extremely high pressures. "That's why everyone is behind that line," said Kula, pointing to a group of workers standing off to the side. "Something could fly out if there's a leak."

Engines whirred and metal banged in the background. There were many types of tanks and liquids on site: a nitrogen tank, two tanks for flowback water, a half-dozen tanks of fresh water. Kula showed me the reel house, or the "dog house," where the coil operator sat and controlled the speed and direction of the coil tubing and monitored pressure levels.

Almost every job on a well site was contracted out, which insulated the big oil companies that owned the well from liability. If an accident happened on site, small companies like C&J were typically stuck with the fines and legal proceedings, while the owner could often walk away from any responsibility. At the site that evening, there were at least six independent-contractor companies at work—frackers, coil tubers, water haulers, tool guys, crane operators, and flowback hands, who monitored how many barrels were coming back out of the well and alerted the team of any leaks or clogs.

A man's voice came over Kula's radio. "We got 2,000 pounds on the line," he said, referring to the pressure level at the well. "Let us know when you want us to open."

"We're moving on to get one barrel out," someone replied, meaning one barrel should return through flowback if everything was working properly.

"Got it."

"This is the life of a coil tuber," Kula said. "It's a lot of hurry up to sit and wait for hours and hours, days and days." Many times, the crew arrived to the site ready to go, but the fracking crew hadn't finished. "Today they weren't ready," said Kula. "But we'll rig everything up and get as far as we can." Kula guessed they'd be done the next night, if nothing went wrong.

"I don't know where our safety guy is. He's supposed to be out here," Kula said. "We've got to be careful. Before there was just one OSHA oil field guy coming around, but they put more money into it because of all the deaths around here. You got more of them running around. If they show up on site and you're not spaced out, you'll be fined. Our equipment is supposed to be 100 feet away from the flowback tanks," he explained. They usually eyeballed the 100 feet, he said, or a ground hand walked 100 steps to measure the distance. At Kula's former company, Cudd, his crew stationed a pump too close to the well, and it was fined $25,000, he said.

"When I was first out here, it was harder for me to trust my guys to do what I know they know how to do," Kula explained. "I used to come and sit here till the job was done. There's a lot of factors you have to watch. You have to watch everything closely because if you have one screw-up, it could be a big disaster. A lot of times the flowback crews are so green, you've got to constantly watch them."

One mistake new workers often made was not measuring the gas levels. They'd see the flare burning and think everything was fine, but they weren't monitoring exactly how much gas was spewing from the well. There could be a gas leak and no one would know. "Gas is heavy so it's sitting there and anything can ignite that gas," said Kula. "That's how locations blow up and you kill everybody on the location. That's why it's hard to sleep when I know there's a lot of green people on location. It's nerve-wracking. You triple-check everything. If you keep doing that, you'll be safe. But it's like anything you keep doing over and over—it gets so redundant, then you get relaxed, and that's when something happens." Kula had been lucky in his career so far—he'd never seen another man or woman die on site.

Technically, companies weren't supposed to have more than two new workers, or greenhands, on a crew. But the rule was often overlooked to expedite drilling, explained Kula. Having a crew full of new workers was particularly common among smaller service companies. "They just hide it," Kula said, talking about his experience working with many oil companies. "They give them red hats because people aren't going to check." A red hat signifies more experience. "At a certain point, they don't care. They just want to get the job done." Many companies handed out bonuses for finishing a job ahead of schedule.

Kula saw a man wearing a hard hat walking in the direction of his truck. "Is he coming over here?" Kula asked. It was the company man, he explained. Kula didn't want him to see me. The company man oversaw the entire operation—from drilling, to fracking, to completion. He was also an independent contractor hired by the larger oil company, but he was in charge of what happened on the site. Marchello called them big babysitters. They typically sat inside a mobile trailer and watched everyone work.

"We'll go back over here," Kula said, and drove to the other side of the well. I slid lower in my seat.

The radio crackled. "You guys got any coffee over there?" a man's voice said.

"I can go check. We have a coffee maker in here," someone replied.

"There's a lot of chewin' and a lot of coffee out here," said Kula. "You get into a lot of bad habits."

Kula opened the truck door and yelled over the loud hum of equipment. "Sam! Sam!"

Sam came running up to Kula's truck.

"What are we doing here?" Kula asked. "Are we getting ready to go in the well?"

"Yep," Sam replied.

As he walked away, Kula said, "He's one of the hardest workers here. He's ready to be a supervisor. He knows how to run all the equipment here—down to the fine details—but his English is not that good. I feel bad for him. We're trying to teach him."

A few minutes later E, Kula's good friend and the supervisor on site tonight, approached the truck. E needed printer paper located on another well site a half hour away. Kula agreed to drive him there.

E jumped into the backseat.

"Has everything gone okay?" Kula asked.

"Yeah," said E. "There was a lot of safety meetings so it took forever."

We drove down a dirt road and the rotten-egg smell from H_2S gas became stronger. It was nauseating.

"Oh, sorry, that was me," Kula said. He and E laughed at the joke. "Makes you want an egg sandwich, doesn't it?" Kula said.

"It's okay, we won't die until tomorrow," E joked.

"You want to use the bathroom here, Blaire?" Kula asked, laughing.

Kula suspected a well nearby was leaking. E said he felt close to passing out when the crew drove past it earlier. "I was like, dude, I'm outta here. Good thing the wind wasn't blowing our way." H_2S could escape during the drilling process, but it was especially potent around large volumes of stagnant oil. Deadly clouds could sit in holding tanks, pipelines, and semi trucks. In 2013, a 24-year-old rig hand died after he inhaled a cloud of gas from a broken pipe. I covered my mouth as we drove by, but I knew that without a gas mask, it was pointless.

Around 1 a.m., Kula and I headed back to the man camp. I yawned and dozed off during the drive, but Kula seemed alert. He chewed on sunflower seeds to stay awake. He used to guzzle energy drinks, he said, but they only made him crash. He also sometimes sang along loudly to Bob Marley. For this drive, he simply talked a lot, telling me more about his family. Kula hadn't dated much since he separated from his ex-wife. His first year working in North Dakota, he only spent 10 days back at home. Kula had considered moving his children to North Dakota, but he didn't think he'd see them much with his busy work schedule. "I hope to eventually move my family to a place where I'm working," he said. "But they know that this is what we have to do, what I have to do, for our family."

25. TOM STAKES

The week after the campground closed for the season, I called the Andresen family. They were living in the woods a few miles from the campground. Tom Stakes was still with them. I attempted to find the location, but after driving 30 minutes on a dirt road and finding no one, I eventually turned back. Soon they had to leave there too. A wildlife management ranger came by and gave them a $100 ticket for illegal camping. The family decided to return to Utah, and Stakes bade them farewell. Soon the cell phone numbers I had for the family stopped working. I never saw them again.

After Stakes was evacuated from the woods, he went back to sleeping in his truck near the train station in Williston and painting decks for $10 an hour. Sometimes it was difficult to sleep in the parking lot. Trains roared by at all hours of the night. Almost every night when the bars closed at 2 a.m., drunken crowds walked past his car, waking him. Other nights, he was part of the drunken crowd. Fights often broke out in the parking lot. "They'd be fightin' outside my truck and I didn't know who they were," Stakes said. "Then I'd have to try and break 'em up." Stakes was known in the Williston bar scene for breaking up fights—he hated seeing people be violent with each other. One night, Stakes said he broke up a fight between two men and one guy was so thankful, he handed Stakes a $100 bill and took him to the strip club to buy him a lap dance. Stakes took it as a sign from God that he should continue breaking up fights.

For meals, Stakes usually kept sandwich supplies and milk in a cooler in the bed of his truck or gathered donated canned food from the Salvation Army. A mobile church van, run by a man named Pastor Larry, often drove by the parking lot and handed out sandwiches to the men sleeping there. One friend of Stakes's who was leaving Williston to go home for the winter bequeathed Stakes his camp cookstove, but Stakes didn't want to draw attention to himself by using it, so he kept it packed away. Stakes missed the serenity of living at Trenton Lake, but he liked being closer to the bars. "It was a prime spot 'cause all the bars were right there," he said. "You just walk right over, get drunk, and walk back."

During this time, Stakes frequented KK's Korner bar almost every night. He made friends easily when he was drinking. One was Eddie Bergeson, whom he met at KK's when Bergeson yelled at Stakes across the bar: "Hey, Moses!" referring to Stakes's long white hair and beard. After chatting and discussing their favorite bands, they found out they were both sleeping in the same parking lot. Bergeson had come to Williston from Mississippi to find work as a painter. Back in Mississippi, Bergeson was a drummer in a band. He usually manned the jukebox at KK's while Stakes simulated the guitar parts for each song. They became fast friends. Then Stakes met Greg Mackie, who came from Portland, Oregon, at KK's, and the three of them started hanging out.

Mackie was a younger man who liked to smoke marijuana. He wore a bandana wrapped around his forehead and jean shorts and sandals. When he was younger, he once attempted to follow the wind, he said. Literally. He waited until he felt a breeze, then walked in that direction until he felt the wind shift. But the wind didn't bring him to Williston. He came in 2011 because he needed a job like everyone else.

Mackie was another refugee from the housing market and construction industry collapse. He used to make a decent living working in construction, but ever since the recession, he'd been living off food stamps in Portland, hanging out at the park playing chess and basketball and watching fire dancers. When he ran out of money and heard about the oil boom, he decided to give it a try. He'd been in Williston the longest out of all his friends. When he first arrived, he quickly found a job doing construction for $14 an hour, but the job didn't provide housing. He slept in a tent behind a grove of trees by the railroad tracks. It seemed like a good spot at first, but he soon realized he was sleeping next to a police shooting range. He didn't stay there long because he grew tired of being jolted awake every morning by gunshots. Next he hid out illegally in an abandoned, bedbug-infested man camp trailer for a few weeks but worried about getting caught. He then bought a rusted-out Chrysler minivan for $275. "It ran but it didn't have no brakes, so you had to drive with the e-brake," he said. "It was pretty scary." When that broke down, he sold it for parts and purchased an old, 16-passenger school bus to sleep in. He renovated it with the help of his friends, pulling out the seats and installing a fridge, a stove, a stereo system, a heater, and a solar panel on the roof to power everything. The fridge, however, worked only when the bus was perfectly level, which was rare. He parked it near where Stakes and Bergeson slept.

Though the area was mostly empty during the day, by around 9 p.m., the parking lot and adjacent street filled up with sleeping men, feet sticking out of car windows and pillows scrunched up against the doors and seats. Trash from the car sleepers littered the parking lot. Stakes and Bergeson always parked their cars backward in the lot, up against a chain-link fence and under a few tall cottonwood trees. Parking backward helped hide their tags and, for Stakes, deterred stragglers from picking through his belongings in the bed of his pickup. He and Bergeson liked to park in the corner if spots were available. They felt this was the most hidden area of the parking lot, though if anyone was looking for sleeping men in cars, they wouldn't be difficult to find. Looming over the parking lot was a sign that read VIDEO SURVEILLANCE with a picture of a video camera, but no one seemed to worry about who might be watching them.

Another man named Nate Beatty, in his late 40s and a father of five, soon joined their crew. Beatty came from Seattle, Washington, after he lost his home in the mortgage crisis, went through a messy divorce, and lost his construction business. He also slept in his car when he arrived to Williston. The four men parked next to each other and met up at KK's Korner nearly every evening after work to drink, talk, and sing along to the jukebox. With Budweiser pints at KK's costing only $1.50, their daily earnings lasted longer. Beatty and Bergeson started a band called Soul Shaker with two other guys and played a gig at a biker bar called the Shop. It was the only show they played, however. Many nights they ended up at the strip clubs, which Stakes called "the titty bars."

Soon all of their vehicles were "tagged." Police officers came by and slapped notices on their windshields. They'd be towed if they didn't vacate the parking lot within 24 hours. Or sometimes an officer would come by in the middle of the night, tap on a window, and tell the men they couldn't sleep there. They'd disperse for a night or two, parking closer to the train tracks or in the adjacent parking lot, and, after a few days, return to their original spots. Stakes called them "gypsies, just wanderin' around." He paused. "I guess I should say tipsy, kinda stumblin' around."

By October, however, temperatures had already dropped significantly. The first snowfall of the year was on October 21. A light dusting of snow covered Williston's streets. With each passing day, temperatures fell. Anyone who had ever survived a winter in Williston knew what was coming.

Police officers began handing out tickets more often in the parking lot, and eventually the group dispersed. Beatty rented a room about a mile away from the bars, and Mackie moved his little yellow school bus to different parking lots around the city, sometimes hiding out in a junkyard.

But Stakes attempted to stay, rotating where he parked his truck. He collected more blankets and sleeping bags from men who were heading to warmer locations, and wrapped them around himself to stay warm. Sometimes he kept his car running to use the heater, but he didn't want to burn through too much fuel. He'd warm up the truck and, when it was nice and toasty, turn off the engine and fall asleep. About an hour later, he'd wake up shivering, turn the engine back on, crank up the heater, then turn it off again and fall asleep. He repeated this all through the night. Sleeping with the engine running was common practice for anyone attempting to outlast a Williston winter in their car, but it could be dangerous. People could asphyxiate from exhaust fumes if they left the car running without proper ventilation. But, if they slept for too long without a heater, they could freeze to death or wake up with frostbite.

One night in December, the temperature was around minus 30 degrees. Nate Beatty left the bars at closing time and began walking home to his apartment a mile away wearing only a thin jacket. His hands soon lost all feeling, the hairs in his nostrils froze, and he began shivering uncontrollably. He realized he might not make it back to the apartment without becoming hypothermic. He saw Stakes sleeping in his truck and pounded on the window. Stakes let him in and blasted the heater. "Tom helped save my life that night," said Beatty.

When Shorty, the owner of KK's, found out Stakes was still homeless and living in his car, he said, "Tom, you can't live out there in your truck, it's too cold. You're too old to be out there. Come up here and sleep on the floor." There was floor space in Shorty's apartment above the bar, so Stakes started sleeping there. Eddie Bergeson sometimes crashed there as well, but he finally decided it was too cold for him in Williston and left to go to Austin, Texas, for the winter.

The construction industry typically slows down during winter, even in a boomtown, and soon Stakes's boss had no more decks to paint. Stakes spent his days drinking at KK's and looking for work. Occasionally he'd meet a guy at the bar who would hire him for a day of work, but the stretches without work were growing longer. After one particularly long stretch, Stakes was down to $2. He didn't know what to do. In the morning, he prayed. "God, please help me. I don't know how it's gonna happen but if you can jus' bless me and help me somehow." That night, Stakes's friend drove him to Champ's Casino on the north edge of town to buy him a drink. When Stakes stepped outside to smoke a cigarette, in the corner of his eye, he saw something sticking out of the snow. It was a dollar bill. Then he saw another dollar bill. He dug in the snow a little more and found two $100 bills. He looked up toward the sky and said, "Thank you, Lord."

Soon Stakes felt like he'd outstayed his welcome at the apartment above KK's. Six people were regularly sleeping in the two-bedroom apartment—two in the bedrooms, three on the floor, and Shorty on the couch. And since it was connected to a bar, people were walking through the apartment all the time, at all hours of the night. Stakes could hear the *thud thud thud* of the music coming from below until 2 a.m.

In December, Stakes found a new job. He was hired by a man named Gary Westerman, who paid him $18 an hour to work construction jobs, his highest wage yet. Then Stakes heard his friend Jesse, another man he met at KKs, had found a trailer to live in and wanted a roommate to help split the $900 rent. Stakes agreed. It was a 34-foot camper, but the water and sewage lines weren't hooked up, so he and Jesse used a five-gallon bucket for a toilet, but it had electricity, heat, and a TV. Compared to where he had been living, it was heaven. The problem was it was a 30-minute drive from Williston, just outside of a town called Alexander, and Stakes had to spend more money in gas to drive back and forth.

I saw Tom Stakes again when he was living in the camper near Alexander. It was Valentine's Day, and nighttime temperatures were dropping to minus 35 with the wind chill. I bundled up in every piece of warm clothing I owned and met him at KK's Korner. He looked a little worn and tired but about the same—his white hair was still long and wiry; his beard longer and fuller. He wore a beige winter coat and faded jeans, but no hat or gloves.

He was upset when I arrived. Shorty had died two days ago. He'd been arrested for sexually assaulting a woman while she was sleeping. The day after, he died of alcohol poisoning in jail. Stakes heard that Shorty went through alcohol withdrawal, and the guards didn't get him medical attention in time. I tried to confirm this, but the only thing it said on Shorty's death certificate was that he had died of "chronic alcoholism, pulmonary emphysema and pneumonia."

"He was a drunk and he'd stay drunk all the time," explained Stakes, "but he was harmless as a flea. Oh, bless his heart. Shorty was a good man." Stakes nursed his beer. "Man, it's been a tough winter. It's been bad. I've lost all these people." Stakes heard that another friend, also a KK's Korner regular, had committed suicide a month before. "He'd come in every mornin' when the bar opened. Every mornin'," Stakes explained. "He was a millionaire here. He had all kinda money. Anyway, he shot himself. He killed himself."

I told him I was sorry and we sat in silence for a bit.

Stakes continued. "A lot of people left because it gets too cold. But they'll be back in the spring probably. But luckily, thank God, I've been blessed, and I haven't had to be out in the cold. Every job I've had's been inside. I've been nice and warm and everything's been good. I'm gettin' too old to do that stuff outside."

Suddenly he perked up as if he'd just remembered something important. "And a cat came into my life!" he said, his blue eyes lighting up. "I was outside my trailer and I saw this cat walkin', and I said, 'Here, kitty kitty kitty.'" He reenacted the scene, leaning forward with his hand stretched out. "She ran over and now she stays with me. This cat, oh my God, when she stretches out, she reaches from here"—he stood up from the bar stool and marked the spot on his thigh—"all the way down"—and slid his hand down his leg. "She's the length of my damn leg!" He named her Baby.

Stakes had come to Williston with his cat named Miracle from New Mexico, but one day when he opened his truck door, the cat scurried away and he never saw her again. Now he was worried he might lose Baby. His boss planned to send him to a job in Mandaree, North Dakota, 80 miles away, where Stakes would live in a man camp that didn't allow pets. "When you got an animal, you got somebody to talk to, you got somebody to take care of, you know, jus' show your love. Rather than jus' sittin' by yourself and watchin' TV."

Twenty years before, when Tom Stakes was homeless in Atlanta, it was one of the loneliest times in his life. His family still didn't speak to him, and the drugs had completely taken over. He made several attempts to stop but always fell back into the suffocating grip of addiction.

In 2009, it had been more than 10 years since he'd seen his sons. He lived south of Gainesville, Georgia, and was arrested one day for writing bad checks. As he sat in jail, waiting out his sentence, a new inmate walked in. Tom immediately recognized him. It was his oldest son, Jay. Jay had been arrested for a probation violation. "It's funny how God is," said Jay. "God has a way of bringing people back together sometimes." Jay could tell his father had been through a lot. "He was pretty much a skeleton," Jay said. "His eyes sunk in—he looked terrible." They were ecstatic to find each other and spent the rest of Tom's sentence catching up.

Tom discovered that his sons, Jay and Dan, had been searching for him for years. They searched online to see if there was any address or record for Tom Stakes but found nothing. "We'd look for telephone numbers or anything at all, but we couldn't find anything because my dad likes to live under the radar," said Jay. Jay was released soon after Tom, and he and Dan went to Auburn, Georgia, where Tom was living, to spend time with their dad.

Tom vowed to change his life after reuniting with his sons. He was done with drugs, he told them. "Once my children found me, that was a big changing point," Tom said. "They says, 'Dad, we love you, we've been looking for you for years.' That was when I decided I'd had enough. I'd had a hard life. I wish it on nobody. Nobody needs to go where I went." He and his sons found an apartment together, and Tom started weaning himself off crack. He turned to alcohol to help with the cravings. They spent a lot of time in Auburn's bars, drinking cheap beer and getting to know each other again.

Tom discovered that his sons had both struggled with heroin in the past. They also lived in Atlanta around the same time Tom was there. Tom couldn't believe they had been so close. Tom was heartbroken to find out that a few years before, Jay's fiancée had been killed in a car accident when she was seven months' pregnant with Jay's child. Both his sons were unmarried. "I felt like . . . that I was a dad again," Tom said, "and I wanted to try and do the right things by 'em." Tom wanted a change of scenery, so they headed to Orlando, Florida, where Jay had a girlfriend. When Florida didn't work out, the three of them moved around and eventually ended up in Red River, New Mexico, after Tom met a traveling preacher named Brother Russell Howard.

Tom had recently become reacquainted with God. Tom wanted to be rebaptized and had the ceremony in a friend's backyard pond. When they arrived in Red River, he attended Brother Howard's fellowship, the Jerusalem Connection, and found a job as a dishwasher at a popular Mexican restaurant in town. Jay fell in love and married a woman with two children. Dan found work giving snowmobile tours in the winters and cooking at a pizza place during the summers.

Though Tom attended church and stayed sober when he first arrived, he soon returned to drinking and struggled to stay in control. Tom would visit Jay and his wife, but he would fight with Jay and get drunk around the kids, who were three and six at the time. "I grew up watching that, and I wasn't gonna let him do it again," said Jay. "I told him he needed to go." Tom left the church and became estranged from his son Dan as well. Once again, his life was spiraling out of control. He soon lost his job, his housing, and most of his friends. With nowhere left to go, Tom took shelter in a cave.

When Brother Russell heard Tom was living in a cave, he helped Tom find a rehabilitation and homeless outreach ministry called the Adullam Project Men's Home in Española, New Mexico. Tom stayed for six months and sobered up.

After rehab, Tom and Jay briefly worked on a construction project together, building a mining town tourist attraction in southwest New Mexico. But during the housing market crash, the project lost its funding. Construction jobs all across the country were becoming harder to find. Jay and his wife divorced after two years together, and he decided to head back to Georgia after an ex-girlfriend called and announced that Jay was a father. But Tom didn't know where to go.

Tom lived with his boss near the mining town, and his boss's wife mentioned she heard an oil boom was happening in Williston, North Dakota. Companies needed people to build houses for oil workers. Tom didn't know how to use a computer, so she showed him a couple of articles about it. That was all the evidence he needed.

Tom threw his few belongings, including his stray cat, Miracle, in the back of the pickup he'd purchased for $1,000. He bought a road atlas and gathered up the $300 he'd saved. He knew he needed every penny for gas and food to make it over 1,000 miles to North Dakota.

An oil train cuts through the prairie near Williston, North Dakota. *(Brad DeCecco)*

Tom Stakes at the Trenton Lake campground in August 2013. *(Will Christiansen)*

The Andresen family cooks dinner with Tom Stakes at the Trenton Lake campground in August 2013. *(Will Christiansen)*

Billy Andresen tends to her daughter while Billy's father, Mike, eats dinner. *(Will Christiansen)*

A gas flare burns on the prairie horizon. *(Will Christiansen)*

The author in front of North Dakota's welcome sign in 2013. *(Courtesy of author)*

The trailer park, Williston Village RV Resort, where the author lived over the summer of 2013. *(Brad DeCecco)*

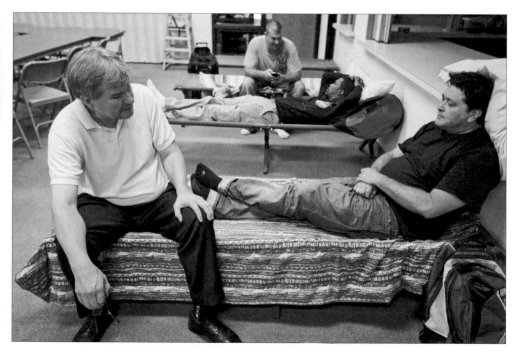

Jay Reinke talks with Overnighter Joe Lee at Concordia Lutheran Church in 2012. *(Gabriel and Carin Photography)*

Williston's welcome sign in 2013. *(Brad DeCecco)*

Donny Nelson and his dog Lucky at Nelson's farmhouse near Fort Berthold Indian Reservation. *(Ashley Panzera)*

Lisa DeVille on Fort Berthold Indian Reservation. *(Living With Oil and Gas, a project of the Western Organization of Resource Councils)*

The man camp, Rough Rider Housing, where Cindy Marchello, Mana Kula, Curtis Kenney, and Scott Morgan lived near Trenton, North Dakota. *(Brad DeCecco)*

Cindy Marchello and Curtis Kenney in Marchello's man camp trailer. *(Brad DeCecco)*

Mana Kula and Curtis Kenney during poker night in August 2013. *(Brad DeCecco)*

Cindy Marchello on a coil rig at C&J in 2012. *(Courtesy of Cindy Marchello)*

Cindy Marchello's daughters Jennie and Elizabeth at Cindy's wedding in September 2015. *(Courtesy of Cindy Marchello)*

26. DONNY NELSON

It wasn't easy to find Donny Nelson. When I first arrived in the area, I wanted to find someone who was outspoken against the oil and gas companies, but when I asked people who that might be, I received blank stares. Having grown up in the mountains of northern California, where a new water bottling company in town prompted protests and angry letters, and our elementary school curriculum involved pretending to be trees and singing about recycling, I was shocked. "Are you *sure* you haven't heard of anyone?" I asked. Finally, I called blogger Jim Fuglie, who wrote about environmental concerns in the state. Without hesitating, he blurted out Nelson's name. "He's your guy."

As I soon discovered, having an opposing opinion is difficult in a pro-drill state. I expected to see frequent protests against fracking and arrived early to my first city council meeting in Williston, thinking there might be hundreds of angry locals crammed into the small room. But what I found was much different. I followed Nelson to a local county commissioners' meeting in Watford City. Standing behind a group of developers and builders presenting their cases to receive permits (which seemed like a courtesy, as not a single one went unapproved) were three farmers, there to express their anger and concerns with the development—an elderly man with white hair who spoke in stuttered sentences, Nelson, and Nelson's 39-year-old nephew, Troy.

Donny Nelson was considered a troublemaker, according to most North Dakotans—though he was the kindest, most softest-spoken troublemaker I'd ever met. Nelson spoke out publicly against the lack of regulation over the oil companies. He wrote op-eds about the dangerous trains transporting Bakken oil throughout the country and became the oil and gas chair for the pro-environment advocacy group, the Western Organization of Resource Councils. The local chapter, the Dakota Resource Council, called itself "the watchdogs of the prairie." When he was in his mid-20s, Nelson participated in protests at the Canadian border to support farmers' rights, and in 2010, he attended an anti-fracking rally in Washington, DC, where he met *Gasland* director Josh Fox. Nelson didn't raise genetically modified crops on principle. Nelson wouldn't call himself an "environmentalist," though. He and other farmers who agreed with him called themselves "conservationists," because they wanted to conserve the environment. There was a difference, they told me.

In some ways, Nelson was not atypical of North Dakota farmers—he struggled with wanting to conserve and protect the land around him while reckoning with his conservative upbringing that championed the free market. In an overwhelmingly Republican state, Nelson voted Independent in the 2012 presidential election because he didn't like either candidate ("I don't even remember who the Independent was," he said, laughing), voted for a Democrat in the 2008 race for governor, then voted for Republican Jack Dalrymple in the 2012 governor race.

Dalrymple had taken the post in 2010 after Governor John Hoeven resigned to become a senator, and he was thrilled to inherit an oil boom. He successfully ran for reelection two years later. Though Nelson voted for Dalrymple, he regretted that decision after the governor seemed to favor the oil companies over the farmers. "He was enamored by the amount of money coming in, and I think there was some funny business going on," said Nelson.

ExxonMobil, Continental, and Marathon Oil all contributed to Dalrymple's campaign, and in total, he collected about $550,000 from oil-related groups. These types of contributions are not uncommon for elected officials in oil-producing states, but North Dakota was unique in that Dalrymple was also the chairman of the Industrial Commission, which was responsible for promoting *and* regulating the industry, creating many potential conflicts of interest. In addition, Dalrymple and his wife owned oil stock in ExxonMobil, which frequently did business with the Industrial Commission.

Other government agencies in North Dakota didn't provide many checks and balances. The state's Department of Mineral Resources, headed by Lynn Helms, tended to approve the Industrial Commission policies. According to a *New York Times* review of Industrial Commission meeting minutes from 2011 to 2014, there were zero failed motions related to oil and gas. Helms also worked for Hess and Texaco for years before joining the North Dakota Department of Mineral Resources. Nelson heard Helms call the people impacted by oil development "collateral damage."

"I've heard people from both sides of the aisle say they've never seen a more arrogant, disrespectful legislature than this one here in North Dakota," said Nelson. "They belittle people and don't listen to 'em. We've filled the room before trying to get something passed, and they've just ignored us."

State agencies are supposed to fine companies for spills and other violations, for example, but in a three-year span, regulators issued fewer than 50 disciplinary fines for all drilling violations, including thousands of spills. And many times, the fines were later dismissed or reduced significantly. The Department of Mineral Resources increased its staff by 30 percent but still had only 19 inspectors in 2012, fewer than other oil states; Oklahoma, for example, had 58. The Environmental Protection Agency wasn't much help. The agency investigated spill complaints only on federal lands; it referred any incident on private property to the state regulators. Helms himself admitted that while the EPA technically oversaw their underground injection of fracking wastewater, its presence was limited: "The EPA has oversight over our program, but the last time an EPA person came to Bismarck, North Dakota, and checked our records was in September of 2001," he said in 2011.

When I asked Nelson why more people didn't fight back and protest, he shook his head. That's not the North Dakota way, he explained. "They call it 'North Dakota nice.' If you disagree, maybe you walk away and do it your own way, but you don't cause waves." The slow way of life in the plains didn't foster much urgency to create change. "The farmers and ranchers of western North Dakota can wait years for rain," wrote Kathleen Norris back in 1993. "Time is defined not by human agency but by the natural rhythms of day and night, and of the seasons." Among a peer group of stoic noncomplainers, Nelson stood out. "People come to me because I tell the bad side," he said.

In 2013, Nelson began fighting a legal process called unitization. Companies typically broke up drilling areas into 1,280-acre parcels, but unitization combined those parcels into a mega-unit of 30,000 to 40,000 acres in an attempt to increase profits for everyone when a well aged and less oil (and thus money) flowed. Unitization was promoted in the early 1990s when North Dakota's oil production had plummeted. During that time, the state legislature lowered the percentage of mineral owners required to form a unit. In theory, the law was supposed to help the company and the landowner. The company cut costs, and landowners still received profits because they'd be part of a larger parcel with more wells, though the revenue would be divided up between more families. The downside was that once you agreed to unitization, companies could create a new lease on their own terms, potentially giving them more power.

Nelson saw the reality of what happened under unitization in 2012. The Industrial Commission approved a deal to combine smaller units into a 30,000-acre mega-unit near Corral Creek, not far from Nelson's property. Many landowners within the mega-unit had no say in the deal because only the owners of 60 percent of the unit's mineral owners were needed for approval, and the state government owned many of the mineral acres within the unit. Nelson's neighbor, who was involved in the deal, lost his original lease and 70 percent of his monthly royalty payments. ConocoPhillips, which had purchased 50 percent of the mineral acres in the new unit, argued that unitization would allow the company to protect more land and drill fewer wells, reportedly telling landowners it planned to drill only 83 wells in the entire spacing unit. But after the deal was approved, ConocoPhillips revised that number to 200 wells. Nelson worried that the company would do the same with his land. "They'd basically be able to do whatever they want," he said.

A 30,000-acre plot is about twice the size of Manhattan. I decided to climb up Thunder Butte on a clear, sunny afternoon to get a better idea of how much land could be in jeopardy. There was no trail to the summit, so I pushed past sagebrush, reeds, and prairie grass to get there.

The butte has been a sacred landmark for Native Americans for hundreds of years. When I reached the flat top, there was a single tree branch in the center with faded red fabric tied around it, almost like a flag. It was the only remnant of the tribal ceremonies that once took place here. Nelson and his brother used to climb to the top as small children and carved their names next to hundreds of others, some dating back to the 1800s.

I could see in every direction, and I spotted Nelson's house. I also counted at least 15 oil wells, two of which were directly below the butte, as well as about a dozen more holding tanks storing either oil or brine and a large waste pit to the east. The number of wells here would likely double or triple within a year—almost as if the oil wells were soldiers slowly invading, and, once again, those living off the land were caught in the crossfire. The days when this land was remote and sacred seemed like a long time ago.

I scrambled down some rocks and saw the carvings, though I couldn't find Nelson's or his brother's name. I started to head back down, but when I reached the edge, the path looked much steeper than I remembered. I walked to the opposite side of the butte and the land dropped off to a sheer rock face. I suddenly felt an overwhelming fear of heights. After a brief panic, I decided to return the way I came, sliding down on my rear the entire way and inching through the tall grass. Only later did Nelson tell me the grass was crawling with rattlesnakes.

The next day, Nelson and I drove along a highway that followed the Missouri River to one of his durum fields a few miles away. A few years ago, on this same highway, he used to ride his motorcycle and not meet another vehicle for miles. "This used to be the most scenic drive in the U.S., and now it's all oil wells," he told me. Today, with 50,000-pound semis continuously roaring by at 70 miles an hour, it had become too dangerous to take his motorcycle out. "[The area] is full of natural springs, but now I don't even recognize it," he said. All drivers could see now were oil wells and their flares, burning off natural gas, 24 hours a day. Waste disposal tanks speckled the landscape. The tanks were frequent targets for lightning strikes and easily caught fire. It wasn't uncommon to see black smoke billowing up into the open sky on clear days. "It will never be the same in my lifetime," said Nelson.

27. CINDY MARCHELLO

Ultimately, it was Richard who asked for a divorce. In 2006, they were living in an old, 12-bedroom, 8,000-square-foot former boarding house that they purchased in Cornish, Utah, a tiny town close to the Idaho border. Cindy had created a mildly successful acupuncture business for herself 40 minutes away in Logan, making about $2,500 a month, but lately it hadn't been doing so well. Gas prices were high, the local economy was struggling, and business was slowing down.

The kids had moved out a few years earlier. Elizabeth had turned 18 and rented a house with roommates, and Jennie had decided to live with her brother Ricky, who had moved into his own apartment. As they described it, Richard quickly fell into a downward spiral after the kids were gone.

Cindy was gone often—at acupuncture conferences, working as a cook for a hunting camp in the summers, hiking the Pacific Crest Trail—and Richard was left to himself a lot. They had long been sleeping in separate bedrooms, and they did their best to avoid each other. "He'd be alone in the big house and it just made him go crazy," said Elizabeth, their older daughter. He began taking money out of Cindy's acupuncture business account, stopped hiding his affairs with other women, and the house deteriorated. He had remodeling projects all over the house—he'd want to redo the floors so he'd scrape off all the paint, then abandon the work and move on to something else. He'd bring in junk, such as saddles and car engines and hundreds of milk jugs from a garage sale, and leave them all in the living room.

At one point, he wanted to cut out the floor of one room and build a trout pond. "That's crazy, Dad!" Elizabeth remembered telling him. He wouldn't listen to her, or anyone else, but fortunately he moved on to another project before he sawed away any floorboards.

One time, before Cindy departed for a long trip, she cleaned the house thoroughly and gave Richard instructions on what needed to be done while she was away. But when she returned, none of the bills had been paid, so there was no power and no phone connection. Mice had gnawed into everything, and piles of dishes were all over the kitchen. She had to borrow money from her father to keep her car from being repossessed.

Richard and Cindy sought counseling at their Mormon church to work on their marriage but didn't make much progress. To Cindy, it seemed like the church simply wanted *her* to be a better wife, and their marriage would be fixed. Richard was charming, and it was hard for anyone in the church to believe he would do anything to contribute to their unhappiness. They also didn't know about his past. Cindy lost many friends in the church during this time. "I think a lot of people were uncomfortable," said Elizabeth. "What do you say to someone whose life is falling apart? In most religions, you hide problems in a marriage. If the bishop's coming over, you make sure there are pictures of Christ in the front room and laugh when the kids misbehave, because company's over. That's how my parents were. You couldn't see the mess they left behind closed doors."

One morning, as Cindy prepped to travel to California for another acupuncture conference, she and Richard started arguing about money. In the heat of the argument, she said to him, "So, are you just done with me?" What she meant was, should she leave the room so they could have some space? But Richard took it a different way. As Cindy remembered it, he replied, "Yeah, I'm done with you. Take the dog and your canning jars and get out." Their dog at the time was a Doberman and Rottweiler mix named Zeus. She left to go to the conference that day, hoping maybe Richard hadn't meant it. But when she came back, he confirmed he wanted a divorce. She moved out soon after.

"She was really, really sad when she and my dad finally split up, even though it was 20 years of splitting up in the making," said their younger daughter, Jennie. Elizabeth agreed. "She didn't want the divorce. At all. Even though he was unbearable. It just wasn't in her to divorce. When she makes a commitment, she follows through."

At first, Cindy stayed with her son Ricky in his basement apartment, but the space was cramped. She reached out to the church to see if they could help her find her own apartment since she had no rental history, but when the bishop found out she was divorcing, he told her he couldn't do anything. Cindy was devoted to the church, and this stung, especially since the church helped Richard pay his utility bills. "If they'd helped me, I wouldn't be in North Dakota right now," she said.

Cindy moved around a lot during this period. She slept on the couches of friends and family, but much of the time her kids didn't know where she was. She lived in a trailer for a while in Logan, Utah, then found a dingy, two-bedroom apartment in a rough neighborhood for $500 a month. Some floorboards were missing in the bathroom, but the landlord didn't care about Cindy's rental history.

Richard moved out of the Cornish house and had stopped making the payments. The mortgage was now under water—the amount they owed was higher than the value of the home. Though Cindy would've liked to keep the house, she couldn't afford the payments on her own. In 2008, they lost the house to foreclosure, along with millions of other Americans who were hit by the housing crisis. Before the bank repossessed it, Jennie went and grabbed all the photo albums she could find.

"It was in an awful, awful state. It was just rubble, just destroyed," she said. Richard liked to hunt and had left a deer's headless carcass strung up and bleeding onto the bathroom floor.

Around the same time, Cindy's acupuncture business collapsed, and she was forced to file for bankruptcy. Afterward, she took any job she could find. She worked weekends at a cell phone billing company, sorting and processing mail, and worked the swing shift during the week at a circuit board factory, both for $8 an hour. But she wasn't making ends meet. She paid around $400 a month to the court for her bankruptcy, a payment she would have to make for about three years, and many times she only had $200 or $300 left over to live on for the month. She also hated the jobs. She hated having a supervisor stand over her, watching her constantly. If she clocked in two minutes late, she'd get in trouble. She hardly had time to take bathroom breaks. At 50 years old, this was not how she had pictured her life.

One day she logged onto the computer and Googled "what job makes money?" The oil field came up in her search, and she saw open positions in Rock Springs, Wyoming. Most of the jobs didn't require a college degree, but a commercial driver's license or heavy-duty diesel mechanic certification was recommended. She thought, *I can do that.* They both cost around $2,500—she didn't have the money up front, but the diesel mechanic certification offered a monthly payment plan.

While in school, she began living out of her 2001 Ford Taurus to save money. She would leave the billing center job at 3 a.m. and head to the college parking lot where she'd sleep for a few hours. Class started at 7:30 a.m., so just before class, she'd clean up in the school restroom to look presentable. After class, she'd go to Elizabeth's house for lunch, then head to her next job at the circuit board factory, then do it all over again. "I didn't really sleep then," she said. "Nobody realized I was living in my car."

When she finished the eight-month class, she applied to oil field jobs close to home in Wyoming and Utah. She sent out some 100 applications, but no one contacted her for an interview. One day, her uncle introduced her to a driller who worked up in Williston, North Dakota. She shared with him how many applications she'd sent out, and he told her the only way she'd get hired is if she applied to jobs in Williston because a boom was happening.

Cindy didn't want to leave her family—Jennie was 26 and had a three-year-old at home. Elizabeth had two young children, and Ricky had three kids. Elizabeth had also recently come down with pancreatitis and almost died. Cindy didn't want to work 800 miles away from them. But after more silence from jobs at closer locations, she decided to give Williston a shot. The second application she sent to North Dakota—to work in fracking at Halliburton's Williston location—resulted in her being called in for an interview.

She drove to Williston over two days and arrived on a brisk afternoon in late March. She checked into one of the few hotels in town, the Airport International Inn. The next morning, she wore black slacks, a white blouse with a sweater, and wore her long blond hair down with the top half pulled back. She drove to the Halliburton equipment yard on the outskirts of town for her interview. The office was in a portable building, and when she walked in, she immediately felt out of place. The only other people in the waiting area were two guys wearing coveralls splattered with grease and dirt. She walked up to the window and told the receptionist who she was. As she remembered it, one of the guys in the office turned to her and said, "So you're here for a job interview?" She nodded.

"Are you going into dispatch or payroll?" he asked.

"No, I'm here to be a frack hand."

He looked surprised. "Do you know what frack is?"

"Of course I know what frack is," she said, annoyed. "Why would I apply for a job if I didn't know what it was?"

Finally, they called her in. Her interviewer was a woman. One question Cindy remembered the woman asking was, "What do you know about Halliburton?"

"I know they don't kill people because they give them better training," Cindy said. She'd been studying how fracking and directional drilling worked for weeks—her friend who worked as a driller even used straws one night at a restaurant to demonstrate what happened underground. So she explained to her interviewer the exact mechanics of a fracking operation.

Afterward, the woman said, "We'd like to offer you the position."

Cindy was shocked. "Does this mean I'm Halliburton?"

"Yes, if you'd like to be Halliburton, I'm offering you that opportunity."

"Just like that?" Cindy said.

She nodded.

Cindy stood up, slid back her chair, and threw up her arms in celebration. "When do I get my coveralls?"

The woman laughed and told Cindy she would need to come back for training in April. She had two weeks to go back to Utah and pack up her life. They told her she would be the second woman to work on oil wells in Halliburton's North Dakota yard.

28. TOM STAKES

Two nights after Valentine's Day in 2014, I saw Tom Stakes at the bar called Hard Ride Saloon near his camper. He had exciting news to share. He had heard from his son Jay. Jay was planning to come to Williston.

"My son's gonna come up here!" Tom said. "I talked to 'im today and he said, 'Only about two more weeks, Dad!'" Jay was living in Gainesville, Georgia, but was struggling to find work and thought he'd have better luck in North Dakota. Tom sat up straighter when he talked about his son, like a proud father. "He's a good man, got real short red hair. Long sideburns. Oh, he's awesome. He's an awesome guy, I tell ya. I love 'im. He's a third- or fourth-degree black belt. He's gonna come up here. 'Cause I need some help. I'm gettin' old." Tom wanted me to talk to his son.

He called Jay while I was sitting next to him. "Hey, buddy, what you doin'? Yeah? I want you to talk to somebody," he said as he handed me the phone.

I said hello and Jay confirmed what Tom told me. He planned to come to Williston to live with his dad. I said I hoped to meet him soon, then handed the phone back to Tom. Jay told Tom he would take a bus up to Williston the next Monday, but he needed more money for the ticket.

"Okay, I'll send you the rest," Tom told him. "I love ya, son. I'm lookin' forward to seein' ya again. And if you need any money, you let me know. I'll send it to ya. There's a lotta money to be made up here if you get in the right position. Okay, lookin' forward to it. I love you so much. Okay, bye." He hung up the phone. He took out his wallet and pulled out pictures of his sons when they were little boys and showed them to me. Then he ordered another beer.

When I called a few months later, Tom said his son still hadn't made it to Williston. Jay had been asking for more and more money and continued to delay his move to North Dakota. Jay called Tom about once a week to explain why he needed more money for the trip. One time, Jay claimed he bought his bus ticket and would arrive on May 16. But when Tom went to the bus stop to pick him up, he wasn't there. When Tom called him, Jay's reason was that he found more work in Georgia and decided to stay. He told Tom he'd need more money to be able to quit the job and travel there.

"Son, I can't keep sendin' ya money. I got bills to pay. It's hard enough as it is," Tom told Jay.

Jay seemed to understand, but then he stopped calling and didn't return Tom's calls. Tom hadn't heard from his son in nearly a month. "I've been tryin' to call him," Tom said, "but he's not answerin'. I don't know what I did. It's messed up. I tried to help him." Tom turned to drinking for comfort.

Construction work, however, was going well for him. Tom Stakes's boss, Gary Westerman, had taken a liking to him. A few years ago, Westerman had come from Kennesaw, Georgia, to Williston to seek his own fortune after the recession wiped out construction work in Georgia. "This was the only place with work in most of the nation,"

said Westerman. "I came up here with just the clothes on my back."
The first day Stakes showed up for a painting job, Westerman could
tell he'd had a hard life, but Stakes's charm and charisma won him over.
Stakes also had decent skills as a painter. Westerman wanted to give
him a chance. "I've had a soft heart for Tom since day one," he said.
After a few months of employing Stakes, Westerman raised Stakes's pay
to $20 an hour. To celebrate the raise, Stakes went to Walmart to buy
an $89 mini DVD player and a bottle of vodka.

On May 29, 2014, Stakes was arrested again. A cop pulled him over
because Stakes's registration had expired back in November. When the
police officer ran his plate, the cop saw his DUI license suspension was
still active. Stakes's 11-month probation was scheduled to end a month
later, on June 23. The officer charged him with driving on a suspended
license and booked him in the local jail for four days. He slept on a
metal bunk bed in a small cell with one other man. According to Stakes,
everyone he met had been arrested for more serious crimes—murder,
rape, assault. *This is a bad place,* he thought at the time. *Why am I
here?* On the day of his release, he was issued a $350 fine for violating
his suspension.

Afterward, Stakes moved out of the trailer in Alexander and slept
in his truck. Work was more sporadic, and he didn't want to pay $450
in rent to share a trailer anymore. Plus, the weather was warmer. He
wouldn't freeze to death in his truck.

But by this time, the Williston Police Department had cracked down
on overnight parking in the city limits. Few people were able to stay
undetected. Stakes's friend Eddie Bergeson returned to Williston, and
Westerman hired Bergeson as well. Stakes and Bergeson found a place
to camp on wildlife management land, tucked away in a grove of trees
across the Missouri River. Bergeson was happy to be back with his old
buddy, but he was concerned about Stakes's drinking, which had accelerated since Bergeson last saw him. "Before I left, Tom really wasn't
drinkin' vodka—he was drinkin' beer," he said. "We'd have a few

pitchers at the bar. But when I came back, he'd buy a bottle of vodka and it'd last him maybe two days. He was drinkin' it straight. I was like, 'At least put some orange juice in that and get some vitamins out of it!' I worried about him." After only a few nights in the tent, a ranger came by in the middle of the night, issued each man a $100 ticket for illegal camping, and told them to vacate the area.

Westerman let Stakes and Bergeson park their vehicles on the RV lot Westerman rented for $50 a week each at a place north of town called Fox Run. Williston now had four RV parks, but Fox Run had become the town's largest and most disorganized. It was a sprawling dirt field of 300 campers. Every space filled soon after it opened, and there was now a waiting list. Westerman had been lucky to snag such a coveted space. The park was known for having higher crime rates than the other RV parks, however. In the past few years, a camper was stolen, two campers had burned down, a semi truck driver ran into another trailer and nearly killed a nine-year-old boy, a woman's dead body was found in a pool of blood in one camper, and five registered sex offenders lived there. Essentially, it had become Williston's shanty-town. Unlike some of the other trailer parks, there were few rules or regulations at Fox Run. Many residents added particle-board mudrooms to their trailers, weeds grew around campers, and a large, overflowing dumpster sat at the park's entrance. One dweller had raised an American flag high above his camper, and it flapped in the wind.

A few weeks after he moved to Fox Run, Stakes called me. He sounded hysterical. He wasn't making much sense, but said his truck had been stolen.

I asked him to slow down, take a deep breath, and explain what happened.

A few days before, Westerman had driven him to work, and Stakes had a strange feeling that something was wrong. When he went to a truck stop to buy a sausage breakfast biscuit and milk, the total at the cash register came to $6.66. The man in line behind him said, "Oh, no, you better head home. Somethin' bad's gonna happen to you today." Stakes laughed, but the feeling didn't go away. He felt anxious for the rest of the workday and took extra caution when walking around the construction site. When he and Westerman returned to the RV park that evening, Stakes's truck was gone. His neighbor had seen a man drive off with it, and Stakes thought the physical description sounded like an old roommate. He called him, but no one answered.

Stakes didn't want to involve the police—he'd been in enough trouble with the cops. He also figured his old roommate was long gone by now, probably in another state. Stakes felt there was nothing he could do.

Stakes sounded dejected on the phone. He wanted to give up and leave Williston. He was done with this place, he said. He wanted to be with his sons again but still couldn't reach either of them. "I wanna leave, but I can't make 20 bucks an hour anywhere else in the country," he told me. "I'm gonna pay off my tickets, buy a van, work through the summer, and get the hell outta here."

Stakes drank heavily the night after his truck was stolen. Since Stakes no longer had a car to stay in, Westerman let him sleep on an old mattress in his van. When the men went downtown to do laundry at Bubba's Bubbles, Stakes walked across the street to Williston Brewing Company and went on a drinking binge. Stakes said he ordered a prime rib and a couple Long Island iced teas and gulped them down. Westerman told him to rest up and take the next day off.

"I'll do better tomorrow, I promise," Stakes told him.

But the next day, Stakes wasn't much better. Westerman could smell alcohol on him and worried he was drunk at work. He knew Stakes was an alcoholic, but Westerman also liked to drink. He'd even share a drink with Stakes after work sometimes. Westerman said he didn't care what Stakes did at night, but he'd send Stakes home for the day if he smelled alcohol on him at work. That day, Westerman kept a close watch on Stakes to make sure he was getting the job done right. They were remodeling Pierce Auto Body and putting new tin on the outside walls, which required a lot of hammering and precision. Other bosses might have fired Stakes, but Westerman wanted to give him another chance. Westerman drove him back and forth to work every day and stopped by the gas station if Stakes wanted cigarettes or a bite to eat. Stakes wouldn't stop talking about the theft of his truck. Stakes later admitted that he owed his old roommate money, and he may have stolen the truck as collateral. But whatever the reason, Stakes felt lost without a vehicle. He retreated to Westerman's van every evening after work and stayed there until morning.

Soon Westerman needed his van back to store tools, and Stakes had to find another place to stay. Bergeson was also tired of living in his car. They discovered that Westerman's neighbor had an empty trailer on the other edge of Fox Run. The man offered to sell it to Stakes for $2,500, to be paid in $200 increments. The lot rent was an additional $800 a month, so Bergeson agreed to be Stakes's roommate and pay $400 toward rent.

I visited Stakes and Bergeson a few days after they moved in. Their trailer, a Nomad Century from the 1970s or 1980s, was at the edge of the park, overlooking Love's gas station and not far from where I had lived the previous summer. The trailer had particle board strapped to the side to keep the pipes from freezing in winter. With temperatures regularly dropping to minus 20 degrees during winter months, noninsulated pipes could freeze and burst within 10 minutes. Two-by-fours had been laid on the ground to keep the mud and dust at bay. Debris was scattered about—a discarded cooler, empty Natural Ice beer boxes, a metal chair. As I drove through the camp, a group of children rode bicycles in the dirt and played with toy guns.

Stakes welcomed me in and I sat on a ratty couch across from him. Bergeson was away taking a shower—the trailer had no running water, so Bergeson typically showered by filling up an empty vodka bottle and pouring water over his head. Stakes preferred to walk to the shower house on the other side of the park. "He's a big boy, he sweats a lot," Stakes said of Bergeson. "That's his bed," he said, pointing to the couch I sat on. "But he ain't happy here. I don't think he's gonna make it much longer. Pro'lly head to Texas or Mississippi."

I asked him why Bergeson wasn't happy.

"What's to love?" Stakes said. "There's nothin' here. Jus' dirt. He come from North Carolina; I come from Georgia. There's mountains and beautiful trees. There ain't nothin' out here. It's a dirty trailer park and there are no trees. The only thing that's out here is jobs. That's it."

Stakes had given up on the idea of leaving at the end of summer. He wanted to save up money before he left. So far, he'd only saved a few hundred dollars.

Stakes wore jeans and an oversized T-shirt with holes in the neck. His long hair had been chopped off—his mustache and beard were trimmed short, making his big ears stick out. He showed off his new look. "My boss said, 'Tom, you gotta clean up a little bit. I don't want customers thinking you're a homeless bum. You can't work for me if you look like that.' I said, 'All right, all right.' So I got a haircut last week. I felt naked. I was never gonna cut it off but I thought, well, I guess I gotta change," Stakes said, then coughed and hacked for a long moment. Instead of clearing his throat with water, he grabbed a half-gallon plastic bottle of Silver Wolf Vodka and gulped some down.

The trailer smelled of cigarettes, dust, booze, and stale A/C air. The fan for the A/C whirred above us, and dishes were piled up in the sink next to empty plastic Mountain Dew bottles and a jug of Red Diamond Sweet Tea. Stained curtains hung haphazardly on the camper's windows, which were lined with duct tape to prevent air and dust from entering. A bath towel was fastened over one window to keep the light out.

Stakes sat in an orange 1970s armchair. He held up the vodka bottle and offered me some. I declined. "It's my drug of choice," he said, taking a swig. Stakes still hadn't heard from his son. And work was once again drying up. He was in between jobs. A month ago, he was making $800 a week, but he'd only worked one eight-hour shift this week, earning him $160. The week before, he made $460, and two weeks ago, $370. "Sometimes I got a thousand bucks in my pocket, sometimes I don't," he said. Most of his earnings went to rent and booze.

Stakes said the trailer's owner had wanted to sell it because his wife had killed herself inside. He pointed to the couch I was sitting on. "His wife sat right there, and when he got out of bed she had a gun in her hand. BAM!" Stakes yelled, and I jumped. "Killed herself right there." I followed his finger to the spot he pointed at above the couch, and sure enough, there was a bullet hole in the wall. I felt nauseous and sat closer to the edge of the couch, wanting to be as far away from the gruesome scene as possible.

"We got her dead ghost runnin' around here somewhere," Stakes said. "But she ain't bothered me yet."

Stakes's roommate, Bergeson, barged through the camper's rickety door. His thick belly could barely fit through the narrow entrance. Bergeson's skin was a deep copper after too many hours in the sun, and his hair resembled a mullet. He wore white plastic sunglasses on his head and a beaded choker around his thick neck.

"There he is!" Stakes said. "You look like a new man!"

"I don't look any better but I feel a hell of a lot better," Bergeson said, his voice gruff and scratchy. He warned us that a storm was coming in tonight from eastern Montana, bringing hail and 70-mile-an-hour winds.

"Oh, shit," Stakes said, sounding more excited than concerned. "Want to go out tonight and have a beer?"

Bergeson leaned back, resting his hand on the rusted kitchen sink. "I don't know. We went out last night."

"Well, hell, this is a new day!" Stakes said. He wanted to go to a local bar called Cattails for karaoke night. Stakes's old hangout, KK's

Korner bar, had closed soon after Shorty died. "You sang two songs last night. Oh, man, I loved it."

"I don't really remember," said Bergeson.

"You sang 'Wild Thing,'" Stakes said. Then he began singing. "Wild thing! You make my heart stink!"

"You made my wiener stink," Bergeson said in monotone. "You gave me everything."

Stakes laughed. "This guy don't drink much," he said, gesturing at Bergeson. "I get up at like five o clock in the mornin' and I got to have two or three shots jus' to get bright-eyed and bushy-tailed. They think I'm an alcoholic. The way I do it ever'body says, 'Oh hell, he drinks that shit straight!' I said, 'Well, it's what you get used to I guess.' 'Cause in the mornings if I don't drink somethin', my skin starts to crawl." Stakes moved his fingers up his arm. "Oh yeah, I'm addicted. I start gettin' sweaty and clammy, and my skin starts crawlin' on my back. Fuck, it's like I'm going through DTs or some shit. But once I've had two or three drinks, I'm good. Then I go through the rest of the day and come home and drink.

"My boss told me, 'One thing I ask, Stakes. What you do after hours is your own business, but do not drink in the mornin' before work. But there's been a time or two where I stayed up most the night and drank and he smelled it on me. He said, 'You been drinkin'?' I said, 'Nope, not this mornin'. I did all night.'" He laughed.

Stakes's boss, Westerman, had brought homemade chicken and rice soup to the camper the previous night and picked up DVDs for Stakes. Stakes watched *The Angriest Man in Brooklyn*, starring Robin Williams, on his mini DVD player. "Yeah, ever'body looks out for ol' Tom. I'm jus' an old fart. The smell that won't go away," Stakes said. He showed me the books he was reading. *Redeeming Love* by Francine Rivers, *Affliction* by Laurell K. Hamilton, about zombies, and a couple of western novels from North Dakota author Louis L'Amour. He bought them each for a nickel at the thrift store downtown.

The novels helped him escape. When he was arrested in May, the guards let him pick out a novel to read in the cell. It kept his mind off the alcohol detox he was going through. "I sat there and concentrated on that damn book and tried not to think about drinkin' somethin'," said Stakes. "Not think about what I was feelin'."

Stakes often thought about his old bartender friend, Shorty, detoxing in jail before he died. Two more people from the bar had died recently. There was "little short Jeff," who allegedly died when he left his gasoline generator running in a garage and asphyxiated from the fumes. Then a friend of Bergeson's and Stakes's named Steve reportedly fell down the stairs at his house and broke his neck. Bergeson said there were rumors that someone had pushed him. The tally of friends who had died this year was up to four. "I don't know what's going on in my life," Stakes said. "It's a crazy world."

Bergeson said he almost died a year ago when his roommate stabbed him.

"It wasn't me!" said Stakes, holding up his hand like he was swearing on the witness stand. Then he giggled. The vodka bottle was more than half empty now, and Stakes wasn't slowing down.

When Bergeson first arrived in Williston, he lived in an apartment closer to downtown with a roommate. One night, an argument escalated. The roommate pulled out a knife and stabbed Bergeson in the face, stomach, and back. "I hope he's dead, I think he's dead, I'm glad he's dead," he said as he stood over Bergeson. Bergeson later discovered that the man had served time in prison for strangling his wife to death.

"We live a strange life," said Stakes, pulling a cigarette out of a Marlboro pack. He took a long puff, blowing the smoke toward the fan to keep it away from me. The smoke dispersed and filled the small trailer.

Bergeson heard another story about three men dying on an oil rig. "The pipe shot out of the ground and skewered one guy," he said.

"That's a scary job. I don't care how much they pay ya. Ain't no job worth dying for."

"They're dyin' at jobs all the time," said Stakes, then he began coughing again. A deep, guttural cough that sounded as if 40 years of cigarette smoke was trying to escape his lungs.

"If someone said, I'll give you a million dollars, but you're going to die over this thing?" Bergeson asked.

"I'd do it!" said Stakes. "Jus' let me live to be 90 first." He laughed.

"I'd be like, give me the money first, then I'd get outta there. Flee the country," Bergeson said. They both agreed that construction work, though not exactly safe, was a better option.

There was a knock at the door. Bergeson opened it and a man with a wide-brimmed hat, leather jacket, and cowboy boots walked in. He introduced himself to me as Richard, tipped his hat, and called me "ma'am." Stakes had met Richard that morning. He was standing outside the bar trying to find a ride home when Richard walked by. Stakes paid Richard $20 to drive him home.

Richard had arrived in Williston a few days ago from Oklahoma. He was a "third-generation roughneck," he said, and, at 51 years old, he'd been working in the oil field for 16 years—in Oklahoma, Louisiana, and Texas and on an offshore rig on the Gulf of Mexico. "This ain't my first rodeo," Richard said with a southern drawl. "It's my third oil boom, and this is the only time I've had trouble gettin' a job. I filled out so many damn applications. I feel like I just wrote a book. Nobody wants to hire me 'cause I got *too* much experience." Richard slept in his truck, hiding in an old junkyard downtown to avoid the police. "I look like another piece of junk," he said. "There's a bunch a crackheads down there. I gotta sleep with a gun in one hand. And the skeeters'll drag ya off and kill ya." Stakes had offered him a parking spot outside their camper so the cops wouldn't bother him.

Richard leaned against the kitchen counter. He declared that

Williston's boom was about to go bust. "All dem boys on the drillin' rigs who went and bought $40,000 cars are about to get a rude awakenin'," he said. "This is just another oil boom to me. There's jobs here, and in the middle of a recession, ever'body flocks here. But people like me who ain't got a lot of money, can't pay rent that's thousands of dollars, and then they arrest ya for sleepin' in yer truck. It's the same ol', same ol'. Just like the ol' gold rush." To save money, Richard liked to hunt for his food. "If it can't swim fast enough, run fast enough, fly or slither fast enough, it's food," he said. He wanted to set up some snares by the lake to catch wild turkeys, but he was worried there were too many children around.

Stakes looked around the trailer, the cigarette dangling from his lips. "Rich, can you hand me that bottle?"

Richard looked on the kitchen counter, but there was no bottle.

"Rich, Rich!" Stakes yelled at him, not realizing Richard had heard him and was already looking. "Dammit, I know you can hear me. Where'd that damn vodka bottle go?" Stakes stumbled around the camper, picking clothes off the chair, looking for his vodka bottle. He finally found it behind his chair and sat back down, taking another swig.

Stakes stared out the window and flicked his cigarette butt into a glass flower vase. "I drink, I carouse, I'm old. I lived a hard life. I'm turnin' 60 soon, how far am I gonna get?" He let the question hang there for a moment but continued before anyone could respond. "This is it—this is my last shot at life. Ten more years, I don't know if I can even live that long. But I can still drink a bottle of vodka. That's one thing I can do," he said as he put the Silver Wolf bottle to his lips.

29. CHELSEA NIEHAUS

A few days after I visited Chelsea Niehaus, the family's trailer's sewage hose had a leak. They needed to replace the hose with sturdier PVC pipe. She and Jacob spent an entire day trying to install the pipe with no luck. Will wore Jacob's hard hat and made a pretend blueprint out of construction paper. He declared himself "project foreman." Jacob spent the afternoon smoking and cussing, working to connect the trailer to the sewage disposal hole with PVC pipe. It didn't take. In the meantime, they had to manually empty sewage from the toilet's holding tank. "The whole exercise has been exceptionally frustrating for Jacob since a large part of his job involves putting together metal pipe," Chelsea wrote on her blog. "At the outset of the project he made the comment that if he couldn't put this together easily he might as well go work at McDonald's. I think he's ready to go work at McDonald's now. Ah camper life. Never a dull moment!" She posted a photo of Jacob sitting next to the camper with pipe in his lap looking dejected.

After 18 years together, Jacob and Chelsea had finally decided to marry. They had their ceremony on Saturday, September 28, in Deadwood, South Dakota, five and a half hours from the trailer park. They found their wedding officiant from an advertisement in a shop window. Her name was "Reverend Faith," and on her website, she touted her services next to photos of herself on a motorcycle. Jacob's parents were the only wedding guests, and they all stayed at Black Hills Inn & Suites. The ceremony was held by a creek outside the hotel. Chelsea wore a red dress with spaghetti straps and a shawl draped over her shoulders. She had a red pendant around her neck and red Indian jewels on her forehead. Jacob wore a bolo tie borrowed from his father. To celebrate afterward, they dined at a casino.

Two weeks later, Chelsea discovered she was pregnant. She woke up in the middle of the night and had a feeling she couldn't explain. "I just knew," she said. "I was like, oh my God, I'm pregnant." In the morning, she found an old pregnancy test in the camper, and sure enough, it was positive. She was excited—she and Jacob had talked about having another baby, but they didn't expect it to happen so soon.

Meanwhile, Jacob's job at DuCon wasn't going well. His boss wasn't booking work for the company, and one day he disappeared completely. After the wedding, Jacob found a job with a new company called Oilfield Support Services, Inc., another roustabout maintenance company. In November, Jacob's boss gave them less than 24 hours to pack up the camper and move it over 60 miles to another location on the reservation called Skunk Bay.

Skunk Bay is a remote summer camping and boating resort on a picturesque cove of the Missouri River and in the midst of the North Dakota Badlands. The closest town, Mandaree, was 40 minutes away, though it only had one small convenience store and a registered population of 596. There were no gas stations for miles, and the nearest hospital was more than an hour away in Watford City. Chelsea was glad to leave the rude neighbors of the Parshall trailer park, but she worried about how remote the new location was, especially now that she was pregnant. She tried to prepare as best she could for the move; it was not a location where she wanted to forget anything.

On moving day, to get to their new camper location, they had to drive past Mandaree, a town of withered homes, junkyards, and mobile trailers. They then turned down an unmarked dirt road and drove for about 25 minutes, swerving to avoid potholes. They passed sweeping views of the Missouri River with its stark blue water, curved through canyons and cliffs with layered multicolored rock. They drove past abandoned farmhouses that leaned from the wind, a flat metal road sign pockmarked with bullet holes, and the Wolf Chief Recreation Area, considered a "native grasses sanctuary." At a vista point turnoff was a sign with faded, peeling wood. Carved into the wood was a quote from when Meriwether Lewis visited the area in the early 1800s: "This scenery, already rich, pleasing and beautiful, was still further heightened by immense herds of buffalo, deer and elk, which we saw in every direction feeding on the hills and plains. I do not think I exaggerate when I estimate the number of buffalo which could be comprehended at one view to amount to 3,000."

Beyond all this, speckling the barren, moonlike landscape was oil well after oil well, a cluster of them around every bend. Most were being actively drilled or fracked. At the end of the dirt road was a bar called the Rooster, the only business at the Skunk Bay resort. During the summer, the owners hosted bands and parties, but the bar was all but deserted after Labor Day. It had icicle Christmas lights hanging on the awning year-round. Out front next to picnic tables stood four electronic palm trees—in red, green, and blue—an odd choice since the closest palm trees to Skunk Bay were hundreds of miles away.

Once there, they took a right on Rabbit Road. They passed a mobile home with tires placed on the roof to keep the sheet metal from blowing away and the words SKUNK BROTHERS spray-painted on the siding. They maneuvered the camper down a steep hillside to their small lot at the edge of a cliff. It took them nearly an hour as dusk fell over the landscape. They dented the underside of the camper in the process. There were only about 10 other trailers parked out there. At night when the sun went down and the 360-degree panorama of stars appeared, at least 50 methane gas flares were visible on the horizon.

Their new location was eerily beautiful, but they again had no water, no Wi-Fi, no laundry facilities. Chelsea woke up to daily morning sickness, the weather turned colder, and she was miserable. "I hated living in that camper," she said. "I wanted to go home." She didn't want to have her baby there. The overcrowded hospital in Watford City was too far away, so she prepped to return to Kentucky. Jacob planned to stay in Skunk Bay for the winter, and they would transition to a long-distance relationship again. "I was ready to go back to Kentucky and lick my wounds and start over," Chelsea wrote on her blog.

Chelsea and Will left North Dakota on November 13, when Chelsea was six weeks pregnant. The next day, the first blizzard of the season swept over the prairies of western North Dakota. They had barely made it out.

30. CINDY MARCHELLO

It was a chilly spring day in the middle of May 2010 as Cindy Marchello drove to the Halliburton yard to report for her first day of work. She had recently completed about four weeks of classes and safety training. After this training, Halliburton put new hires, known as green hats for the color of their hard hats, in "field trials," where they worked on an active well location with supervisors to watch over them.

Marchello was told to show up at the Halliburton bus, a company-branded school bus that took workers out to location, at 4 a.m. When she stepped onto the bus, it was chaotic, with no assigned seating. She walked to the back of the bus and recognized one other guy from her training class. She waved to him and they sat next to each other. He seemed as scared as she was. The two-hour bus ride was a terrifying place for newcomers, and especially a female newcomer. People called it "the prison bus." Guys would throw bottles at each other, and if anyone fell asleep, which happened often early in the morning or after a 12-hour workday, men would spit or write things on the faces of slumbering workers.

To her knowledge, Marchello was the only woman working as a frack hand for Halliburton's North Dakota operation at that time. She heard about one woman before her—a petite, younger woman the guys talked about. But that woman had moved up into management and no longer worked on well locations. Most of the men on the bus were surprised to see a woman there. For Marchello, even though the oil field is one of the most dangerous industries in the United States, she lived in more fear on the bus than on active well locations. "The bus was probably the most dangerous place in the oil field," she recalled. "I learned very early on to sit in the back seat so nobody was behind me."

When they arrived at the well location, Marchello slid men's red coveralls (there were no female versions) over her clothing and fastened a green hard hat over her ponytail. A supervisor told her to wait by the bus for further instructions. An hour later, she was still standing there. Finally, she caught someone's attention and asked what she should do. He told Marchello to sit by the frack tanks, a long line of steel shipping containers, each one filled with 21,000 gallons of water. She looked over to the frack tanks and saw no one there. "And?" she said. "Is there somebody over there?" He told her someone would come by eventually. She waited there by herself, but no one came. About 10 hours later, someone told her it was time to get back on the bus.

The next day, there was a different supervisor at the well location. When the supervisor saw her in the lineup of green hats, he grumbled at one of his men, who happened to be Curtis Kenney, and told Kenney to "get that girl out of here." Kenney introduced himself and gestured for Marchello to follow him. Kenney had noticed her the day before. She was hard not to notice. "Every guy there knows when there's a woman on location. I might be gettin' older, but I'm not gettin' blinder," said Kenney. "There was nothing Cindy could do that wouldn't cause attention." Kenney had been working there for three months.

For the first few weeks, Marchello followed Kenney everywhere. He taught her how to assist whoever was running the sand pump. They mixed sand, made from fine particles of quartz, with frack fluid before it went into the well. She'd stand by the belt and turn it on and turn it off when someone on the radio told her. Kenney taught her how to stay safe and what to do and where to stand when they had to disassemble the pump trucks and iron piping, move them to another location, and reassemble them. She'd haul hoses and pipes from the truck to the well hole and help bang iron together as they set up. She learned to operate the crane and drive the mountain mover. She kept her head down, worked hard, and tried not to draw attention to herself. "When I first got there, I felt like I didn't belong and I was very apologetic," she said. "I was like, I'm really sorry, I'm just trying to earn a living."

Every night after her shift, Marchello studied for hours to learn the terminology for the tools and procedures on the well. There were so many different types of valves and iron piping—dart valves, check valves, double swing valves, chiksan swivel joints. She practiced hand signals for operating the crane and studied Halliburton-specific acronyms. Hundreds of them. In an email to her daughter Jennie, she wrote: "I do math and vocabulary till I can't see and fall asleep. I have to learn about fluid volumes and weight of fluid and tons and tons of specific math formulas! Math follows you everywhere . . . so does computer stuff."

She cried herself to sleep most nights because she missed her family and felt out of place. One night, when one of her grandchildren was sick at home, her daughter Elizabeth called her in the middle of the night to ask her advice. Her grandson was hysterical and took the phone. Marchello sang him lullabies and tried to soothe him. "I'll be home in a few weeks, baby. This big work isn't gonna keep me away for too long," she remembered saying. By the time she hung up the phone, she only had three hours before she needed to leave for work. It killed her that she couldn't be home to comfort her grandson. "I thought, I'm 1,000 miles away. What the freak am I doing?"

Sometimes immediately after a shift, even though she was exhausted, she walked along Williston's only bike trail by the river to decompress, still wearing her greasy coveralls and steel-toed boots.

She often considered giving up and going home. "I will never be tough enough for this job," she remembered texting Elizabeth one night after work. Elizabeth replied: "Then you need to be smart so you can come home."

Being smart meant earning enough money to pay her debts and get back on her feet. Her goal was to cover her bankruptcy bills, build credit, and maybe even buy her own home. Her first paycheck for one week of work (40 hours at $14 an hour plus 10 hours of overtime) was about $800. Back home, there were entire months when she hadn't earned $800. This was her chance to get ahead. "When things got tough, I kept thinking about my kids and how much they needed me," she said. "Because even though my kids are big, I'm still a single mom. I'm the only backup person they have." She also hoped to find love again one day, but wanted to wait until she was financially stable to become seriously involved with anyone. Never again did she want to depend on a man for money and allow him to control her life.

Every day, she felt herself becoming physically and emotionally stronger. Her "pec muscles were getting a serious workout," she told Jennie. It was easier to pick up tools and lift heavy machinery than when she first started. She was also learning how to manage her strengths and weaknesses. She didn't compete with the guys on the heavier jobs but figured out how to move her body in a certain way to create more torque or haul chemicals in a more efficient way. Though she constantly felt others on the crew doubted her abilities, she was becoming more confident in herself. She wrote to Jennie: "Boss made me mad a couple times but I bit my tongue. He kept taking tools away from me. He doesn't do it to the guys. I've decided to be LOUDER tomorrow and stick up for myself."

After two weeks of training, she passed the trials, and Halliburton sent her to receive her commercial driver's license, or CDL, a symbol that the company was investing in her. Not everyone made it that far.

Marchello was glad to be moving forward, but she also felt exhausted. This was just the beginning.

At CDL school, Marchello had more challenges. She remembered one of her teachers, an older man in his 70s, telling her, "There's only been two girls to come through this school and they didn't pass." Marchello knew it was going to be a difficult three weeks of working with him. In June, she wrote on her Facebook wall: "Why o why. . . . 5 more days of CDL School. This had better be worth it. I'm too old for this crap! I will refrain from adding any of my man-bashing thoughts."

When she returned with her CDL, she was once again assigned to the same crew as Kenney. One of the supervisors was furious he'd been given a woman on his crew, which typically consisted of 18 men. Although the supervisor told Kenney to mentor Marchello, he pulled Kenney aside and whispered, "Don't teach her anything because she's only here for a lawsuit." He didn't think Marchello would last long. Kenney regularly heard guys talking behind her back about how she was a worthless addition to the crew or making inappropriate comments about her body. "Most of the guys on the crew treated her like she was . . . unwanted," Kenney said. Sometimes the supervisor told her to shadow another guy for the day, so she did. Eventually she found out that she was being passed around as punishment. If the supervisor was mad at somebody on the crew, he'd say, "You're on the shit list today and you get the girl."

One of the toughest challenges for her was learning how to back up a semi truck. Marchello had passed a series of tests in CDL school but still had difficulty on site. Setting up the equipment required maneuvering the semis into tight positions. Many times her coworkers yelled and screamed at her while she was backing up, which only added to her nerves. Later she found out members of her crew had made bets about who would be the first to make her cry. They paid one guy $150 to see if he could harass her to the point of tears. "Every time you were on shift, we made bets," a coworker told her months later. "I'm talking thousands of dollars. I'm talking about company men involved."

She stopped him. "And who collected on the bet?"

"Nobody," he replied. "Not one person. I knew every time they were having that conversation that no one was going to break you."

In addition to facing direct insults, there were subtle ones as well. Even the men who were kind to her didn't always trust her with equipment, or blamed her for things that went wrong. Other men avoided her for fear that gossip would travel back to their wives that they were spending time with a woman at work. She wondered if some men were trying to force her into quitting. One day she walked over to her assigned semi and the windshield wiper arm had been broken off. The truck had already passed inspection for her trip, so she figured it must have happened recently. When she started the engine, the radio blared at full volume and heat blasted out of the vents. She couldn't adjust them because the knobs had been pulled off.

Her experiences on the bus also weren't improving. One day, a guy they called Mincoff was preparing to draw on a sleeping coworker's face, and Marchello woke up the coworker before Mincoff could do anything. He was furious and came up to her with the marker in his hand and snarled, "I can make you disappear."

"Well, my ex-husband couldn't do it in 28 years, so good luck with that," Marchello snapped back.

A few weeks later, even though she was sitting in the back trying to stay out of the way, a half-full Gatorade bottle came flying across the bus and hit her in the eye. It came from Mincoff, though he allegedly wasn't aiming at her. Afterward, she walked up to where Mincoff was sitting, shook the bottle in his face, and said, "I can make you disappear." Then she threw the bottle in the trash can. He stopped harassing her after that, but she had a black eye for a week.

Most of the fracking locations they went to had a portable toilet or two, but they were rarely cleaned and were used by hundreds of men. She dreaded going to the restroom and at first removed her coveralls behind the Porta Potty before entering to avoid dragging them on the disgusting floor. But after a couple days of this, she noticed a group of guys watching her remove her coveralls. She had clothes on underneath, but it still gave her the creeps. From then on, she began removing her coveralls inside the restroom, carefully maneuvering in the small compartment to avoid touching anything.

She also stopped wearing any makeup or nail polish. One day, however, she returned to work after attending a wedding in Utah and forgot to remove the nail polish she'd worn. While she was duct-taping cardboard over a bin with the help of a male coworker, he suddenly reached over and began touching her hand. She pulled away, confused. She looked down, saw her nail polish, and quickly put her gloves back on.

Though Kenney had a wife and family, this didn't stop him from being flirtatious with Marchello. At first, the two didn't share a living space. The Halliburton man camps were full, so the company put Marchello in a hotel, and Kenney lived in a company-rented apartment building.

Kenney often asked Marchello if she wanted to go for drives. He'd tell her how much of a friend she'd become. He started bringing her cookies while they were out on location. She appreciated his kindness and friendship, but at times worried he was developing feelings for her. He came around when he wasn't needed just to spend time with her. Then she received notes under her hotel room door. "I like your butt" was scribbled in messy handwriting. The note was written on scrap paper from Halliburton equipment labels, so she was certain it was from a Halliburton employee. Another note scared her. "If you had been here I would've come into your room," it read. Based on

Kenney's behavior toward her at work, she suspected it was him, but she couldn't be sure. (Kenney continues to deny it was him.) She didn't want to falsely accuse him, and she didn't believe management could do much about it anyway, so she stayed quiet. "I didn't want to cause trouble," she said.

Soon space opened up for her to move into a man camp called Target Logistics, located north of Williston. The huge, 1,000-person camp was practically a mini-city where multiple companies housed workers. It was surrounded by a gate with a full-time guard, and workers weren't allowed to have any visitors, including spouses or children, and no drinking, drugs, or roughhousing was tolerated. Besides a few housekeepers and cooks, Marchello counted only eight women employed by Halliburton living at the camp, most of them engineers or warehouse coordinators, and they were all housed together in one trailer.

The camp had a massive cafeteria where everyone lined up to eat for breakfast, lunch, and dinner. Marchello hated the group meals. "Men would look at you like you had no clothes on," she said. "If you sat by yourself, guys would flock around you like flies. It was awful." This was also the camp where men stole her underwear out of the washing machine. She began taking all her laundry home to Utah on her days off, stocking up on extra underwear and bras, or trekking to the local laundromat. Because several companies were there, she didn't know whom to complain to when incidents happened. Even if she did complain, she didn't think it would matter. "There was nobody there who cared," she said.

Marchello lasted in Halliburton's frack department for about four months. For reasons she never entirely understood, she was transferred to Halliburton's warehouse, where a number of other women worked. She guessed it had something to do with her supervisor, who never seemed to like her. They had argued one day. He claimed she was too hard on one of the new male hires, who quit. Marchello disagreed. She became so angry, she kicked the side of her supervisor's desk. Upper management soon told her she would no longer be working in frack and she was transferred to the warehouse.

Marchello was furious and upset, but at the same time, she realized she could have easily been fired for losing her temper. She posted on Facebook after the incident: "EMOTIONS. It would be wonderful if I were capable of learning the lesson life keeps throwing at me. Although I am angry at myself for not being tough enough to endure, I am pleased with myself. I bit my tongue instead of getting fired. I have given up the quest of expressing myself in intense situations without crying. I guess I'm old enough now to say, 'suck it up boys, I'm gonna cry. Deal with it.'"

At the warehouse, there was a woman named Sarah Carpender, and she and Marchello became fast friends. Carpender had four young kids at home. For Marchello, the warehouse work was mundane. She cleaned hundreds of coveralls and hung them according to size, sorted through equipment, and logged inventory. It was a cut in pay since she didn't work overtime, but she liked the consistent schedule.

After a few months, however, the warehouse hired a new employee. The new guy and Marchello didn't get along. He threatened her, saying he would "cut her throat" if she didn't follow his orders. He berated her for her work performance and complained to human resources about her. She tried to speak up about his behavior, but her supervisors didn't believe her. Most of them assumed he was a nice, jovial guy. Carpender believed Marchello but didn't feel comfortable getting involved. Marchello worried about her safety around him and avoided being alone with him.

At the same time, she was frustrated that she'd been at Halliburton almost a year and still hadn't received a raise. She made $14 an hour and discovered new guys with no experience were starting at

$16 an hour. She asked her boss in upper management for a raise, and he said no. She remembered arguing with him: "But why are you hiring them for more than you hired me?" He replied: "I have 400 guys standing outside that door. If you don't want this job, they do." Other former crew members told her Halliburton was notorious for denying raises. The only way to make more money was to transfer companies. Kenney had recently left Halliburton and was now working at a company called Cudd Energy Services, which focused on coil tubing operations, and told her they had an opening. The position was for a nitrogen pump operator. She didn't think she had a chance. "Coil tubing is like the Rolls-Royce of service companies because they are paid a higher wage. It's very unusual for a new person to go into a coil job," she explained. But she applied anyway. To her surprise, she was hired. She sent in her resignation to Halliburton.

On Marchello's first day at Cudd, Kenney had a surprise for her. She arrived at her room in the man camp and there was a pink-and-purple comforter on her bed with Disney princesses on it and a sign on the door that read THE CAMP PRINCESS. She shook her head, crossed out the word PRINCESS, and wrote QUEEN.

31. PASTOR JAY REINKE

I met Pastor Jay Reinke one Sunday during the summer of 2013 when I showed up to his church service. I was late, so I slid quietly into one of the pews in the back. Reinke stood behind the pulpit and wore the traditional black clerical shirt and white tab collar. The Lutheran sanctuary had stained glass windows, and quotes like EAT, DRINK, AND FIND ENJOYMENT IN THE TOIL hung on the wall. Members of the congregation filled about half of the sanctuary, and most were middle-age or elderly. I counted six young men who I guessed were Overnighters. One man with a buzz cut sat with his arms crossed and dozed off during the service. Another man with long hair and a scraggly beard sat stoically and watched the pastor.

During the sermon, Reinke mentioned the Overnighters program. The city had recently asked him to limit to how many people slept on his floor—29 was deemed a "safe" number for fire code. "This past week has been hard," he said. "We had to say no to 29 other people. Many don't even have a car." Reinke explained men of all sorts were showing up to the church's doorstep—three Muslims and one "very nice black man from Ghana" were sleeping at the church. "I told them that life in Williston is difficult," he said. He asked his congregation to join him in being good neighbors, and he assured them that he did background checks on the men.

After the sermon, I introduced myself. He invited me to sit down and chat during the church's coffee hour. He explained that part of the reason his neighbors were concerned about the Overnighters was because of an African man who once stayed at the church. The man had stabbed someone at the local laundromat, Bubba's Bubbles. Reinke had implemented background checks to help mitigate the damage. It was easy for men to lose direction in Williston, he explained. "It's almost impossible to build community here," he said. "It's a very vulnerable population."

I asked him if any women stayed at the church.

He could think of only two who had stayed there in the past: a woman from the Congo in her 30s and a girl from Somalia in her early 20s. "She was very attractive, model-like," he said. "I could tell she was very street smart, but still. It made me nervous. An extremely attractive girl around all these guys?" He said she'd been sleeping in one of the local parks before she came to the church. The pastor invited her to sleep at his house in his parked car, but she didn't stay long. Reinke wasn't sure where she was now. "They're all becoming vagrants," he said. "If they weren't a vagrant before, they're becoming one here."

It was more difficult for women to find a job that provided housing, Reinke said. And he worried about the safety of "cheap rent" situations for them—did they really trust the landlord or the other people staying there?

"Is there nowhere else for people to go for help?" I asked.

Reinke explained the Salvation Army gave out food and gas vouchers but had no way to help with housing. The Salvation Army recently started buying one-way tickets out of town for new arrivals who couldn't find a roof over their heads, hoping they'd become someone else's problem. Reinke often spotted men smoking and drinking outside the back door of the Salvation Army's office, waiting for vouchers. "The Salvation Army is a little bit of a—" He paused to carefully choose his words. "Not a good place. The men there are sliding downhill."

Reinke's wife, Andrea, sat nearby listening to our conversation. She jumped in to help explain what he meant. "I think people start to get worn out," she said.

Reinke nodded. "People start to break down after a while. I had to tell two guys to leave this week. They were working part-time day labor for two and a half months. That just isn't going to work here," he said. Even if a newcomer found a job, he explained, the number of hours he or she needed to work to survive in Williston took a toll. Oil field work wasn't easy, and not having a stable home made the job difficult to sustain. "It's a modest-paying job when you think about all they ask of you," said Reinke about oil field work. "It's a young man's game."

I returned to the church a few nights later to attend a "neighborhood meeting" Reinke had organized. Only one neighbor showed up. She was stocky with short dark blond hair and looked to be in her early 50s. She introduced herself as Nancy and lived a few doors down from the church. Andrea Reinke was there, as were two former Overnighters, both of whom now had jobs and housing but occasionally volunteered for Pastor Reinke.

One of the former Overnighters introduced himself as Steve Tanck from St. Louis. He was 56 years old and had come to Williston in June 2012 after he was laid off from his job as a sales manager at Home Depot and the bank foreclosed on his home. Tanck heard about the church from the YouTube video and slept in his Chrysler minivan in the church's parking lot for about a month. He eventually found an apartment above a dry-cleaning business with about 15 other people, but the city shut it down within a few months. After about a year of living in various sketchy situations—a trailer on someone's property, a mobile home with a leaky roof and mice—he found a job at a furniture store and felt secure enough to bring his wife and daughter to Williston. They were able to find a two-bedroom, one-bathroom apartment for $1,250 a month, a steal compared to other places.

Tanck credited Reinke for helping him survive in Williston. He was grateful for the hospitality Reinke showed him his first month in town and had attended Concordia Lutheran Church ever since, volunteering for the Overnighters when he could. "When you're coming from 1,300 miles away and you don't have anyplace to go, to have the security of a parking lot with other people like you around—as opposed to being on the side of the road—the comfort that brought was tremendous," said Tanck. "I couldn't put a price tag on it. It was a godsend. It was the answer to my prayers."

In the church's gathering room, Reinke stood behind three long tables with his back toward the wall. Outside, sheets of rain poured onto the sidewalk and the wind hissed. There were severe storm warnings for the night, with 40-mile-per-hour winds expected. Reinke's gray hair was matted down from rain, and he wore glasses low on his nose.

Reinke had called the meeting to answer his neighbors' questions about the Overnighters. He hoped to garner their support because the city's Planning and Zoning Department was threatening to shut down the program. It sent Reinke a letter detailing the requirements to continue operating. Reinke needed to have the same features as a homeless shelter: showers, an emergency sprinkler system in the building, and a designated sleeping room, and he had to hire a full-time social worker. But Reinke didn't want the church to become a homeless shelter. He hoped to apply for a temporary housing permit to keep it running and planned to argue his case for the Overnighters at the city's next Planning and Zoning meeting, which was closed to the public.

Reinke explained his plans to Nancy.

She crossed her arms and said she had concerns. "There was a guy staying in the building who was talking on his phone outside about the good hookers in Williston," she said, her tone combative. "It sounded like he was telling his friend to come here for the hookers."

Reinke held his chin and nodded. "I encourage you to speak up when you see that," he advised.

Nancy was not pleased with his answer. "Well, I'm a neighbor being offended by someone staying here."

"Was he a black guy?" Reinke asked.

"Yes, he was black-skinned."

"Was he African?"

"It didn't sound like he had an accent—I could understand what he was saying," she said.

Reinke nodded and begin talking about Christ and redemption. He could guide these men to the word of God, he explained, and they could change their ways.

Nancy pursed her lips. "You're bringing in the wrong part of life here to Williston if you're promoting illegal activity like that."

Reinke didn't address her comment directly but gave her examples of how he was standing up against the unsavory activities around town. Reinke said one entrepreneur started a "Fun Bus" in Williston, for example, which drove bar to bar with strippers, picking up patrons. "I met the guy who started it and told him, 'This is not good for women or men.' I don't think it's functioning anymore," he said. Reinke also discovered that the local college received funding from the pull tabs at Williston's strip clubs. Reinke confronted someone at the college about it. He remembered asking: "Is that the message you want to send young women who are trying to find a place in society?"

Nancy didn't seemed convinced. Reinke tried a different argument: "These are husbands and fathers who are here to serve their children," he said. "They're people who need an income and want to work, and it's our duty to serve them." He paused and leaned against a table. "It's messy, though. I had to kick a man out the other night because he hit another man. One thing I can do is I can tell them not to talk on their phones outside. How does that sound?" Reinke asked Nancy. "I want the neighbors to feel as comfortable as possible."

Nancy nodded but didn't smile. Her arms remained crossed. She had another concern: "How can I prevent people from knocking on my door asking 'Is that the church that lets people stay there?' It's not my job to be the receptionist for the church. My property value might go down. When I bought the property, I had an understanding that I was living next to a church, not a homeless shelter, not a hotel, not a hostel. If I had wanted that, I would've bought next to one. To me, a church is a church, not a place for sleeping."

Reinke nodded, absorbing her argument and preparing his rebuttal. "Okay. There *is* St. Peter's Episcopal that I know has AA meetings. This is what churches are involved with sometimes. I think it's just part of—and one of the burdens—of being a neighbor. There's no way for us to prevent people knocking on your door. But I would ask you to consider it as an opportunity to serve. These people are trying change their lives and need our help. It might not be what you expected, but the whole boom is nothing we expected."

We heard a knock on the door. A woman with red curly hair poked her head into the room. "Hi, I'm looking for a place to stay tonight," she said. "I'm willing to clean or help out in exchange."

Reinke asked her to wait in the hall and he'd be right with her. When she closed the door, he turned back toward Nancy. "I wish I could solicit other churches to help," he said. Reinke had asked other churches in town if they'd take one or two already-vetted Overnighters, but not one had agreed. "Imagine having to turn people away in this?" he said, gesturing to the door while the storm raged outside and hail pummeled the narrow windows.

After Nancy left, Reinke came over to where I was sitting, placed his hands on the table, and leaned forward. "Can you *believe* that lady?" he said, pointing to the door where she'd exited. "That's the same lady who called the cops on children in the parking lot. They were doing a craft project using matches. For a *craft project*. And she called the cops! They call her the playground Nazi at the park. She says she didn't sign up for this. Well, welcome to Williston!" he yelled, throwing his arms out wide. "It really pisses me off, excuse my French," he said. "There's just so much fear. I wish people would stop making decisions based on fear."

It was nearly 9 p.m., and Overnighters were arriving at the church for the night. Men huddled by the back door waiting to be let in. Reinke unlocked the door, and a half-dozen shuffled in, removing dripping-wet coats and hats. They unrolled sleeping bags and blankets to claim their spots on the ground. They tucked their bedding between tables and hung wet T-shirts and socks on the backs of chairs. One man kept his clothes in a black garbage bag. A few men had purchased fast food and ate their meals quietly at the tables. I met Derek MacDonald, a skinny 28-year-old with glasses, who came from the small town of Smith Center, Kansas. Before coming to Williston, he took care of his sick grandfather and struggled to find steady work. He'd snag the occasional construction gig, but it wasn't enough to support himself. He also had a DUI on his record, which dissuaded many employers from hiring him. "I only had a couple jobs the whole year," he said. Broke and unsure of what to do next, he had packed up two duffel bags, a sleeping bag, and a tarp and bought a one-way bus ticket to Williston. "I found a job within the first hour of being here," he said.

Reinke invited in Carol, the redhead who'd interrupted the meeting, and a young man named Brian, who had arrived earlier that day and needed a place to sleep. Brian looked to be in his mid-20s and wore a baseball cap over bleached blond hair. Reinke sat down at a table across from them to give an orientation.

He handed them the list of rules, printed out on computer paper. "This is not a luxury hotel," he said. "We're a church, so we'd like you here on Sunday morning. It's very difficult for women here," he said, looking at Carol. "Women sleep in the hallway. It's some privacy, but not much." Carol had red-lined lips and dainty hands. I found out later she came to Williston from Maine to produce a radio news show.

Reinke continued: "You'll sign in each evening, and we'll give you a name tag. Lights out at 11 p.m. No drinking. Anything I can smell or find with a Breathalyzer is grounds for you to leave. No profanity. If your feet stink, I will tell you. You need to wash them. There are no showers here. You have to use the sink. For showers, there's the community center, or for private showers, Elite Gym for $60 a month. Shirts need to be worn at all times. We ask you to do some cleaning in the mornings. You can use the microwave but no stove. The city doesn't want us to do much cooking. Don't eat or drink by where you sleep.

"And. You. Have. Got. To. Be. Looking. For. Housing," he said, punctuating every word with his pen pointed at their faces. "It's a hard life here," he said, softening his tone. "Two guys who stayed here have committed suicide. Another one has gone missing and I think he's dead."

Carol said she brought her own bedding, but Brian didn't have anything. Reinke handed him a blue blanket and a quilt. He said the blankets were first come, first served.

Reinke stood up suddenly, as if he'd forgotten something. He walked to the edge of the room. "Gentlemen, I have a new rule!" he yelled. "Weeee! A new rule! We had a neighbor that heard one of you talking about prostitutes in Williston."

One guy in the room let out a snort of laughter but silenced himself quickly.

"No more talking on your cell phones in front of the church!" Reinke said. He asked them to make phone calls in the rear parking lot or off church property.

He returned to where I was and sat down, then leaned forward and lowered his voice. Reinke discussed Brian's chances of surviving in Williston, even though the man sat nearby. "He seems like a good guy. I think he has a chance of making it here. But I'm not sure about Carol," he said. Carol was no longer in the room—she likely left to set up her bed in the hallway. Reinke was concerned about her mental state— but from what I could tell, she was fine, just a little quirky.

Suddenly, Reinke remembered he wanted to give Brian and Carol a speech. He couldn't find Carol, so Reinke sat across from Brian. "This is a hard place," he started. "When things go south, plan B means plan Blessing. Jesus was broken on the cross, and that's how he saved us," Reinke said as he grabbed Brian's arm and looked him in the eye.

Brian began to cry. "I used to be a bad alcoholic, things were really rough," he said as he wiped away tears. "I've crisscrossed the country at least a dozen times trying to find an opportunity. I just want some-one to give me a chance to see what I can do."

Reinke took Brian's shoulder and told him it was going to be okay. He held Brian's gaze. "You are welcome here."

32. TOM STAKES

Tom Stakes passed by Concordia Lutheran Church often. He knew the church offered a warm place to sleep, but he never went in. For one, he heard the pastor didn't allow drinking, and he wasn't willing to follow that rule. He also hadn't attended church in a long time. His church-going friends often invited him to sermons, but he declined. "I don't feel like I deserve to be there," he told me once. He felt embarrassed about his drinking, and the longer he stayed away, the harder it was to return. He still had faith in God, though. His oldest possession was a worn leather Bible that he kept zipped away in a black protective case. Inside, the pages were well read, with highlighted passages and notes scribbled in the margins. Stakes liked to read over his favorite verses at night. He didn't miss the responsibility, stress, and packed schedule of being a pastor—always preparing for sermons, performing baptisms, marriages, and funerals, and visiting members in the hospital. It had taken a toll on his family life. But at the same time, he missed feeling needed.

One summer evening, I picked up Stakes from Fox Run RV Park, and we met Greg Mackie near the train station at Mackie's yellow school bus. They planned to get tipsy on cheap beer before going to the bars downtown. Inside the bus, the floor space had been converted into a giant sleeping area, with old couch cushions piled together. A sticky fly strip with dead flies hung by the entrance, fishing rods leaned against the window, and piles of clothes were scattered near the bed cushions. Stakes, Mackie, and I sat at a small table near the front.

Stakes lit a cigarette, and Mackie cracked open three Miller Lights for us. As we chatted, a young man, barefoot and wearing overalls without a shirt, poked his head through the bus's open door. He asked if we were on our way to the Rainbow Gathering in Heber City, Utah. Stakes said no, but he invited the young man inside for a beer. The man ducked into the bus and sat down on the couch cushions. He said his name was Eric and he'd hitchhiked to Williston from Utah a few days before. He aspired to be a roustabout on an oil rig, but in the meantime he was applying to fast-food restaurants.

As the sun set, the streetlamps cast dim spotlights on the asphalt parking lot. We sat and talked in the faint light. Every so often a car drove by, and slowly more people walked by on the sidewalk near us. The strip clubs were located across the street, and people congregated outside. This part of downtown Williston, typically deserted during the day, was waking up for the night.

Suddenly, Stakes cried out, "Girl! What the hell you doin' over there?"

We all stopped talking and looked over to where he was facing.

"No, this ain't right," Stakes said, shaking his head.

"Who is it?" Mackie asked.

Stakes pointed through the open door to a girl in the distance, a few feet away from the train tracks, slouched against a cement wall with a red duffel bag next to her. She looked young, with long brown hair, a black T-shirt, and fitted jeans.

"It looks like she's hurt," Stakes said. "She got her hand over her face. It looks like she's been cryin'."

Mackie, Eric, and I stood up to see better.

"No no no, girl. You havin' a hard time, but dammit, girl. You ain't alone," Stakes said as though she could hear him. "If you need help, we're gonna help ya however we can. We ain't gonna mess with ya."

Mackie turned to me. "We see a lot of this. People get dropped off at the train." He said he often saw couples fighting—sometimes people would yell and scream at each other in front of onlookers. He thought maybe that was the case with this girl. "I've seen more fights up here than probably in my whole lifetime."

Stakes interrupted. "Ah, fuck, she's over there cryin'. I got to go see what it is." He left the bus and made his way over to her, with the rest of us close behind. As we neared her, it was obvious she was crying. Her face was in her hands and she was sobbing.

Stakes approached her slowly. "Hey, how long ya been here?" he asked gently.

She looked up at him, her eyes red and puffy. "Like . . . an hour," she managed to say before crying again. "I'm scared."

Stakes knelt down and spoke to her softly, as if she were a young child. "Well, I'm Tom. You want to come over to the bus? We're just sittin' there drinkin' a couple a beers."

She sniffled. "The boys over there were yellin' at me."

Stakes stood up and raised his voice. "Who was?"

She burst into tears again. "I don't know," she said in between her sobs. "The guys at the strip club, or whatever that is."

"What?" said Stakes, becoming angry. "They were messin' with ya? Well, nobody's gonna fuck with you 'round me. Nobody."

She continued crying, trying to catch her breath. She wiped her damp cheeks.

Stakes softened his voice again. "Girl, it's okay, it's all right," he said, trying to console her. "Just breathe a little bit. We're not gonna hurt people. We love people. We take care of each other. We all been in the same boat. Come on over there and we'll figure somethin' out. You ain't gotta sit out here like this with all these wild motherfuckers runnin' around."

Eric, who'd been standing by quietly, chimed in. "Yeah, this town gets crazy at night. That's why I don't hang out over here."

She wiped away more tears and sniffled.

"What's your name?" Stakes asked.

"Tori."

"Aw, like Tori Amos. I like Tori Amos," Stakes said, and patted her on the back. "Come on now, nobody's gonna mess with ya. You only been here for like an hour. You don't even know what the hell's goin' on 'round this town. How old are ya?"

"Twenty-one," she said, her sniffles becoming quieter.

Stakes coaxed her to stand up and we all walked back toward the bus. Tori looked suspiciously toward the bus and stopped just outside of the entrance. We stood around her in a circle. She told us she was from Waterloo, Iowa, and had boarded the train yesterday. She was supposed to have a job waiting for her in Williston and planned to get picked up by her new boss, a man she'd never met. "I texted him at 8:30 p.m. and told him I was here and he's still not here. Then the guys at the strip club were screaming at me, saying 'Don't get raped' and all kinds of shit." Her voice became mouselike as she held back more tears. "I don't want nobody to get me," she said, bursting into tears again. She heaved, trying to breathe through her tears.

"You came up here by yourself?" asked Eric. "You need somebody else. Because there's like 12 guys to one girl out here," he said confidently, seeming proud he knew such information.

Stakes glared at Eric for his comment, and Eric shrugged. "Don't worry about it, Tori, it's gonna be fine," said Stakes. "Take a breath, let it go, 'cause we all been here before. We're all scared sometimes, and you're a young woman. You say you're 21? You ain't even lived life yet. I know it's a scary proposition to walk into an oil town and they got all this crazy crap goin' on. And you don't have a clue what you're gonna do. You got no money, you got no job, no place to live. It's tough. I only been here a year and a month. I had to sleep in my truck, had to make do. I found a job there, a job here, tryin' to make it. This guy's been here for three years," he said, pointing to Mackie. "But we figured it out. You got a place if you need one. Even if you gotta stay at my place, I'll sleep on the floor outside. You can have my bed. That'll give you somethin' for right now. Nobody's gonna mess with you, I promise you. I won't. I'm 60 years old." He chuckled. "But I tell ya, ain't nobody gonna bother ya."

"Do you know anyone else here?" I asked her.

She shook her head and looked down at her feet. She said the job she'd been promised was door-to-door sales for $200 a day. But she'd only spoken to her boss over the phone. She had his phone number, but the battery on her cell phone had died.

"You need to call somebody?" asked Stakes. "I got a phone that works." He pulled out his flip phone and Tori read aloud the number she had for her boss. It started ringing and Stakes put the phone on speaker.

A man's voice answered.

"It's Tori. Are you guys coming?" she said, the words rushing out.

"Oh, shit. I'll come right now. What time is it?"

"Almost 10 o'clock and I'm scared," Tori said meekly.

"All right, be right there," he said, and hung up.

Tori looked dejected. "They freakin' forgot about me," she said, sniffling.

Stakes moved closer to her and lowered his voice. "Are you sure you're safe with these guys? Do you know these guys, Tori?"

"No, I don't know nobody. I know nothin'," she said softly.

"You be careful, because you don't know what the hell you're gettin' yourself into up here," said Stakes.

Stakes and Mackie started arguing over where she would sleep tonight. Mackie offered her a place to sleep on the floor of the bus, but Stakes said he'd already offered her his mattress in the camper while he slept outside. Stakes explained the homeless situation in Williston to her. "It used to be you could camp in the park over there," Stakes said. "But they disbanded everybody because everybody was gettin' drunk and stealin' things outta people's tents, gettin' in fights. Then it used to be you could camp out at Walmart, but they ran everybody off from there. It got to a point where there ain't nowhere to go."

Stakes wanted her to know that he always protected women. "We take care of our ladies," he said. "I may flirt, but I'm not gonna make a move. I ain't gonna let nothin' happen to no woman. Hell no. You're in good hands, Tori. We're not some strangers out here tryin' to hurt people."

"If somebody's abusin' a woman, you have to stand up," said Mackie, agreeing with Stakes.

Stakes tried to convince Tori to come with us to the bars. Tori said she didn't like beer. A loud truck rumbled by our group, the headlights momentarily blinding us.

"Maybe she can have a rum and Coke instead," Mackie said.

Tori stayed quiet, looking down at the asphalt.

"Well, I don't know what she likes. But we'll take care of ya," Stakes said to her. "We're gonna adopt ya."

Suddenly Tori looks up. "Is this Williston?" she asked, looking around frantically.

"Yeah, this is Williston," Stakes said.

"I'm supposed to be going to Alexander," she said, referring to the small town a half hour away.

"Oh, I know a pastor there," Stakes said, excited. "He helps us out sometimes. But we're not big Christians," he said, shaking his head. "No, no. We get drunk."

"We're Christian drunks," Mackie said. A loud motorcycle sputtered by in the distance.

"Well, Noah was a drunk," Stakes said, referring to the Old Testament story. "I'm a former preacher, and I still know the Word."

Tori ignored them and asked to use Stakes's phone again. She called her new boss, and he said he'd driven around the parking lot but didn't see her. She told him to look for the yellow school bus.

After she hung up, Eric told her that if this job didn't work out, she could always apply to the fast-food restaurants or do housekeeping.

"Yeah, they're always looking for housekeepers up there by the Vegas Motel," Mackie said. He suddenly seemed bored with the conversation and walked back into the bus, turning on some music.

"You be damn careful with these guys," Stakes said, lowering his voice again. "This is a boomtown, an oil town. There are bad people out here. There's a lot of people who disappear around here. I ain't tryin' to scare ya, but you're 21 years old in a strange place, and these are some wild boys 'round here. Don't let them abuse you. Don't let them touch you unless you want it. It's your choice."

Tori looked away from Stakes; she watched a car that was driving by the road above us. She hugged herself tighter and shivered. Her thin coat offered little protection from the breeze.

Around 11 p.m., a white Dodge van pulled up next to us. The van's door slid open, and the interior light illuminated the passengers inside. Two men sat in the front. In the backseats were two other young attractive women and a young man. The man driving apologized to Tori. "Another guy was supposed to be here at 9:30," he said. Tori put her bag down on the carpeted floor and pulled herself inside, sitting next to one of the young women.

Stakes told her to take care. She thanked us and waved before sliding the van's door shut. The van accelerated, driving out of the parking lot, and turned toward downtown. Soon it was out of sight. Stakes, Eric, and I stood in the parking lot and watched the van leave in silence.

Finally Stakes said, "It's good there were other girls in there." He paused. "I think she'll be all right." He sounded uncertain. "It was the best we could do."

That night, the Williston bar scene was in full swing. As we made our way from the train station to the bars, a group of drunk girls stumbled past us, giggling and yelling at two guys standing behind them. We walked through the alley behind Main Street, where people spilled out of the back doors of the bars. Most of the men wore stained T-shirts and loose jeans; the girls wore tank tops and jeweled designs on the back of their fitted jeans. They stood together in groups, smoking cigarettes and holding bottles of Coors or Budweiser; their voices and laughter carried into the warm summer night.

Stakes wanted to go to Cattails, but first we stopped at a bar called the Shop to check out the scene. A young man wearing a baseball cap stood outside smoking a cigarette, watching us closely. Stakes opened the heavy, opaque door and peered inside. The hazy glow from neon lights lining the walls filtered onto the sidewalk. Three men sat at the bar in silence and stared at the TV above them. Stakes turned back to us and shook his head. "There's maybe one person in there," he said.

The man smoking outside spoke suddenly. "What the fuck does it matter?"

Stakes looked at him, surprised. "Well, it does, 'cause we can go somewhere else."

The man shrugged, obviously annoyed. "There's alcohol, so what the fuck does it matter? I've been in that bar, that bar, and that bar," he said, gesturing to the establishments all around us. "It doesn't fucking matter." He put out his cigarette and walked back into the near-empty bar.

We headed north to Cattails, designated by a Budweiser sign above a green fence. There was a large crowd outside the back entrance.

It was obvious the party was here. Stakes said he heard a rumor that the bar had become so successful, the owner wanted to sell it for $2.5 million. Stakes waved to a guy standing outside whom he called Scrappy, a Cattails regular. We made our way through a black door into a small fenced-in area packed with people—about 80 percent of them men. Country music blared from the speakers, and we pushed through the crowd to buy three pints of beer from the outdoor cashier. As we paid, Stakes asked Mackie if he had the $200 he owed him. Mackie told him not yet.

"It's all right, I know you're good for it," Stakes said, patting him on the back. "But I got rent to pay next month."

We took the beers and found a table in the corner. As soon as we sat down, a young woman with short blond hair stumbled over to Stakes and threw her hand on his shoulder to stabilize herself. She was intoxicated. A blond man came up behind her and apologized to Stakes. Stakes asked if the woman was okay, and the man nodded.

"How long have you been in town?" Stakes asked.

"Since January," he said in a thick European accent. He explained he came from Norway to work in the oil fields.

"It's boring here!!" the woman yelled, stumbling into her Norwegian friend. "This guy is, like, totally cute," she said, leaning into him. She started singing quietly, looking down at the ground as she swayed.

Stakes chuckled. "Well, you know what, girl? I'm kind of totally cute too," he said, imitating her cadence. "And I'm 60 years old!" He laughed.

"You are not cute," she said, pointing at him sloppily. "You're, like, butt ugly." She giggled and leaned onto the Norwegian guy.

"Well, if I'm butt ugly, kiss my ass!" Stakes said, and laughed at his own joke.

The girl suddenly seemed to realize what she said and frowned. "I'm sorry. Actually, you're, like, sexy."

Stakes waved her away. "Nah, I understand what you're sayin'. I know I ain't cute."

"I apologize," she slurred. "I'm drunk and I'm being a bitch."

"Don't apologize," Stakes said. "I agree with ya. I'm an ugly son of a bitch. I've heard it all before. I've been a long time livin'."

Her Norwegian friend was now chatting with some other men. "I'm gonna go get another beer," she said as she stumbled away.

Mackie, who'd been staring into his beer, watched her leave and looked over at Stakes. "Rockin' the Bakken!" he yelled, and pumped his fist.

Stakes smiled and raised his glass. "Rockin' the Bakken!"

Mackie and Stakes wanted to check out the karaoke inside the bar. We opened the door and heard someone singing. Stakes bobbed his head to the music. We sat at a table closest to the stage. People drank beer out of plastic cups, and a group of men huddled over a blackjack table in the corner. A rifle was mounted over the bar next to a SUPPORT OUR TROOPS sticker. Mackie wrote his name down to sing a karaoke song.

We sipped our beers—Stakes was on his second one—and watched two heavyset women sing off-key to Adele's "Someone Like You" ballad. Then it was Mackie's turn. Mackie took the mike and guitar music came over the speakers. "There are starrrrrs!" he yelled along to the tune. "In the south-ern skyyyyy!" Stakes leapt up and cheered. He went over to the stage—he was the only one standing in front of it—and sang along with Mackie, air playing the guitar and rocking his head to the music.

When they returned to the table, it was almost midnight and my beer was empty, so I announced it was time for me to go.

"I'm gonna miss ya when you leave," Stakes told me.

"I'll see you again soon," I said as I stood up.

"Yeah, but I might not be alive," he said softly, taking a sip of his beer. I wasn't sure how to respond to his comment, so I stood there in silence. Then Stakes insisted on walking me back to my car. Mackie reluctantly finished his beer and followed us.

We walked back down the alley and weaved our way through an unlit parking lot of used Ford pickup trucks to get to my car. The night was quieter now, but the music from the bars pulsed in the background. Stakes hugged me good-bye. He said he was headed back to the bar to "see what fight I can get into." He laughed. "Just kidding."

"Yeah, right, you're an instigator," Mackie said.

"Well, dammit, it's a tough town. Especially when everyone gets fucked up and drunk," Stakes said.

I told him to get home safe.

"Well, I don't know if I'll get home safe," Stakes replied, "but I tell ya what, we're gonna do somethin'."

Mackie laughed. "Yeah, we'll find something to do."

They waved good-bye and headed back toward the bars.

The next afternoon, I visited Stakes in his camper. He had slept in Mackie's bus and Eddie Bergeson had given him a ride back to the camper that morning. Around noon, Stakes started drinking again. When I arrived, he appeared worn out—the bags under his eyes were more prominent, and he slouched over in his chair holding a vodka bottle. But despite the drinking, he seemed lucid enough to sit down and chat with me. He was worried about Tori. He said he'd been thinking about her. I agreed—I'd been doing the same. I had tried calling her that morning, but her phone had gone to voicemail. I promised him I would keep trying.

"I'm just curious to make sure she's all right," he said. "To me, she's a child. Just turned 21 years old. It's like . . . damn. Doesn't know anybody, never been here, and ain't got a pot to piss in." He looked out the window and was silent for a moment. "It gets to me sometimes. 'Cause I can remember times when I really . . . when there were people that came up to me and helped me too. So I try to pay it back, or pay it forward."

I nodded and we chatted more about the previous night. Worried about the comments he had made about death last night, I asked him how he was feeling. He said other than some numbness in his finger that wasn't going away, he felt fine. The last time he visited a doctor was when he lived in New Mexico. The doctor determined he was in good health. "She just told me my potassium levels and my blood pressure," Stakes said. "I've smoked for 50 years, drank for a lotta years, done drugs for a lotta years. I always joke I'm gonna live to be a 150. I'm not goin' anywhere. But sometimes you don't get a choice. Sometimes—I'm gettin' to a point now where I can't remember certain things. I'm forgettin' things, like I can't remember people's names, or there's a word I can't remember. It's like a fog. And I know I've gotta keep workin', 'cause I've got no retirement. I don't know if I can get Social Security because most of the time I worked under the table. I may have 10 more years if I'm lucky. Maybe I can make it to 70. I'm gonna try. But it gets harder to find work, 'cause your body starts breakin' down; you become a little more brittle. With this kinda work, you're not just sittin' there all day. You're paintin', you're buildin'."

The other day, Westerman promised Stakes he'd keep employing him as long as he could do the work. Stakes hoped he could start saving money. He calculated that if he worked 40 hours a week at $20 an hour, he could make $800 a week. After his expenses, he could put $500 a week away in savings, and after five years, he'd have $130,000— a solid retirement fund. So far, however, he'd only saved a couple hundred dollars in the past two weeks, and he needed that to pay rent. He also wasn't working anywhere close to 40 hours a week.

What about family he could live with as he aged? I asked. Old friends back in Georgia or Louisiana?

"All my relatives have pretty much died by now," he replied. "Nobody would remember me anyway. My older brother won't even talk to me. His wife doesn't like me. And every time I call—well, he's not there, or he's kinda short with me if I talk to him. My younger brother and I had a fallin' out, and I haven't seen him since Mom's funeral. I've tried to find him, but I don't know if he's alive or dead, or what." Last Stakes heard, his younger brother was living in Barstow, California.

"For now I'm just livin' week to week and day to day. And I'm gettin' older, and there ain't much I'm gonna be able to do about it." Because he was adopted, he didn't know what health risks might lay ahead. "I don't have a record of my hereditary stuff. I don't know if I've got heart disease in my genes, or other stuff like certain types of cancer. I live a crapshoot every day. I just live from one day to the next."

After two hours, I told him I had to go—I was driving back to California the next day.

"Well, I hope it's been a little enlightening. If that's the only legacy I've got, for you to include me in a book, then that's the legacy for me. It'll be somethin' people can remember me by. 'Cause other than that, I got nothin' to offer the world, other than just being old Tom." He suggested I title his story "The Rise and Fall of Tom Stakes," because he rose up early in his life, did well for a time, and then fell.

I told him I would be back in Williston that November.

"Well, I might not be alive if you come back in November," he said. Then he laughed as if it were a joke and gave me a hug. I got in my car, and he stood on the crooked steps of the trailer and watched me drive away.

33. FORT BERTHOLD

On the morning of July 8, 2014, Edmund Baker, the environmental director for the Fort Berthold Indian Reservation, arrived at his office and received an urgent call from a colleague at the tribe's energy department. The man told Baker there had been a spill and requested his presence on site immediately. Baker grabbed his safety gear, jumped in his car, and drove 20 minutes to the spill location near Lake Sakakawea.

He arrived to a chaotic scene. "There was no site control, no one in command to follow protocols. It was a nightmare," he said. Baker toured the site and learned what he could about the incident. A pipeline owned by Crestwood Midstream Partners had burst and released an estimated 1 million gallons of brine saltwater, an oil field waste product. It was one of the largest oil field spills in the state's history. It had likely happened a few days before, but no one knew for sure. The pipeline had been built in 2010 and didn't have monitoring equipment that could alert the company of a leak. Though these monitoring systems are widely available for pipelines, they're not required under North Dakota law. The spill was discovered only as the company combed through production loss reports.

After it ruptured, the pipeline had released toxic salty brine, which snaked down a hill, killing all vegetation in its path, and into a small creek that fed Bear Den Bay, a tributary of Lake Sakakawea (though the company denies the spill ever reached the bay). The path of the brine was nearly two miles long. The site was also dangerously close to a nearby water intake system, which supplied the town of Mandaree and the surrounding population with drinking water. Baker wasn't sure what to do—he had never dealt with a spill of this scale. His first thought was to secure the water supply. The water intake system was still pulling in drinking water less than a mile from the affected area—Baker couldn't believe it hadn't already been shut off (it was finally turned off around 3 p.m. that day).

Often referred to with the less-ominous term "saltwater," the brine that spilled that day is fracking wastewater laced with chemicals (sometimes including lead, lithium, methanol, hydrochloric acid, boric acid, and tetrakis phosphonium, a pesticide) and is about 10 times saltier than ocean water. Some batches even contain traces of radium, a naturally occurring radioactive element. About 10 barrels of wastewater brine are produced during flowback for every barrel of oil, and each well creates millions of gallons of this brine. "The general public thinks, oh, it's just a salt spill. No, it's a lot more than that," Baker explained later. "You can have a mixture of contaminants and all kinds of nasty stuff—the stuff they put down the hole and want to get rid of."

At the site, Baker was concerned about water contamination and requested assistance from North Dakota's State Health Department, which is typically in charge of public safety in the aftermath of spills throughout the state. However, after the representative made one short trip to the spill scene, he was asked not to return. An Environmental Protection Agency representative was also denied access to the site at first. Baker later heard that these orders had come from a tribal coun-

cilmember. Baker was shocked. "There was the need for the EPA's guidance because there was risk of water pollution," he said.

In addition, Baker's superior requested that he not talk to the press.
A couple of reporters had showed up, including an Associated Press
reporter named Josh Wood. Wood had read a report from the Forum
News Service that an eyewitness had seen oil sheen on the Missouri
River downstream from the spill. When Wood arrived at the site on
July 9, he wasn't permitted to see the spill and was told to come back
the next day. But the next morning, officials had roped off a "media
zone" and wouldn't let reporters near the affected area, threatening to
arrest anyone who stepped past the zone or snapped unauthorized photos. Wood and his photographer eventually received a guided tour of
the site with a Crestwood representative, but besides viewing a small
area of dead vegetation, they couldn't see much. "The tribe had au-
thority on who was doing the spill investigation, giving them complete control with what seemed to be very little oversight," said Wood.

Meanwhile, citizens of Mandaree had no idea if the source of their
drinking water had been contaminated.

Lisa DeVille, a tribal member and environmental activist on the reservation, wasn't surprised by the lack of information. The day of the
spill, DeVille was cooking dinner at her home in Mandaree. Around
5:30 p.m., she received a text from her friend Denise. "There's something going on," her friend wrote. "I think there's been a spill." DeVille
quickly finished cooking and drove around town to see if there were
any clues to where the spill was located. She saw a helicopter land in
a clearing north of town and saw one of the tribe's pro-oil councilmen emerge. She knew it must be bad if the tribe's councilmen were
responding to the scene—spills happened nearly every day on the reservation, and no one paid them any attention.

DeVille, a youthful 41-year-old with long brown hair, a strong jaw, and piercing eyes, had been fighting with oil companies for over four years. She and her husband, Walter DeVille, also an environmental activist, grew up in Mandaree, and they had five children and two grandchildren. DeVille's family had been on the reservation for generations. Her grandmother, Julia Charging White Eagle, was born in Elbowoods in 1919. In 2010, when oil drilling intensified on the reservation, a friend showed DeVille something suspicious next to an oil well on her property—snow around the natural gas flare was stained yellow. DeVille didn't know what it was or if it was toxic. She called the tribe's environmental division, then run by Baker's predecessor, but no one could give her an answer. She began researching on her own and contacted a science professor at Fort Berthold Community College, Dr. Kerry Hartman, for help. He told her about oil field brine and explained that much of its content is unknown. Dr. Hartman encouraged her to return to school to answer some of her questions and become an advocate for the reservation.

"My grandmother taught us how important the environment was," said DeVille. "The air, the grass, the land, the water. It's all life. If you contaminate or destroy it, you're not going to live."

Once DeVille began speaking out against the oil development at community meetings, she found a small coalition of other tribal members who were upset by the changes to their reservation. The most vocal among them were women—particularly two sisters named Theodora and Joletta Bird Bear. They formed the Fort Berthold Protectors of Water and Earth Rights (POWER) and joined forces with farmers, including Donny Nelson, through the Dakota Resource Council.

Some women, such as Marilyn Hudson, showed her support but felt conflicted at times. The money Hudson received from her mineral rights allowed her to pay expensive medical bills and feel more secure in retirement. Many of her friends had benefited financially as well. Even Lisa DeVille had some oil money coming in from Walter's family's land. Though he split the royalties with his siblings, the amount was nearly enough to support their whole family. Others signed away rights but later regretted it and joined forces with environmental protection efforts. Theodora Bird Bear, however, didn't want well sites anywhere near her home. Mineral plots on the reservation hadn't been sliced into tiny pieces to the same extent as on nontribal lands, so owners had more power to stop the oil companies from drilling—though few did. As of 2015, she was one of the few mineral-owning tribal members to successfully deny the oil companies access to her land.

After the Crestwood spill, DeVille's anger toward the oil companies and the regulatory agencies only intensified. The tribal council claimed it was testing drinking water sources in the area but gave no indication that it planned to release the results to the public or even to the tribe's own environmental director, Edmund Baker. Baker found this highly suspicious—why not release the results if there was nothing to hide? Baker's department had little leverage with oil companies, and within a few weeks, cleanup efforts had all but ceased. "The company doing remediation was giving biased reports, understating certain things, and doing things on purpose to slow things down," Baker said. "And politics reared its ugly head. There is a tendency to minimize the scarring environmentally because this is revenue for the tribe."

The public, for the most part, didn't seem fazed. This was what typically happened after spills. Though more local and national media covered the Bear Den Bay spill because of its size, location, and possible contamination of a major drinking water source, they quickly moved on. A few weeks later, on August 22, another pipeline spill occurred near Mandaree—126,000 gallons of brine leaked from a different Crestwood-owned pipeline. But the media barely covered it. Crestwood spills were old news.

More than 4,000 brine spills have been documented in the state since the boom began. Leakage into rivers or fragile wetlands is especially harmful to local wildlife. A 2006 spill that leaked more than a million gallons of brine into a North Dakota creek near the town of Alexander caused a massive die-off of fish, turtles, and plant life. The creek still showed damage 10 years later. Longtime farmers and ranchers in the region know this phenomenon all too well. Donny Nelson still has sections on his farm that have never fully recovered from saltwater spills in the 1950s and 1980s. "They've tried rehabbing it, and it'll grow weeds for a while and then they start dying off. It will never grow anything in probably tens of thousands of years," said Nelson. "Up in the northern counties in the state, it's unbelievable. There's hundreds of acres, and nobody's doing anything about it. Bankers and lenders are starting not to lend money to buy the land because it's contaminated."

Unfortunately, state records and industry documentation of how much oil and brine spills is poor. In July 2011, the company Petro Harvester reported a 12,600-gallon brine spill near the 700-person town of Mohall, but after further inspection, officials revised the spill to 2 million gallons. However, state records still list the original 12,600-gallon amount. Kris Roberts at the state's Health Department told reporters he saw no point in changing it. "If we try to go back and revisit the past over and over and over again, what's it going to do? Nothing good." Between 2009 and 2011, oil companies reported dozens of spills totaling about 1.7 million gallons of brine, but companies often don't know how much spills and base their estimates on the amount recovered after much of the liquid has already soaked into the soil. Many companies report zero barrels spilled—which could mean either nothing spilled, or they simply could not come up with an accurate estimate.

What's more, the radioactive waste from brine isn't limited to radium in the soil and water. Small nets called filter socks are used on pipes to sift out solid material from the brine during the disposal process, and an estimated 75 tons of those filter socks are generated every day in the state. Before 2016, the North Dakota health code did not allow the disposal of radioactive materials higher than 5 picocuries per gram in state landfills; however, filter socks can contain as high as 70 picocuries per gram. Companies therefore trucked them out of state to dispose of them—an expensive task that led to frequent illegal dumping incidents. Piles of filter socks were found in dumpsters, ditches, or abandoned buildings; one was found at the entrance of Theodore Roosevelt National Park. In 2016, instead of cracking down on illegal dumping, the state simply raised the disposal limit to 50 picocuries per gram.

Of course, as in many areas where oil development takes place, oil spills are also common. In the fall of 2013, one of the largest inland pipeline oil spills in U.S. history happened about 60 miles from the reservation. More than 865,000 gallons of crude oil gushed onto a farmer's field from a broken pipeline run by Tesoro Logistics. The farmer, Steven Jensen, didn't discover the spill until days, or possibly weeks, after it occurred, and the Health Department didn't report the spill to the public until a week later (after a reporter asked about it). The spill contaminated about 15 acres of Jensen's cropland, and cleanup efforts were still under way two years later. In 2015, after a pipeline burst and 50,000 gallons of Bakken crude spilled into the Yellowstone River near Glendive, Montana, traces of benzene from the oil were found in Glendive's drinking water. State officials trucked in bottled water for residents until the contamination cleared a few days later. Smaller oil spills happened daily in the region. But Edmund Baker isn't nearly as concerned about oil as he is about brine spills: With oil, "companies will take extra measures to protect their product in terms of leak-protection systems," he said. "They've got all these bells and whistles to counteract losing the product. But with a brine pipeline, that's not the case. We've seen a lot of efforts to save money."

In addition, there's little regulatory oversight when companies install pipelines. North Dakota had only a few pipeline inspectors and didn't require companies to reveal any data about smaller pipelines, even basic things like their location, until April 2014. Fines against companies are limited to $12,500 a day and often go uncollected. Companies have been known to take shortcuts. More than 50 percent of pipeline incidents were due to either equipment failures or corrosion, according to a report by the Pipeline Safety Trust, an independent nonprofit organization. "Some of these pipes were put into place too soon, too fast," Mark Fox, the tribe's chairman after Tex Hall, told reporters. Fox, who was more critical of oil development, continued, "The integrity is questionable in many areas."

Nearly one year after the Crestwood spill at Bear Den Bay, DeVille was finishing her degree in environmental science at Fort Berthold Community College and had turned her attention to opposing new pipeline projects, such as one through the ecologically fragile Missouri grasslands. Then one day, a researcher at Duke University named Dr. Avner Vengosh called her. He wanted to travel to North Dakota with a team of researchers and conduct a water contamination study at the Bear Den Bay site, among other brine spill sites throughout the state. Dr. Vengosh chose North Dakota because he was unable to locate any peer-reviewed studies on the environmental effects of fracking in the area. Most researchers had focused on other drilling hubs in the country. He was surprised so little research had been done on North Dakota, given the magnitude of oil activity there.

DeVille agreed to show him the spill site, and they went out on a blistering hot day in July. To enter the site, they had to pass a check-point manned by a single guard, but he waved them through after DeVille told him they were simply visiting the waterfront. They hiked down a steep slope to the spill site, and when they arrived, Dr. Vengosh was shocked by the destruction. Large swaths of grass were tinged brown and small ponds of brine stood stagnant, glistening with a metallic sheen in the sunlight. They snapped photos of the dead vegetation and collected brine and water samples. "We were surprised to see that you could still find brine," said Dr. Vengosh, "because it was almost a year after the spill. You could easily see the spill pathway."

DeVille was grateful for the researcher's attention to the issue because yet another spill from a Crestwood-owned pipeline had happened a few months earlier, not far from Bear Den Bay. And North Dakota's largest brine spill to date had occurred in early 2015 north of Williston—some 3 million gallons of salty brine spilled into a creek that fed the Missouri River, a drinking water source. The pipeline was only six months old and had a monitoring system installed, but no one had bothered to turn it on. Then DeVille discovered that approval of the Dakota Access Pipeline was near.

The Dakota Access Pipeline would begin in North Dakota, travel through South Dakota and Iowa, and end in Patoka, Illinois, extending some 1,170 miles in total. The $3.7 billion pipeline would have an initial capacity of 470,000 barrels of oil of day, and its company, Energy Transfer Partners, claimed it would create 8,000 to 12,000 construction jobs and generate $156 million in sales and income taxes to state and local governments.

Though the pipeline wouldn't directly cut across any reservations, it would border two—Fort Berthold and Standing Rock—and the only places where the pipeline would cross under the Missouri River in North Dakota were near the reservations. The original path was closer to Bismarck, but the Army Corps of Engineers ultimately decided against it, partly because of its proximity to a large population and their water supply. Many Native Americans were furious that the corps would choose to endanger their lands and water instead of those of the mostly white population of Bismarck. DeVille was particularly angry because the pipeline would pass Mandaree by fewer than 10 miles and cross under another tributary of Lake Sakakawea, Fort Berthold's main source of drinking water. For those who had lived through the Garrison Dam flooding, it felt as if history were repeating itself. The U.S. government would once again decide the fate of how the Missouri River would impact the reservation.

DeVille traveled down to Killdeer, North Dakota, to speak out against the Dakota Access Pipeline in June 2015. Joletta and Theodora Bird Bear were also there to speak. DeVille stood in front of the North Dakota Public Service Commission and read a letter she had prepared. Her voice shook at first, but she continued reading: "I, Lisa DeVille, and environmentally concerned citizens of the Mandan, Hidatsa, and Arikara Nation oppose the Dakota Access Pipeline Project. We have witnessed many pipelines malfunction in North Dakota causing toxic environmental impact." She mentioned the Bear Den Bay spill, the 3-million-gallon spill near Williston, and evidence of long-term contamination from a 2010 pipeline spill in Michigan's Kalamazoo River. "We know 'Big Oil' and its supportive political leadership will continue to chip away at sovereign nations' rights and the environmental laws already in place," she said. "We are counting on you to help stop them."

The Standing Rock Sioux Reservation south of Fort Berthold had not yet dealt with intense oil drilling activity—the boom hadn't hit that far south yet, and many Fort Berthold tribal members wanted to warn Standing Rock members of the downsides before it was too late. Reservations across the country saw Fort Berthold as a cautionary tale of what could happen when tribes allowed oil companies to invade with little regulation. "I never would've expected, prior to 2006, a big energy project like this on Fort Berthold," said Theodora Bird Bear. "None of us did. But if it can happen here, it can happen to anybody, anywhere. All the pipelines that have failed are a warning. People need to become knowledgeable and not to be afraid, not to be intimidated. Our children will be dealing with the pipelines in 20 years. What will be the integrity of the pipelines then? Crestwood's pipeline was just a few years old, and it's already failed four times. So what's the future mean?"

Despite the women's testimonies, the North Dakota Public Service Commission gave a green light to the Dakota Access Pipeline in early 2016, and construction began in the state. However, Energy Transfer Partners still needed approval from the Army Corps of Engineers to cross public waterways. The pipeline would cross hundreds of waterways, but the places of concern were closest to large drinking water sources for the reservations: the Missouri River northwest of Fort Berthold, the Little Missouri River near Mandaree, and Lake Oahe, 500 feet from the Standing Rock Reservation.

Finally, in April 2016, Dr. Vengosh and his team published a report that they had found widespread water contamination at spill sites in North Dakota, including the million-gallon Crestwood spill. They found high levels of ammonium, selenium, lead, radium, and other toxic contaminants exceeding federal guidelines for safe drinking water. Dr. Vengosh concluded there was "clear evidence of direct water contamination from fracking" across the oil patch, and at the Bear Den Bay spill site, a particularly concerning accumulation of radium was found in the soil. Dr. Vengosh's team couldn't determine if toxins had entered Mandaree's drinking water supply (since their data was taken nearly a year after the spill), but recommended continued monitoring.

The Duke study was a game-changer for DeVille. She carried copies of it everywhere she went. The day after it was released, she brought the study to an Army Corps of Engineers meeting in Mobridge, South Dakota. "This is proof that pipelines are not safe," she told them. At a tribal council meeting about a pipeline that would cross under Lake Sakakawea, she handed over the study, and the council members seemed to finally listen to her. More tribal members, particularly the youth, were joining her efforts to fight pipelines on the reservation. Native Americans at Standing Rock launched a global protest against the Dakota Access Pipeline in 2016, with thousands of people, including DeVille, mobilizing to stop the pipeline from crossing the Missouri River nearby.

Though the Standing Rock protesters were making headway and gaining momentum, at Fort Berthold, 150 miles north, daily spills continued even after oil prices fell and drilling activity slowed. And the protesters' demands to stop the pipeline from crossing under Lake Oahe wouldn't prevent the pipeline from crossing waterways elsewhere in the state, including those on Fort Berthold. In the summer of 2016, the Army Corps of Engineers approved the portion of the Dakota Access Pipeline that crossed the Little Missouri River, eight miles from DeVille's home in Mandaree.

34. CHELSEA NIEHAUS

Litha Carole Freya Niehaus Klipsch was born on July 3, 2014, at 9 pounds, 11 ounces. She had two middle names and a combined last name from both her parents. Jacob made it home in time for the birth. He coached Chelsea through labor at their home in Louisville, Kentucky, with two doulas and a midwife present. A few days later, he returned to North Dakota. Chelsea was left alone with a four-day-old newborn and five-year-old Will.

In the middle of December that year, on one of my trips to North Dakota, I called Jacob and asked if I could meet him in Skunk Bay.

He and I planned to meet at his trailer after the workday. I followed his directions and drove through Mandaree, past signs Lisa DeVille posted that read RESPECT MOTHER EARTH and WATER AND AIR IS LIFE. PROTECT OUR FUTURE GENERATIONS, then 20 more miles to Rabbit Road, where he said his trailer was located. I saw his blue Ram pickup, so I knew I must be in the right place, but I barely recognized Jacob's trailer—it was the same one I visited when I met Chelsea over a year ago, but it looked completely different. For one, it appeared abandoned, and debris was scattered everywhere—almost like the inhabitants tossed all of their belongings outside and left in a hurry. Kitchen items were strewn across the frozen mud— utensils, bowls, plates caked with mud, a rusted mini fridge. Nearby, there was a dead plant, a black mound of trash bags, and a ripped awning blocking the front door. My foot crunched on an empty container of tobacco chew, and I almost tripped over a piece of wire as I walked over to the trailer. The trailer's windows were plastered with particle board, and duct tape sealed the vents to keep out the wind. Ten yards away was a plastic blue tricycle, turned over in the snowbank and missing a wheel. *Was that Will's tricycle?* I wondered. *Was this the right place?*

At that moment, I saw Thor. The Great Pyrenees bounded over and greeted me excitedly, panting and licking my hand. His leash was hooked to a wooden shipping box, a makeshift doghouse.

I returned to my car, cranked up the heater, and waited. I had arrived early, and Jacob was late coming home from his shift. Frozen, crusted patches of snow blanketed the ground. The wind whipped and whistled past my car window, and I didn't see another human being for hours. After about two hours, a young woman in a gray hoodie and pajama pants stumbled out of her trailer and walked over the frozen mud. She eyed me suspiciously as she walked by. She approached another trailer, opened the door, and it banged shut behind her. I never saw her reemerge.

At one point, I needed to use the restroom, so I drove over to the bar, the Rooster, with plastic palm trees out front. It looked closed, but I figured I might as well knock on the door to see if anyone was inside. I knocked and knocked and there was no answer. I squeaked open the door and saw a woman in her late 50s with tan and wrinkled skin sitting at the bar. There was no one else in the room. She wore a tank top even though it was below freezing outside. She stared at me and didn't say anything.

"Hi, is there a bathroom in here I could use?" I asked.

She shook her head. She told me there was an outhouse up the hill. She pointed to a small cement dwelling tucked between two trailers. "It should be open," she said.

After I used the restroom, I realized I had forgotten to bring anything for dinner, and the closest place to buy food was more than 40 minutes away. I dug through my car and found a box of Cheerios I'd purchased earlier in the week. I munched on the cereal as I waited.

A few minutes before 9 p.m., after sitting in my car for five hours, Jacob arrived. His own pickup truck didn't run, so he'd caught a ride with a coworker. He wore a black T-shirt, a beanie over his scraggly hair, and dirty jeans and had a bushy beard that grew in every direction. He apologized for his tardiness and invited me in. We stepped over the awning and the trash bags to get to the front door. Inside, the trailer looked equally unrecognizable. A large bag of Pedigree dog food spilled out into the hallway. The dimly lit room was filled with what appeared to be mostly trash—plastic bags, empty cardboard boxes, clothes hangers, and medicine bottles scattered about. An overflowing trash can was in the corner by Will's old bunk bed, and a large propane tank blocked the pathway. Clothes, towels, and more plastic bags were piled high on the couch—a laundry basket teetered on top. The only remnants that indicated Chelsea and Will had ever lived there were a paper printout Chelsea pinned to the wall listing "5 Reiki Principles"; Chelsea's handmade curtains, now faded and dusty; a milk-carton birdhouse that Will made; and handwritten notes on construction paper that were strung along the window. I asked Jacob what the notes were about—he explained that before Chelsea and Will left, they had all written down what they were thankful for. "Being able to pay the bills," wrote Jacob on one square. "All of us together," wrote Chelsea on another. "Pumpkins," wrote Will.

Jacob immediately pulled out a bottle of whiskey, poured himself a shot, and threw it back. He pushed aside some clothing for me to sit on the couch. He sat on the steps to the master bedroom. He pulled out a cigarette and let it dangle from his lips. A smoke detector with a low battery beeped loudly. A dog—most likely Thor—barked outside.

I asked to use the restroom. Inside, dust and grime lined the sink and floor, and empty water jugs filled the bathtub. The overhead light was broken. The door barely shut from the junk in the hallway so I moved a few items out of the way and held the door shut to give myself privacy.

Jacob was not the most talkative person and mumbled the answers to most of my questions. He told me he had no running water because the pipes had frozen. He typically showered at a truck stop in Watford City, but ever since his truck broke down last week, he didn't have a way to get there. It had been at least a week since his last shower. "This will be my third winter living like this. My tolerance is higher than most," Jacob said, chuckling. "Most people up here live like this—because the money goes home." Jacob usually ate food from gas stations or grilled meat on his electric skillet and microwaved potatoes. Most of his neighbors were undocumented immigrants from Mexico. He didn't want me to write down their names. They looked out for each other. "When the wind rattles and you're out in the middle of nowhere, it can be a little scary," he said, throwing back another shot of whiskey.

He was still working for Oilfield Support Services, Inc., which was contracted by Marathon Oil. He typically left the camper at 5:45 a.m. and returned by 8 p.m., but his crew was putting in extra overtime to boost production numbers before the end of the year. Tonight he'd worked on a well site installing flow lines—the pipes that funnel the gas, water, and oil out of the well. The oil was piped into storage tanks, the saltwater to wastewater tanks, and most of the gas was flared into the atmosphere.

Oil prices had recently fallen, but Jacob didn't seem worried. "They're gonna get all of the oil," he said. "It's just a matter of when." Many of his coworkers talked about heading to Texas, where costs were lower to produce oil and "not everything's gonna break on you in the wintertime," said Jacob. He considered heading south as well but planned to stick it out in North Dakota for the time being.

I asked if he ever frequented the Rooster and he said he'd been a few times, but he tried to stay away. "I have a past history of problems, you know."

Jacob talked about the home birth of Litha. "It was wild. I didn't pass out when Will was born, but they say that guys will just fall on the floor. I can see how," he said. "There was a white light around everything, in that one little moment." He planned to travel to Louisville for Christmas the next week. The past two years he had stayed in North Dakota over the holiday. "I'm not missing any more Christmases," he said. "That first year sucked. I stayed here and drank my sorrows away—or whatever the cliché is."

After an hour, I bade him good-bye. He told me to be careful on the icy camper steps and poured himself another shot.

When I told Chelsea I'd visited with Jacob, she sighed. "I'm so sorry for whatever horrible mess you walked in on."

35. CINDY MARCHELLO

At first, Cindy Marchello didn't have a crew at her new company, Cudd. She was stuck doing grunt work at the yard. Curtis Kenney's crew included Mana Kula and the other Tongan guys. Though Kula and his crew didn't hang out with many white guys, Kenney snuck his way in when Kula was short on men for a job and Kenney tagged along. Kula eventually took a liking to him. He made Kula laugh. He nicknamed Kenney "the cracker" because he was the only white guy around. Other times they called Kenney an anorexic, albino Tongan, which Kenney took as a compliment.

To Marchello's surprise, Kula and his Polynesian crew were friendly to her when they saw her in the equipment yard. They treated her like an equal and would stick up for her when other men didn't. She discovered many were also from Utah, like her. She offered to help them with odd jobs, such as rebuilding one of their pumps, which she had learned how to do at Halliburton. When their crew was on a well location, hours from any town or grocery store, she drove to the location with pizza for everyone. "I didn't say 'Please let me on your crew,' but I also know how politics work," Marchello said later. "If you need somebody, you're going to call somebody you like."

Her efforts eventually paid off, and she became close friends with Kula and joined his crew. With the camaraderie of the Polynesians, Marchello felt more like herself. She joked with the guys more, impersonating the Wicked Witch's laugh from the *Wizard of Oz*. "You and your little dog too!!" she'd squeal, sending everyone into a fit of laughter. "To be part of that group, especially up here, was way different," Marchello said later. "You have a family. You have friends—they're your buddies."

But at the same time, Marchello began having more issues with Kenney. The man camp they lived in was one long trailer with about 60 rooms, most with two beds. Marchello had her own room because she was the only woman. Kenney somehow obtained a key to her room, and she found him lying in her bed when she came back from her shift one day. She yelled at him to leave and asked to have the lock on her door changed. But even after her lock was changed, Kenney still found ways to access her room. She sometimes came home and found evidence he was there, such as his favorite beers or soda discarded in the trash. Every time she confronted him about it, he acted like it was no big deal and she was overreacting. In his defense, Kenney admitted he had a key to her room, but he said other employees did as well. He claimed he only entered her room to drop off or pick up something.

When she worked on well locations with him, she'd nap during her breaks in one of the semi trucks parked on location. She'd lock the doors and crawl into the sleeping cab, but when she'd wake up, Kenney would be sleeping next to her. She had no idea how he got in; she assumed he found an extra key. Most of the guys, even Kula and her Tongan friends, laughed off Kenney's behavior. They figured it was harmless flirting and Marchello seemed to enjoy Kenney's company at times, so they thought maybe she reciprocated the affection.

"Curtis was infatuated with her, and wanted to be around her," Kula said about Kenney and Marchello's relationship at Cudd. "He would text and call her all the time, and try to get together with her. But there'd be times I'd hear her tell him to stop and then she seemed to lead him on. Marchello would complain about Kenney, then afterward she'd be on the phone with him, or text him back."

Marchello argued she was nice to Kenney only because Kula liked him and she wanted to support Kula. She vehemently denied she ever had feelings for Kenney, a married man whom she described as a "dweeby mouse." "I finally quit over it," she said. "I didn't know how to fix it." On her job application, she wrote "hostile work environment" as her reason for leaving.

After she left Cudd in August 2011, she went to a company called Killer B Trucking where she worked as a sand coordinator for $18 an hour. She was in charge of overseeing the frack sand trucks and monitoring the sand as it went into the well. The position was more solitary since she wasn't part of a crew, but she enjoyed the responsibility. Other, male, sand coordinators seemed to receive the choice jobs, but it didn't bother her much at the time.

Then one night in late fall, upon returning to her parked pickup truck, she pulled herself up into the driver's seat and suddenly felt a thick arm around her neck. A man whispered in her ear: "I won't leave until you scream for me." She moved her hand to the steering wheel, hoping she could honk the horn and alert someone. She recognized his voice. He was a trucker who had targeted her before. He once asked if she wanted to go fuck behind the fracking water tank. She had yelled back at him, loud enough so everyone could hear: "We don't have to go behind the tank, I can beat the shit out of you right here in front of all these boys." Now his arm was around her neck. She didn't want to think about the other things he might do to her if she didn't get out of the truck. She remained silent, and he tightened his grip. "I bet I can make you scream," he whispered. Though it was hard to speak, she sputtered out: "I can take your job. I can kill you. Do what you're gonna do." Finally, after a few tense moments, he let go and left. She immediately ran to another truck on the well site to find a coworker and spilled out everything that had happened. When she was done, the man replied,

"It wouldn't have happened if you weren't such a dirty whore." Marchello never officially reported the incident.

Soon after that, she left Killer B because the company wasn't booking enough jobs. But she struggled to find another oil field job. She went home to Utah, unsure of what to do next. She was denied unemployment insurance, so she took temp jobs at a phone solicitation company and at a cheese processing factory for $8 an hour. In addition to worrying about bills, she remembered how much she hated factory work. Her children encouraged her to stay home, but she missed her oil field paychecks. She wanted to find a way back. The glistening shimmer of black gold, with its promise of financial independence, drew her back in.

In Utah, none of her friends or family believed she would return to North Dakota. But she persisted. She continued to apply and interview at oil field companies. She wanted to leave the oil field on her own terms. Plus, she hadn't accomplished what she set out to do. She wanted to buy a home. "I was still stuck," she said.

Marchello first heard about a company called C&J Energy Services when she worked at Killer B Trucking. The company was headquartered in Texas and had recently opened its first yard in North Dakota. She knew it was looking to hire employees.

In October 2012, Marchello, Kula, and the Tongans applied together as a 12-member crew so they could have more negotiating power. Kula was considered one of the best managers in the coil tubing industry. If C&J didn't agree to their terms, all 12 of them would go elsewhere. The strategy worked, and they negotiated their best terms yet—a per diem bonus for every day they worked on a well job, paid housing in the Trenton man camp, a three-week-on, three-week-off schedule, and all expenses covered to travel home. Marchello was given the title Pump Operator B and received $21 an hour, plus a $35 per diem. The crew would work three weeks straight, clocking in at least 12 hours a day, every day, then have three weeks paid leave. In Marchello's case, she would make $840 a week to be home with her family. In addition, like her other jobs in oil, she'd work overtime often and be paid well for it. It was the type of package that she'd lusted over when she first applied to the oil field more than two years ago—the type of job that motivated thousands of American workers to abandon everything for the oil field. With her anticipated work schedule, she was on track to earn $120,000 that year.

They told her she was the first woman to be a coil tubing field hand for the company, and with Kula and the Tongans by her side, she had high hopes that this job would be different from her others. Even upper management at the corporate headquarters were thrilled to include her in their "diversity" numbers, and when a supervisor from the Texas corporate office stopped by the C&J yard in Williston, he told Marchello she was a legend. "It's especially rare for a woman to be in coil," Marchello explained. "Women usually can't survive frack long enough to make it into coil tubing."

The downside was that Kenney was coming along as well because Kenney had become a good friend to Kula. Marchello knew if she wanted to work with Kula, Kenney was part of the deal. "At that point, I needed to go back to work. I wanted oil money, and I was willing to do whatever," she said. She told Kula she was okay with it but requested she not be on the same schedule as Kenney. Days before training at C&J began, Kula was in a car accident. He stayed with his old company and worked light duty to recover, while Marchello, Kenney, and the Tongans began working at C&J.

Marchello and her crew quickly realized the small company was disorganized and the regional management had little knowledge of North Dakota's unique oil industry environment. There was little oversight from the corporate headquarters and no clear hierarchy at the North Dakota location. One manager would tell the crew to position the trucks a certain way, then another manager would yell at the crew to position the trucks a different way. One of the regional managers had frequent clashes with the crew, and he had a hard time with a woman in the ranks. "From the day I started, management didn't like me," Marchello said.

One day, the manager overheard a male employee call Marchello a "fucking cunt." Marchello complained to the manager afterward, asking why he didn't reprimand the coworker or stick up for her. She remembered him saying: "If you can't be one of the guys, then don't be here at all."

The manager's days were numbered, however. He was the first in a long line of a revolving door of C&J regional managers in Williston, and he left six months after Marchello was hired. The supervisors who followed him didn't last much longer.

The schedule at C&J was also unpredictable and draining. Because C&J wasn't yet a respected company in North Dakota, it often couldn't secure enough work. When the company did have a well job, Marchello worked some 100 hours a week. A day shift could start at 4 or 5 a.m. and end around 11 p.m., when the crew arrived back at the man camp. Other times, she'd be on location for 24 hours, off for 12, then back to location for another 24 hours. She wondered, at age 56, how long she could maintain such intensity.

C&J often asked employees to drive semis with illegal load amounts or drive without the proper permits. "They're always asking you to do illegal things in this business," said Marchello's son-in-law, Matthew Anderson. Overweight or nonpermitted trucks can receive fines from the state, and any violation goes on the driver's record. In addition, crew members technically aren't supposed to drive more than 10 hours in a 24-hour period or drive without a 24-hour break if they'd worked more than 70 hours in a week, but the company skirted the rules frequently. "They'd ask you to lie on the logs nearly every single time," said Anderson.

Despite the downsides, Marchello was excited about her paycheck. With her higher wages, in May 2013, she finally achieved a lifelong dream: buying a home by herself. It was a five-bedroom, two-bath house built in 1912 in Ogden, Utah, and a short drive away from where her children lived. It cost $94,000, and she provided the down payment and secured the loan all on her own. "I worked really hard to get that," said Marchello. "Because when I grew up, the women I associated with didn't own property. The fact that I bought a house all by myself—my credit, my money, my choice—is a huge deal."

But after only six months of working at C&J, Marchello's crew decided they wanted to switch jobs. They didn't like the company's disorganization and felt some discrimination from the upper managers. They wondered if it was racial discrimination. The Polynesian crew often had to work the night shift, while a crew of white guys had the day shift. "The discrimination was evident from the very beginning," Marchello said. "[Management] would make comments about them and take away their bonuses for no reason . . . things they weren't doing to the white boys." Marchello originally planned to go with the crew to another company, but when the offers started trickling in, she was the only member who didn't get one.

Marchello was devastated that her crew was gone. Kenney asked to stay at C&J, telling Marchello he didn't want to leave her, but he was transferred to a different crew. Meanwhile, Marchello was called to the office to talk to a manager named Mike Hambrick. He said he needed her help in the office and presented it as a promotion. She would still do some field work, he said, and her title would remain Pump Operator B. She remembered him saying: "This has nothing to do with the guys leaving. This has been in the works for a couple months, and we just haven't been able to implement it."

Marchello was fine with the change at first. Working in the field had been wearing on her, and sitting indoors in a comfy office sounded nice—especially since she was receiving the same hours and pay. The warehouse inventory and office organization was a complete mess. Necessary equipment hadn't been ordered, and no one could locate items already in stock. Managers would reorder them and waste thousands of the company's dollars. She began organizing the inventory and streamlining the ordering process. She took pride in her work, and she was good at it. "What I was doing, nobody had done since they opened the yard," she said. "There were $8,000 pieces of equipment that no one was keeping track of."

There was another woman working in the office named Vanessa. She worked at the front desk and was essentially a secretary. Vanessa made significantly less annually than Marchello and didn't receive per diem bonuses or time-off rotations—only a couple weeks of paid vacation. Many people began confusing Vanessa's and Marchello's positions. Marchello made sure to sign all of her office emails as Pump Operator B to clarify she was *not* a secretary.

In many ways, the position also caused her to become more visible in the company. She gained a reputation for being knowledgeable about the company's business dealings in Williston. Workers from other C&J locations knew they could come to her if they needed something done. But a few seemed to have ulterior motives. They'd come by the office to chat with her and invite her to lunch. "It seemed like every dumbass that came up here thought she was the C&J plaything," said her co-worker Scott Morgan.

Marchello replied: "Well, they used to call me Hali Ho when I worked at Halliburton, so I don't know what the C&J version of that is. But, yeah, I get my fair share of opportunities to spit."

Four months after they left, the Polynesian crew members realized they made a mistake moving to another company. The new company made promises to them that were never delivered. They wanted to return to C&J. Marchello pulled some strings with the new manager, and in August 2013, a number were hired back. Marchello was thrilled, but she stayed in the office even after her crew returned. "At least I have my poker buddies back," she said.

Soon, however, Marchello began to realize her transition to the office—a move she thought was temporary—was causing her to earn significantly less money. She wondered if the move was purposeful, to slowly and deliberately demote her, make her unhappy, and cause her to quit. She simply wasn't working enough hours. Though C&J guaranteed her at least 84 hours a week when she was hired, she was now averaging only 56 hours. Her male coworkers were still getting some 120 hours a week when they were in the field. She asked Mike Hambrick if she could return to the field, but he said no—she'd been away for too long and it wouldn't be safe for her, she recalled him saying. He asserted she wouldn't remember how to perform the job well. "I think they were keeping me in the office because I was an old lady," Marchello said. "I never would've chosen less money in the office. I don't care that it was warmer. I don't care that it was more comfortable. I came to North Dakota for the money, and I was never going to make field money in the office. Period."

36. TOM STAKES

I visited Williston again in the middle of December 2014. Oil prices had fallen to around $58 a barrel, down from the high of $107 a mere five months before. Gasoline prices had dropped to below $3 a gallon, and most of the country was celebrating. But not Williston. Rumors of layoffs and bankruptcies spread through town, and with the holidays approaching, tensions were high. Workers traveling home for Christmas worried they might not have a job when they returned. On December 14, *The Williston Herald* splashed the headline OIL PLUNGES AGAIN across the front page, above an image of a thick red arrow pointing dramatically downward.

It was two weeks until Christmas, and the town's central green space, Harmon Park, was crammed with illuminated wire-framed animal figures and lit-up candy canes. Strands of white Christmas lights spiraled around each tree and lamppost. In the middle was a wire-framed Santa in his sleigh and reindeer leading up to the sky with the letters API underneath, which stood for the American Petroleum Institute, and nearby was an oil pump statue wrapped with festive lights. Patches of crunchy snow, which had melted and refrozen many times over, speckled the dead lawn, and muddy mounds of snow, formed weeks ago by a plow, flanked the streets. It was Christmastime in an oil town.

I reached out to Tom Stakes to see how he was doing. Gary Westerman had fired him two weeks earlier for showing up to work drunk. He was now unemployed and sleeping on a couch at his friend Rick Sonstegaard's house near downtown. Sonstegaard was living with his 90-year-old mother and had convinced her to let Stakes stay there. The property was an older two-story house with white siding, a slanted roof, and two large trees out front, their bare, crooked branches reaching up into the gray sky like skinny gnarled fingers.

Stakes spent most days zoned out in front of the TV, depressed. He had given up looking for work since the holidays were approaching, and he figured most employers would wait until the new year to hire anyone. The slowdown in the oil industry had trickled down to the construction business, and since he'd been paid under the table, he didn't qualify for unemployment. He'd completely run out of money and relied on Sonstegaard and Sonstegaard's mother to provide food for him. Occasionally Sonstegaard or another friend would feel sorry for him and slip him a $20 bill or buy him a bottle of vodka, but he hadn't been drinking as much because he simply couldn't afford it.

I picked him up in the early afternoon on a Friday—it was overcast and cold, in the low 30s. When I saw Stakes, he immediately asked if I'd buy him a bottle of vodka. I said I couldn't do that. Would he like some lunch?

"No," he said. He wasn't hungry.

"Coffee?"

"No." A drink, he said. All he wanted was a drink.

I relented and agreed to buy him one drink at the bar DK's, the outside of which Stakes had recently remodeled with Westerman. The job had taken three months, but he'd been fired shortly after they finished. We drove over to the bar and Stakes showed off the new green tin siding he had helped install, staring at the building like it was an ex-girlfriend who broke his heart. "See that, up and down the sides," he said, pointing. "We did all that. We reframed it and everything. It was all nasty rotted wood before."

We walked through the bar's unmarked door into a dark, musty room. The tall, round tables in the center of the room were all empty at this time of the day. Two men sat at the curved bar watching television and drinking, and a female bartender dried glasses. A commercial about natural gas came on as we walked in. "There's 60 percent less pollution . . ." the announcer said. The rest of the commercial was drowned out by clanking glasses and a sports game playing on another TV across the bar. A popcorn machine pumped out a thick smell of melted butter.

We sat down at the far end of the bar, and the bartender sauntered over to take our order. I asked for water and Stakes ordered a Long Island iced tea. He was going to get as much alcohol as possible out of his one drink.

Stakes hunched over on his bar stool and sighed. His beard and mustache had grown scruffier since I'd seen him last. His hair was hidden under a baseball cap with the Cattails bar logo on it. Under the lettering was a cartoon duck lying on its back holding a beer bottle in its mouth. Stakes told me he bought it for $20 at the bar, back when the weather was warmer and he was working outside most days.

I asked if he wanted to talk about why he was fired from his job.

"Well . . . it got to where I was drinking too much," Stakes said. "Gary'd tell me, 'Tom, do not come into work drunk.' And of course, I would. He warned me five or six times, he said, 'Tom, I will fire you.' 'Course I didn't think he'd do it, but sure enough. . . ."

The waitress returned with my water and Stakes's drink. She thunked the tall glasses down in front of us.

"He could smell it on me," Stakes continued. "But if I didn't have a drink, I'd sit there with a screw in one hand and the screwdriver in the other and I couldn't get the screw in." He held up his hands, shaking them as he demonstrated. "But when I had a drink, I could get right to it. So he knew, he knew."

Stakes felt betrayed, however, because many times, he and Westerman drank together after work. When they'd go to the bar, Westerman would order two shots of Crown Royal and a beer, and often he'd have another round. Stakes wondered if the real reason Westerman fired him was to save money. Eddie Bergeson, Stakes's old roommate, had been fired too, back in October. But that was another story. Bergeson and one of his buddies had been caught eating hallucinogenic mushrooms in the men's restroom at DK's bar. He wasn't on the clock at the time, but Westerman was furious. He fired Bergeson immediately. "He thought we were sellin' drugs," Bergeson said later about the incident. "But we weren't sellin' anything, we were just eatin' 'em." Bergeson left North Dakota in early November and returned to his home state of Mississippi.

"I just been kinda depressed," Stakes said, as he sipped his Long Island iced tea, seeming comforted by the mix of vodka, rum, gin, tequila, and triple sec. "'Cause anytime something dramatic happens in my life, and I don't know how to fix it, it's just, what do I do? What do I do? So now, I'm waitin'. I guess that's why I been vegetatin' on the couch. But God's always taken care of me, and if he doesn't, well, it's my time to go," he said, pausing. "But I'm not gonna do anything drastic. I'm not suicidal or anythin' like that. Death scares me in a way. But I know I'm comin' up on it pretty quick. I've been smokin' and drinkin' most of my life . . . can't be good for your body.

"I'm thinkin' about givin' it a good shot to go to AA or somethin'," he said, looking up at me.

I raised my eyebrows. "Yeah?"

"You know, get things worked out that way. Get a new start. I've talked to some AA people around here and they seem to think it's a great program. Nobody's judgmental of you because they're all in the same boat. They understand that if you make it for a while without drinkin' and you fall off one day then it's okay. They've all been there. You can network there too. There's the old saying 'Birds of a feather flock together.' And that's what we do as alcoholics, we all flock together. So now if I can get with this group and maybe fit in, maybe that'll pay off. I could meet somebody—maybe they've been sober for a long time and understand my situation. They might give me a shot at a job, you know? That's not the primary reason I'd like to do it, but it's time for me to change my life. See what I can do." He took a deep breath. "Since I lost my job because of the drinkin', it's best if I quit drinkin', if I can."

One of the "AA people" Stakes talked to was a man I'll call Randy (he requested that I change his name) who lived down the street from the Sonstegaard property. Last week, Randy invited Stakes to an AA meeting, but he said no. Now he was reconsidering the invitation. "He got to that point to where his hands were gettin' all jittery, but now he's 100 days sober," Stakes said.

Stakes had attended AA meetings once before in his life—back in 2009 at a Christian-based homeless shelter, the Adullam Project Men's Home, in Española, New Mexico. Before that, he had been living in the cave in Red River and drinking every day. He'd walk down the mountain about a mile to go to the liquor store, and the owner would let him sweep up or do an odd job in exchange for a bottle of booze and some food. But when winter came, he worried he might freeze to death in that cave. He'd bundle up with three or four coats but couldn't stay warm. His old church friend, Brother Russell, told him about the Adullam Project. Stakes lived in a converted old dance hall with 15 to 20 other men for about six months. They'd clean, cook, attend church, and do day labor to raise money for the organization. Only three or four men attended the AA meetings, and they became close. But as soon as Stakes left the Adullam Project, he started drinking again.

He'd tried to quit a few times since then, but his sobriety never lasted long. A week ago, he even tried to quit when he ran out of money for booze, but it didn't go so well. As soon as he had a few dollars, he bought more. "After a few days I got real jittery, so I started back. Now I'm gonna try to stop again, just see what happens. I love it, but I can't do it 'cause I go overboard with it. It started elevatin' to a point where in the afternoons, when I'd get home from work, I'd drink till I got ready to go to sleep. And that was fine. But then it elevated to a point where in the mornin's, I'd get up and have to have a drink just to function through the day. I could see the gradual acceleration, you know?"

I nodded and sipped my water. He finished his drink, slurping up the last bit of liquid between the ice.

"So it's time—I hear so many stories and it's time to make a decision about it, 'cause I can't just keep doin' it or it'll kill me. I been drinkin' too many years and smokin' too many years. Smokin's gonna be my next issue. If I can control the alcohol problem, then I'll start the smokin' process," he said. He pulled at his mustache as he talked. "But everybody up here drinks and smokes. I look around the bars and I see so many sad people. They come in every night. Every day the same people, over and over and over again. It got to a point where I couldn't afford to go to the bars much anymore. I'd just buy a bottle and go home. I don't wanna become that person. I don't wanna just sit around the bar all the time, sad and worryin' and depressed all the time. Ever'body I hang out with will sit and tell ya, 'Man, I've been drinking too much, I need to stop.' But we never do. That's the thing about an alcoholic. We want to but we can't, because there's somethin' that shuts down in our brain—we can't make a rational decision. It takes over and it becomes the monkey on our back, the devil inside us, whatever it is.

"I'm gonna give it a shot and see what happens. I gotta put my best foot forward and hope I don't stumble. Right now's probably my last day of drinkin,' and I'll give it a shot tomorrow, see how that goes. What do you think? Think it's a good idea?"

I nodded. I wasn't sure how serious he was, but I felt guilty that I bought him a drink when he was on the verge of quitting.

I asked him about the last time he went to AA—what worked for him?

"Well, you've got the 12 steps you go through. I don't even remember what they are, but one was to make amends for all the wrong I've done. Because with alcoholics, we've done a lotta wrong to people. I don't even remember all the people. I don't know where they are anymore. So that's gonna take me a while. You got to admit to yourself and to others that you're an alcoholic, and believe in a higher power, and trust in Him. . . . I think if I get into this AA program, get some sobriety underneath my belt, maybe Gary'll give me my old job back."

Stakes decided to attend an AA meeting that night at 8 p.m. As I drove him in the direction of Sonstegaard's house, he wasn't sure how to get back because he'd never left the house on his own before. I explained how close it was to downtown and showed him which street to turn on. "Huh, it's just straight down this road?" he asked, pointing outside the car.

He leaned back in the passenger seat, still confused on where exactly he lived. When I dropped him off, I watched as he walked back to the house. About halfway down the cement walkway, he slipped on the ice, his arms flailing and his right leg sliding off the path. He caught himself before he lost his balance and hit the pavement. Then he continued walking cautiously, keeping his arms out to steady himself, to the front door of the house, and disappeared inside.

Around 7:30 p.m., as I read in my hotel room, Stakes called and said I could join him at his AA meeting if I liked. Guests were allowed at this one, he said. But no recording and everyone else had to remain anonymous. I agreed.

I drove downtown to where the meeting was held. The location was a weary two-story brick building on Main Street, next to a coffee shop called Daily Addiction that had opened during the boom. I grimaced at the irony. There was a crisp layer of snow on the ground, and Main Street had a few modest Christmas decorations. Red SEASON'S GREET- INGS flags draped the streetlamps. I saw Stakes and another man standing outside smoking cigarettes. Stakes waved. I exited my warm car and stepped into the bitter cold air. A gust of wind stung my face and slammed my car door shut.

Stakes introduced Randy, the neighbor who had first invited him to AA. Randy had been attending AA meetings on and off in Willis- ton for about three months. He had moved to Williston from Wyoming.

We were a few minutes early, but the door to the building was un- locked, so we entered and walked up a steep stairway to a room on the second floor. The space had a linoleum floor, couches, a small kitchen, and a vending machine. Inside, it smelled of bleach and burnt coffee. Eight long tables had been placed in a square formation so everyone could face each other.

Stakes dug some change out of his pocket and bought a Cherry Coke from the vending machine. We grabbed two seats near the door and Randy sat across from us. Eight men and two women were already there, sipping Styrofoam cups of coffee and chatting quietly. Stakes saw one woman he recognized and said hello. Later, Stakes told me they had met when they both lived on the streets during his first winter in Williston.

In the room, posters of the 12-step commandments hung on a maroon accent wall, next to plaques of quotes like A DECLARATION OF UNITY and AA PREAMBLE. Stakes picked up a book called *12 Steps and 12 Traditions*, then placed it down on the table unopened. He looked around the room, then stared down at his lap and fidgeted. He rubbed his palms and picked at his thumbnail. A few more men strolled in and took seats across the room. There were 19 people total now, 3 of them women, not including myself. Stakes looked at the clock. Only a few minutes until 8 p.m. He crossed his arms and stroked his beard. He leaned over and whispered to me: "I'm not going to talk this time. I'm going to wait until I'm more comfortable."

A couple minutes past 8, a man near the front of the room announced it was time to begin. "Let's start with a prayer," he said. Everyone in the room stood and bowed their heads. "God grant me the serenity to accept the things I cannot change, the courage to change the things I can, and the wisdom to know the difference," the man said. The men and women in the room knew the words and chanted along. They finished with "amen," and we sat back down.

Stakes seemed to suddenly realize he was still wearing his Cattails baseball cap, so he took it off and put it on the table in front of him.

The introductions began, with everyone in the room stating their first name followed by "and I'm an alcoholic." Everyone greeted them in return. When Stakes's turn came, he sat up straighter and said, "My name's Tom and I'm an alcoholic." He seemed relieved when his turn was over and they moved on to the Hispanic man next to him. Over the next 45 minutes, people volunteered to share and spoke about the difficulties of working far away from their families and the benefits of being part of the AA community. Stakes listened quietly, shifting his weight or picking at his fingernails.

For the closing prayer, the man at the front of the room asked everyone to stand and hold hands. I took Stakes's hand and we bowed our heads. "Our Father in heaven, hallowed be your name," they said in unison. "Your kingdom come, your will be done, on earth, as it is in heaven. Give us this day our daily bread, and forgive us our debts, as we also have forgiven our debtors. And lead us not into temptation, but deliver us from evil. . . . Amen."

The next day, Stakes planned to attend two AA meetings back to back—one at 12 p.m. with Randy and another at 8 p.m. His roommate, Rick Sonstegaard, had stumbled home drunk from the bars the night before and told Stakes he wanted to join AA as well. Stakes decided he couldn't hang out with his old friends Nate Beatty and Greg

Mackie anymore because they spent too much time at the bars. He knew he wasn't strong enough to resist alcohol around them. He also wanted to buy a new hat. "I'm gonna have to get me another hat. This hat's got a duck layin' upside down with a bottle in his mouth. I don't think that's a good influence." He laughed. He hadn't felt jittery yet; he figured it was a good sign.

Before the 8 p.m. meeting, Stakes, Sonstegaard, and Randy decided to attend a free dinner in the basement of a local Methodist church. The church was adorned with two lonely strands of Christmas lights at the entrance. We walked down a flight of stairs into a gymnasium-like room, and a pudgy woman with short, jagged blond hair stopped us. "Merry Christmas!" she said. The enthusiasm in her voice felt forced. Inside, a dozen round tables were decorated with shiny plastic red-and-green tablecloths, with candy-cane-striped candles as the centerpieces. A statue of Mary and baby Jesus sat by a plant in the corner, looking like items at a yard sale. The blonde woman asked if we'd like a plastic gift bucket. The buckets were old gallon ice cream containers stuffed with toiletries, socks, and thermal underwear. Stakes took one and thanked her as we walked away. "This'll be the biggest Christmas I've had!" he said, and laughed. We sat down on metal chairs under the fluorescent lights. The room was packed with people—mostly men, but a handful of women and one family with toddlers. Stakes dug through his bucket and found soap, a comb, a few pieces of candy, and a card. He opened the card and read it aloud: "Wishing you the best gifts from friends of faith at the Methodist Church and the Life Assembly of God Church."

"A little personal touch," Stakes said, nodding. "That's nice. First Christmas card I've gotten in a long time." At the bottom of the bucket, he found a multicolored rubber bracelet with lettering that said WALK WITH JESUS. Stakes asked if anyone wanted it, but Randy was already wearing one. Stakes shrugged and stretched it around his wrist.

The pastor of the church stood in the middle of the room and announced it was time for dinner, then said: "All right, let us pray!" The room fell silent. "Great House of God, thank you for this food which our friends have made for us this evening. I pray, dear Lord, that its warmth will fill us with warmth as we celebrate this time of year and the coming of our savior Jesus Christ. Help us look for those who need a little bit of extra love and compassion during this time of year. I pray this in the name of Jesus. Amen."

"Amen," the room echoed.

Chairs squeaked on the linoleum floor as people stood and formed a single-file line behind the serving table. A man who looked around 40, with a protruding belly and oversized jacket, walked down the line and held up Colgate toothpaste from his bucket. "Anyone want this toothpaste?" he asked. We all shook our heads no.

We were handed Styrofoam plates and bowls, and a volunteer slopped chili into my bowl. It had chunks of ground beef, garbanzo beans, and hot dog slices in it. There was no vegetarian option, but no one seemed to mind. We filled our plates with saltine crackers and grilled cheese sandwiches layered with salami, and picked up plastic baggies stuffed with homemade cookies.

During dinner, Sonstegaard talked about what Williston was like before the boom. He had grown up here but moved to Seattle after high school. He returned a few years ago to care for his aging mother and find work. He had met Stakes through Nate Beatty, an old friend of Sonstegaard's. Stakes slurped his chili while he listened. As he lifted a spoonful of soup to his mouth, tiny strings of gooey cheese stuck to his beard.

After he finished eating, Stakes walked outside to smoke a cigarette. As soon as he was gone, Sonstegaard leaned in closer and explained how Stakes came to live with him and his mother. On Thanksgiving, Beatty and Sonstegaard visited Stakes's camper to bring him a 21-pound turkey. They noticed Stakes had only a small heater and wore thick layers to stay warm. The temperature was around 12 degrees that day. "He had a little heater, but it was so small," said Sonstegaard. "I could see my breath coming out. I thought, 'Jeez dude. You can't stay here. This is not okay.'" Sonstegaard and Beatty discussed finding Stakes a better place to live. Sonstegaard didn't think his mother wanted to take in a homeless man, but he explained Stakes's situation to her, and to his surprise, she agreed. He wasn't sure how long his mother would let Stakes stay with them, but he was determined to help the man get back on his feet. "We've got to get him a car and help him find work," he said.

Stakes returned from smoking and sat down.

As we cleared our plates, the pastor of the church announced we'd be singing Christmas carols. Stakes leaned over and whispered to me: "Oh, no, let's get out of here!" he teased.

The pastor started with "It Came Upon the Midnight Clear." A woman played the piano. Stakes cleared his throat and sang along. His voice was soft but confident, hitting a range of high and low notes.

After singing six more carols, the same woman who greeted us when we arrived stood up and projected her voice: "If any of you need a winter coat, you can follow me upstairs and I'll see if I have anything! If you did not receive a bucket, see Lynn in the blue sweater and she will help you out!"

A pastor from another church, wearing a purple dress shirt and a tie with a smiling snowman on it, sat down at our table and introduced himself as Dennis. He said that he helped organize another weekly dinner at the First Lutheran Church on Main Street. They started offering the dinner because of the boom and usually had about 70 to 90 people show up.

"Do you ever help people find jobs?" Stakes asked.

The pastor said he could try.

"Could I give you my name and number just in case?" Stakes asked. He borrowed my pen and wrote down his name and number on the back of the pastor's business card. Underneath he wrote: "Looking for work. Met at Methodist church for weekly meal."

At the AA meeting later that night, Stakes spoke up for the first time. "I'm Tom and I'm an alcoholic," he said clearly and confidently, his voice projecting into the quiet room. "I came to the meeting today at noon, and I came back tonight and I'm still sober. I'm grateful for that. I listened to a little sermon this morning on TV, so all in all it's been a good day. I try not to have too many bad days. I learned from you guys the other night that you got to let it go. You got to give it over to God; you can't handle it all on your own. It's like when our lives become unmanageable. Well, mine was pretty unmanageable.

"I drank about a half gallon of vodka every two days. All the time. I tried to quit last week for a couple days and, on the second day, man, I started shakin' so bad and skin crawlin,' cold sweats. Well, I ended up havin' to get another bottle just to get over it. And then when I started comin' to AA and I gave it up, I didn't have the shakes. I haven't had the skin crawlin' and cold sweats.

"It's been a few days now that I haven't drunk anything, and that's a pretty good feelin' for me. I appreciate you guys and what this program means, and I don't plan to give it up because I know it's somethin' I have to do for the rest of my life. 'Cause if I don't and I start gettin' a little cocky, I'm gonna go right back to that bottle. I've got to do everything I can to maintain sobriety, and leave it in God's hands, because I am in the palm of His hands. That's all I got. Thanks," he said, and leaned back in his chair.

"Thanks, Tom," the room said in unison.

37. CHELSEA NIEHAUS

Six weeks after my visit with Jacob, I flew to Louisville, Kentucky, to see Chelsea, Will, and Litha, who was now six months old. Oil prices were in free fall. Jacob's hours had been cut, and the atmosphere at his workplace was tense. Jacob had netted about $83,000 the year before, but with the reduced hours, he was looking to make only $63,000 for 2015—if he kept his job. Nearly every day, Chelsea heard about more oil field layoffs. "A lot of people are scared," she said. "Some were laid off right before Christmas. I have a feeling a lot of those jobs won't come back." Chelsea tried to keep costs down and not hire babysitters unless she had to, but it was difficult to parent alone. "I haven't had an hour to myself in I don't know how long," she said.

I saw her on a brisk January morning before she took Will to school. Two months earlier, she had enrolled him at a Waldorf school, where he seemed to be thriving. At his old day care, his teachers told Chelsea he was "behind" because he couldn't write his name by age three. But at Waldorf, teachers didn't introduce students to the alphabet until age seven. Instead, kids were taught to cook and clean, tend a fire, knit, draw, and sing songs. "It's very new agey," said Chelsea. "They teach them how to be people and to work with their hands." It cost $6,000 a year, however, increasing to more than $10,000 a year at age seven. Chelsea received help from her grandmother to afford it.

Chelsea loaded Will and Litha into the backseat of her Mitsubishi to drive Will to school. Will wore red rain boots and insulated cover-alls that were three sizes too big. Litha wore a knitted shark-shaped hat to keep her head warm. Chelsea fastened Litha into the car seat, and Litha burst into tears. "It's okay, Litha," Chelsea said, soothing her. "She hates the car seat. She's pretty convinced it's where abandoned babies go."

In the car, old coffee cups sat neglected in the cup holders, loose change was scattered on the floor, and receipts were stuffed into a com-partment under the radio. Will had plastered colorful stickers onto the backseat windows.

On the drive to school, we passed a gas station. The price was now $2.17 a gallon for unleaded. Watching gas prices trickle down was hard for Chelsea—every cent decreased Jacob's chances of keeping his job. "It's been frustrating here lately," she said. "Everyone around me is excited about oil prices being so low."

Chelsea felt more isolated than ever living in Louisville. Although she had gone to college in Louisville, she didn't have many friends in the area. Over the years, she'd lost touch with people. Her community used to be her coworkers at the lobster shipping company, but she didn't talk to them much anymore. "I miss my job. I kind of regret letting it go now," she said.

Chelsea entertained thoughts about returning to work but knew it would be difficult with Jacob in North Dakota: "There are a million things I could do, but I can't do any of them with just me here," Chel-sea said. She had a bachelor's degree in arts administration, a fine arts minor, and an MBA. In addition to her degrees, Chelsea was certified as a life coach, a wellness coach, a herbologist, and an ordained min-ister, and she was working toward certification as a birth doula. "I have all these degrees and credentials, but I've never been able to do

much with them," she said. Plus, working full time didn't make financial sense. She'd have to pay for day care for Litha and after-school care
for Will. A full-time job was hard enough with just one child—she
couldn't imagine doing it with two.

Recently, she'd tried to convince Jacob to come home. Financially,
she argued, they could break even. He could attend the Knight School
of Welding in Louisville, a program that promised graduates "$40K a
year!" He could work a welding job and she could supplement. They
could lower their cost of living by not paying for two separate house-
holds 1,300 miles apart. She could garden and raise chickens to cut
back on food expenses, she reasoned.

But Jacob said he wasn't ready to return home yet. He didn't want
to quit a good job—$63,000 a year was less than before but still more
than he ever made in Kentucky. And he knew it could be difficult to
find employment in Louisville. They had some savings, but not much,
and Jacob still had about $30,000 in student loans to pay off.

Chelsea was no longer blogging for Real Oilfield Wives. Her final
post was at the end of October. "I don't know if I ever felt comfortable
with the label of 'oil field wife' to begin with," she said. For one, she
didn't like feeling defined by her husband's profession. "I have all these
other things about me that I do, that make up my personality—is this
really how I want to identify myself?"

Second, she didn't always feel like she fit in with the other wives. "In
some ways I'm very proud of what my husband does—he's out there
doing a hard job and taking care of our family. But some things I see with
oil field wives don't resonate with me." Some wives acted "obnoxious and
spoiled," she said. Others seemed catty and immature. "Some of them
are bitching and complaining and acting really trashy. I wasn't raised
like that. I don't come from a family like that," Chelsea said. She saw one
wife seek help with depression, which Chelsea also struggles with, on the
Oil Field Wives Facebook page. But the commenters told the woman
to "suck it up" and "get off her pity pot." The attitude angered her.

We pulled into the parking lot of Will's school. A kid about age 9 or 10 chopped wood behind a building. Kids darted past him shrieking and playing. The younger children were inside a building called the Kinderhouse. They peeled layers of knitted clothing off their tiny bodies. Chelsea had Litha strapped to her chest and she waved good-bye to Will. "Bye, sweetie, I love you!" she said. We treaded across muddy wood chips and past playground equipment as we made our way back to the car.

Most parents at the Waldorf school were wealthy, liberal, and highly educated. There were a few moms Chelsea could see herself becoming friends with, but so far they were mostly acquaintances. And no one at the school had met Jacob yet. When people asked her about Jacob's job, she replied, "He works in North Dakota," and left it at that. She often wondered what people thought about the situation. "I'm afraid to tell them what Jacob does," she said. "They're going to look at me funny. Or we're going to get into a fight about fracking. They just don't get it." Seeing Will excel in school, however, made whatever uncomfortable conversations she had to endure worth it. "He's really changed and become more outgoing," she said. "It's been the best thing for him."

On the drive home, Litha made spitting noises in her car seat. Chelsea yawned. "Mommy is sleepy," she told Litha, watching her from the rearview mirror. "I know I'm not the best parent in the world," Chelsea said. "I don't have a lot of patience because I'm always having to parent. I never get a break. It's hard to give them both the attention they need." Lately Will seemed to ask about his dad every day. "The last few weeks have been really hard on him. He used to hardly ever tell me 'I miss my dad.' But lately it's been every day. 'I miss my dad,' 'I miss my dad.'"

Back at the house, Chelsea nursed Litha. We looked through her wedding photos on her laptop. Litha pulled on the computer's power cord and chewed it. Chelsea took the cord out of Litha's mouth and held her close. The laptop teetered on Chelsea's knees as she clicked through photos. She explained one reason she and Jacob decided to marry was so they could get health insurance through Jacob's company, DuCon. But Jacob switched jobs soon after. Now Chelsea and the kids had health insurance through Obamacare. "We'd been talking about it anyway, so we just said, 'Let's finally go ahead and get married.' People ask us where and we're like, 'We got married in Deadwood, South Dakota!' " She laughed. "It's kind of a neat little curiosity."

She moved her face closer to the baby's. "And you were conceived that night," Chelsea said in a high pitch.

Litha smiled and cooed.

"Yep, you were a wedding night baby," Chelsea said, looking down at Litha. "You sure were. We talked about having another baby, but we just didn't expect it to happen right then." Chelsea laughed. "Surprise!"

Chelsea set Litha down on the living room carpet. The baby crawled over to a dog toy and chewed on it.

Chelsea picked up Litha and rocked her. She fell asleep on Chelsea's lap. "The last time I slept six straight hours was the day she was born," said Chelsea, shaking her head. "I remember it fondly." It was easier when Will was a baby, she said. Jacob carried him around the house or rocked him on the porch to give her a break. They took turns waking up in the middle of the night to soothe Will. "When one of us would get tired, you could just hand him off," said Chelsea. "Now there's no relief. It's been really hard."

Jacob came home for Christmas but could only stay a week. Chelsea worried Litha wouldn't remember her father, but the baby seemed to recognize him immediately. "He was the first person she saw when she was born, so he's printed on her in some way," she said. Litha's first "words" were "da da da," which pleased Jacob.

While Jacob was away, Chelsea tried to manage with repairs on the house, but some things she needed his help with. The backyard fence was broken, and the storm door needed to be replaced, but it was too heavy for her to move by herself. Other things, such as mowing almost a half acre of lawn, were simply too labor-intensive to do with two kids in tow. She hired outside help instead. "My priorities tend to be elsewhere," said Chelsea. "God help me if I ever had a husband who wanted to come home to a clean house."

Chelsea sometimes worried about crime in the neighborhood. She installed a security system for the house and adopted another dog, Maddock, for extra protection, since their Great Pyrenees was with Jacob in North Dakota. She also kept her .38 revolver in the house. "I've got a gun, a dog, and an alarm system. If they get past the dog and the alarm, they'll meet angry momma," she said. But she still felt uneasy. Many people cut through her backyard on their way to a bus stop nearby. One night as she nursed Litha in bed, she heard a voice directly outside her window. It sounded like a man, or maybe two men. Terrified, she called the police. As she waited for them to arrive, she heard the front doorknob rattle—someone was attempting to break in. Maddock barked and barked and barked. Chelsea took her children and the dog into the bedroom, locked the door, loaded her gun, and stayed on the phone with the police. Finally, they arrived. It turned out to be a woman from down the street with Alzheimer's who had escaped from her home. Chelsea worried what might've happened if the woman had succeeded in breaking in—she hoped she would've recognized that the intruder was an elderly woman before shooting, but she wasn't positive. "In this house by myself with my children—if you come through that door, chances are I'm not going to ask questions. It could've been bad."

At 1 p.m., we drove back to the Waldorf school to pick up Will. NPR played softly on the radio, and Litha cried and cried in her car seat. At the school, chickens clucked and pecked at the ground. We walked into the kindergarten building and saw Will collecting his belongings.

"Hi, girls!" Will said when he saw us. "I have a dirty sock," he told Chelsea, holding up a muddy sock.

Chelsea nodded. "Let's focus on getting ready."

Will dumped dried mud out of his rain boots and slid them on.

Chelsea needed to run a few errands on the way home. She stopped by a drive-through ATM to retrieve cash. She leaned out the window and tapped buttons on the screen. "Your father has not cleaned out our bank account. That's good," she announced.

"Why?" Will asked from the backseat.

"Because your father cannot be trusted with money," she said.

We pulled into the driveway of their house. Chelsea turned off the engine and massaged the area between her right shoulder and her neck. She had strained her shoulder one night while maneuvering around Litha in bed. "Man, I could go for a margarita right now," she said.

We entered the house and Maddock leapt at us, panting excitedly. Chelsea set Litha down on the living room floor and went into her bedroom to change. Litha sat with her chubby legs facing forward and watched her family quietly. Maddock rolled around on the carpet. Will pulled out a small trampoline from the spare bedroom and jumped on it in the kitchen.

Chelsea returned wearing a loose sweater that fell off one shoulder. She plopped down on the chair in the living room and applied Icy Hot balm to her shoulder. The pungent menthol smell wafted through the room. She read the news on her phone. "Ugh. More layoffs. Halliburton, Schlumberger, and now BP are all cutting jobs," she said, sighing loudly. "That is not the news I wanted to hear."

As Chelsea prepped dinner in the kitchen, Will stood with one foot in each of Maddock's empty dog bowls and talked to his mom. "Mommy, I really wish I had gummy bears," he said.

I asked Will if he liked living in North Dakota.

"No, it was disgusting," Will said, contorting his face. "The trailer was disgusting. I hated it."

Chelsea stopped chopping an onion and turned to him. "I didn't think you hated it. What about the rock museum?" she said. A museum with a farmer's 1930s rock collection was within walking distance of their trailer park in Parshall. "And the dinosaur place in Dickinson?"

"Oh, yeah," Will said, thinking about it. "Okay. I want to go back."

"Well, I can't promise anything," Chelsea said. "I don't know what's going to happen. A lot could change. I don't even know what's going to happen by March."

March was the end of the first quarter, a time when many oil field companies made financial decisions about the coming year. Chelsea figured whatever changes were coming, they'd happen then. "I really quit trying to make long-term plans, because it seems like every six months something changes. We're here, we're there, oil prices are up, oil prices are down. It's hard for me because I'm a long-term planner." Jacob had talked about heading back to the military recently, Chelsea said. He was riled up about ISIS and wanted to join Peshmerga, the Kurdish fighters in Syria. The plan stalled, however, when he discovered they didn't pay. "I never know what Jacob's going to say or do," said Chelsea. "Some days he's a loose cannon."

Jacob often missed the military, explained Chelsea. He didn't just leave the Army—he was involuntarily discharged at 23. About a month before his Iraq training, while stationed in South Korea, Jacob went on a drinking binge. He returned to base belligerent. His officers gave him a warning, but it happened again. The third time, they kicked him out. Chelsea said he deeply regretted his behavior and felt as though he let down his Army friends, a number of whom had been deployed to Iraq and died there. "He's got some major issues wrapped up with that," said Chelsea. "It's something he has never gotten over. He feels like it was his fault. But this is what he does—this is his alcoholic behavior. He'll wait until something is about to happen and something in him will flip a switch and he fucks it up every time. I don't know why. It's his pattern."

It had happened again, Chelsea said, four months ago. That September, she, Will, and two-month-old Litha planned to take a train up to Williston to live in North Dakota with Jacob for two months. Chelsea was packed and ready to go, but 24 hours before they were scheduled to leave, she checked their joint bank account and $600, most of the money in the account, was gone. She saw a charge at Skunk Bay bar, a charge at the Mandaree convenience store, and a $200 charge for a hotel in Watford City. She knew this was a bad sign and alcohol was involved—she and Jacob typically discussed any major purchases, and they needed the money to pay bills. She called Jacob's cell phone and the hotel but couldn't reach him. "It was terrifying," Chelsea said later. She decided right then that she and the children wouldn't go to North Dakota. "He beeeegged for us to come. I told him, 'You screwed up, buddy.'" Afterward, she enrolled Will at the Waldorf school in Louisville, and she and Jacob hadn't discussed the incident much since. "It's come up a couple times, but we haven't really dealt with it honestly. Not the way it needs to be dealt with. The only reason that I can even tolerate it is because I'm not there. If he tried to pull that at home, he'd be out on his ass so fast his head would spin."

Now Chelsea worried that with oil prices low and Jacob working fewer hours, he was more likely to get himself into trouble. "It's like, 'What are we going to have to bail you out of this time?'" Chelsea laughed. "All his life, if he's given free time, he gets himself in trouble. He was a great soldier but a terrible civilian. He's good at working; he's terrible at not working."

I asked her if she worried an incident like that might happen again.

"It's always in the back of my mind. I think if he was home around his children, if he was somewhere where he had support, it would be different for him—rather than out there on the cliff with no family. He can not drink around his kids. He can do that. But when he's by himself and given too much time to think, he's a mess."

Jacob drank in high school, but it didn't seem excessive at the time. Everyone drank. She figured he'd grow out of it. "He never quite did," she said. It wasn't until the military incident that Chelsea realized he had a problem. They had been engaged at the time. She was so angry with him that she called off the engagement. They remained apart for nearly three years and even dated other people during their separation. But one day he sent her an email out of nowhere. She received it at work and had to step away from the computer. She waited until she was home to read it. Jacob said he still loved her. "I had missed him a lot when we were apart. It was awful. Then I read it and we started talking," said Chelsea. He was attending Indiana University in Bloomington, and Chelsea went to visit him. Five months later, he moved in with her in Louisville. Two months later, she was pregnant with Will.

She had hoped their three-year separation would encourage him to work through his issues with alcohol, but it didn't. "After the military, it's just gotten worse and worse and worse," said Chelsea. "He needs to deal with it, but he's not going to deal with it until he's darn well good and ready."

Before dinner, Chelsea nursed Litha in the living room. The baby fussed and cried.

"Why you so grumpy, my baby princess?" Chelsea said, cradling her.

Will tried to sit on Chelsea's lap, but she asked him to stop.

"I wish my dad was here," Will said.

"I know," Chelsea said.

Will played with a doll house in the living room. He flipped the house on its side and pretended one doll was being chased by an imaginary Godzilla.

Chelsea's phone buzzed. It was a text from Jacob. "He says the new guys are pissed off about 'treater' work. I have no idea what that means," she said. His company had recently hired three new employees from other states, and she said she didn't understand why anyone would move to North Dakota now with current oil prices.

Chelsea asked Will to help set the table. Will yelled from the kitchen that he was stuck in the refrigerator.

Chelsea put Litha on her hip and walked to the kitchen to check on the Crock-Pot. She stood at the counter and texted Jacob.

"What are you doing?" Will asked.

"I'm trying to communicate with your father and get dinner ready at the same time," said Chelsea. She turned to Litha and kissed her on the forehead. "Is that your da da da on the phone?"

After dinner, Will jumped on the trampoline while Chelsea put away the leftovers and washed dishes. Litha cried in her high chair. Chelsea sat down with Litha in the recliner to nurse her again, wrapping a pink fleece blanket dotted with cartoon frogs around herself and the baby. She had to feed Litha before she could manage Will's bedtime. "Morning and bedtime are when it's really hectic," Chelsea said. "I want to read him a bedtime story, but she'll be fussy."

Chelsea said if Jacob remained employed in North Dakota by June, they'd head back and live in the camper with him over the summer.

Will heard this and threw his head down on the carpet. "No!"

"Why?" Chelsea said.

"Because North Dakota is cold!"

"Not in the summer," she said.

"Oh," Will said. He picked up Chelsea's water glass and sipped it. He pretended to drown from the water, holding his throat and making choking noises.

Chelsea finished nursing and set Litha down on the carpet.

"I've got to go to the bathroom. Will, don't let your sister eat anything she shouldn't," Chelsea said as she walked away.

Will rocked in the recliner and sang a song he made up. "Godzilla! You'll meet him in Tokyo. Godzilla! You'll meet him in France.

Godzilla! You'll meet him in Louisville!" He ignored Litha and she crawled backward under a chair. Chelsea returned and picked up the baby. Military helicopters flew overhead—Fort Knox was nearby. After the whir of the propellers faded, there were voices from people walking down the street. Chelsea sometimes heard people rapping to themselves as they walked by the house. "It's unnerving at first. You hear this male voice, but then when you realize what it is, it's okay."

"Will, go get your pajamas on," Chelsea said.

Will hung his head and pouted.

"Do you want to watch TV tomorrow?" Chelsea asked.

"Yes."

"Then you need to go get your jammies on."

Will pouted and shuffled his feet in the direction of his bedroom.

He returned with his pajamas on. Chelsea told him to pick out a bedtime story. He picked *The Giving Tree* by Shel Silverstein. Chelsea began reading: "'Once there was a tree . . . and she loved a little boy.'"

Will hugged her as she read. He leaned on his mother then collapsed into her lap. "Can you hold me like Litha?" he asked.

"You're too big for that," Chelsea said. "And my shoulder hurts."

Will squeezed next to her in the recliner. "I never want to go to sleep. Can I stay up all night?"

Chelsea ignored him and continued reading. "'And every day the boy would come . . . and he would gather her leaves.'"

Will tried to lie across her again. This time, he slipped, bumping into the book as he rolled onto the ground.

"William James!" Chelsea slapped the book shut.

Will ran out of the room giggling.

"You're about to get no TV!" she yelled, and followed him into his bedroom. Litha began to cry.

Chelsea returned to the living room to retrieve the baby. "This is really a two-parent job," she said, bouncing Litha and trying to soothe her. She tried to nurse her again, but Litha squirmed and fussed. "Oh, Litha, you are all over the place."

Will yelled from the room that he couldn't sleep.

Without looking up from Litha, Chelsea yelled back: "Go to sleep!"

I stopped by Chelsea's house again on Saturday morning. Chelsea was having a "craft day"—she was painting mugs to sell on her Etsy store and helping Will make a hula hoop. He ran through the living room and pretended the hula hoop was a UFO.

Chelsea had talked to Jacob the night before. He spent most of the conversation ranting about Kurdish politics and how the United States ought to fight ISIS.

Will stomped by us and screamed: "Santa Claus is coming to town!"

Chelsea stopped talking. "Will doesn't like when I talk about politics," she told me. "He's sensitive to serious conversations. There's been so many over the years. If you speak in a serious tone, Will starts screaming, anything to stop the conversation."

Chelsea set a pot of water on the stove to make macaroni and cheese for Will.

"I'm going to call your father," she said.

"I want to talk to him!" Will said, jumping up and down.

"He's probably sleeping in his camper," Chelsea said.

The phone rang and Jacob picked up. "Hi," said Chelsea. "Your son would like to talk to you." She put Jacob on speakerphone and handed the phone to Will.

"Have you ever watched the original Godzilla movie?" Will said as he skipped into his bedroom.

"I'm sure somewhere," Jacob said, his voice crackled and garbled over the phone's low-quality speakers.

Will shut his bedroom door to have more privacy, but we could hear Jacob's voice cutting in and out. Will became frustrated. "Why does Mom's phone keep doing that!" he yelled from behind the closed door.

"He really misses his dad," Chelsea said. "He used to not want to talk to him. He said he was mad at him for leaving. But now he could talk to him all day."

Chelsea's long-term dream for her family was to move to New Orleans. She always loved the architecture and culture of the city. She had planned to move there after graduating with her master's degree. She even scouted out the best neighborhoods to live in, but then, life happened. She and Jacob started a family instead. Her dream of living in New Orleans never went away. "It's something I've never been able to get over," said Chelsea. With Jacob's North Dakota oil field experience, he could apply for jobs near New Orleans on offshore oil rigs. A typical schedule was two weeks on, three weeks off. "He'd be around more than he is now," Chelsea said. Her old boss at the lobster shipping company, Paul, used to work in offshore oil, so Jacob already had a connection to the industry. But the plan wasn't perfect. Her boss had eventually quit the rigs because he missed his family too much. "He missed a lot of his kids' growing up," said Chelsea. "He wasn't there and he's making up for that now. I go over his story in my head and I'm like, this is going to be Jacob. He's going to be in his late 30s and be just like Paul, wishing he had spent more time with his kids."

But she figured she shouldn't worry too much about the future at the moment. "Right now everything's so up in the air—whether he'll come home, whether he'll work here. I don't know what toll [working in the oil field] is going to take family-wise."

38. PASTOR JAY REINKE

In September 2013, the Williston Planning and Zoning Department shut down Reinke's Overnighters program. They determined the church was not fit to house people because the building had no emergency sprinkler system, no showers, no designated sleeping area, and no social worker on staff.

Afterward, Reinke discovered a few neighbors and congregation members had met privately to discuss strategies to shut down the program. Some sent letters to the city voicing their opposition to the Overnighters. "I find myself a little confused why people reacted so strongly to it," said Reinke. "Isn't this kind of a simple thing? Floor space. Come on!" Former Overnighter Steve Tanck had his own theory: "They didn't like outsiders and wanted it stopped, so they kept going until they found the right person."

Between 2011 and 2013, more than 1,000 people stayed at the church. On its final night, Tanck couldn't bring himself to go. "I just couldn't. I couldn't. It hurt too much," he said. "We were still trying to figure out what else we could do." Reinke broke down in tears and hugged each Overnighter before saying good-bye. Andrea posted a sign on the door that read THE OVERNIGHTERS IS OVER. In 2012, a filmmaker from California, Jesse Moss, had showed up and filmed the conflict at the church. He named the film *The Overnighters*, and it went on to be shortlisted for an Academy Award.

Soon after the program ended, Jay Reinke stepped down as the pastor. Allegations surfaced that he had had sexual relations with a man in his past. The Concordia Lutheran leadership forbids homosexuality, and Reinke admitted to the allegations and resigned. He called the incident his own "moral failing." It was a hard time for Reinke. Rumors about the scandal spread quickly through town. "My resignation was very, very painful. And my own fault," Reinke said later. His fall is detailed in Moss's film, and when the film premiered in 2014, the entire town of Williston knew what had happened.

After the Overnighters ended and he lost his job, Reinke struggled to find footing in the community. A neighbor told Andrea she should leave her husband and encouraged them to move away from Williston, but Andrea stuck by him and they decided to stay. "I would just as soon build a new story here as opposed to someplace else," said Reinke. "Andrea has a good part-time job, we own our home, and Eric's doing well in school. I might as well stay. Suck it up. A lot of people say, oh, this book is done, but it's just one chapter. In time, a new chapter starts."

Reinke applied to become one of Williston's city commissioners but ultimately didn't receive the nomination. He found employment selling oil field equipment at Pipeline Supply and Service but missed his job as a pastor. "I drive by the church, and I get teary-eyed when I think of the people that slept there. It was a once-in-a-lifetime fraternity of people who were in need. I get emotional when I think about it," he said. "It was so unprecedented. You had people who said, 'No no no, this isn't what a church is supposed to do.' And in one sense, that's true—it's not the church's job to provide housing for people. But if we can help a neighbor in a specific way, let's do it. Let's find joy in that."

39. CINDY MARCHELLO

Home was on Cindy Marchello's mind more often these days.

She was growing increasingly frustrated with her job. She often discussed leaving North Dakota or the oil field altogether. She talked to her supervisor, Mike Hambrick, about different positions within the company for her. She applied for a Department of Transportation job in Williston but didn't receive it. C&J's secretary had transferred to a different office, and Hambrick offered Marchello the job, but she'd receive no overtime and would need to move to Williston permanently. Marchello was shocked Hambrick even suggested such a position. C&J had recently opened a location in Saudi Arabia and was transferring some employees there. Some guys took the Saudi offer, thinking it would be a better deal, but they saw their wages fall once they arrived. Marchello considered going as well, but her parents thought it would be too dangerous there for a woman. She also had her doubts. "Women can't drive over there," she said. "You can't go anywhere without a man."

In the fall of 2013, she missed the birth of her grandchild. Her daughter Elizabeth was due the week before Thanksgiving, so she took time off to be home with her family and witness the birth. But the baby was late. As she was driving back to North Dakota, Elizabeth had the baby. "That drive back was the hardest drive I've done," said

Marchello. "I cried the whole way." Of her six grandchildren, it was the only birth she'd missed.

The event caused her to seriously consider quitting the oil field. She could quit over the summer of 2014 and take back her old job as a cook for a hunting camp for about $100 a day, but the work was seasonal and didn't pay enough to support her entirely. She also contemplated launching an online business to sell acupuncture "meridian" beads to supplement her income when she returned home. The beads were to be worn on specific points on the body to increase energy flow. One night as we were chatting, she gave me a bead and told me to put it below my knee to help with my "chi."

Her other idea was becoming a stand-up comedian. "I told my kids, I have decided on my next career. I think I could be a good stand-up comedian. Do you think I could be a stand-up comedian?" she asked me.

I smiled. "I think you could definitely be a stand-up comedian."

"I'm done with the oil patch," she said, "but I want to walk out with my head held high."

The more I got to know Marchello, however, the more her view on women's equality confused me. She disliked feminism, she said. She and her son-in-law once burned feminist books after he took an online women's studies class. The female teacher seemed to hate men, they said. "There's a reason they call women bitches," she said. "Not all of us, but enough of us." She was annoyed by women protesting to be part of the priesthood at the Mormon church in Salt Lake City. "The man is the head of the household, the woman is the heart," she said. "But we are equal in every way. We have the power to create; therefore, we do not need the priesthood." Marchello believed the protesters had deep-seated issues that caused them to be so angry.

"Do you think discrimination toward women in the past caused some of those church rules to be created?" I asked.

She considered the question. "On an individual basis, yes. I've experienced discrimination myself." She paused. "But then don't go. If you can't handle what's going on, go somewhere else. They don't have to have the priesthood to be equal. We all assume that because the man goes out and earns the living, he's better than us. But there are lots of ways women can serve. Those men sacrifice their life to be the leader of the church, and women don't have that kind of time because they shouldn't. They should be taking care of the young and the sick."

Yet Marchello herself was trying to bring home a paycheck in a male-dominated environment—not caring for the young and the sick. In many ways, she was the strongest feminist I knew. She fought daily to be treated the same as her male coworkers. But like many women, she seemed caught between her desire to be treated as an equal and her traditional upbringing. "I fight and fight to be equal among the men," she told me once. "But when they treat me as an equal it still makes me mad, because I should still get to be a girl sometimes. I should still have two or three buddies who will fix my tire for me." Feeling unsure of where she fit in was isolating and exhausting. Which Cindy Marchello did she want to be, the fiercely independent woman who wanted to be equal in every way to her male coworkers, or the traditional Mormon woman who once looked to a man to provide the paycheck while she cared for her family? The person she identified with could change by the moment. "What do I really want?" she asked once. "Actually, I just really want a paycheck. Just leave me alone. Let me do my job and let me go home."

But Marchello couldn't leave her desire for equality alone. In May 2014, she discovered many of the men on her original crew had been approved for raises and she hadn't. One guy who was receiving a raise had worked at C&J for only five months and had less experience than her. She had worked there for nearly two years. She had a graduate degree (albeit in traditional Chinese medicine), was a certified heavy-duty diesel mechanic, and had years of oil field experience. She'd asked for raises many times but had always been denied. The week before she learned about the raises, she claimed her boss had looked her in the eye and told her C&J could not afford to give anyone raises. She recalled him saying that if she wanted to keep her job, she should "shut her mouth and stay behind the desk" and "quit worrying about her paycheck."

Furious, Marchello asked around and discovered she earned the same or less than numerous men with less experience than her. One recent hire made $20,000 more than her a year. In early August, Marchello contacted the Equal Employment Opportunity Commission, or EEOC, to file a complaint for gender and age discrimination. "By going to the EEOC, now somebody outside of this company knows I'm alive," Marchello said. "I have nothing to lose. I already don't have money. I'm used to being poor."

She calculated that C&J owed her $80,000 in lost wages after she had been moved to the office. Her claims were: She was transferred, denied pay raises, denied training, denied monetary and nonmonetary benefits based on her sex and age of 56. Marchello wanted to limit her claims to items she believed she could prove on paper. Her claims were that C&J violated Title VII of the Civil Rights Act, the Age Discrimination in Employment Act, and the Equal Pay Act.

Later that summer, Marchello was on edge. She was waiting to hear if the EEOC would take her case. She had a new supervisor and they often clashed. She didn't talk about the EEOC charge at work, but she had a feeling her supervisor knew. He'd berate her for ordering too much of one equipment item or too little of another. When she'd try to explain herself, he'd yell and say she needed to "obey" him. But even if he knew about the EEOC case, she figured C&J couldn't fire her because it would be perceived as retaliation by the company for speaking up. "They can't really fire me," she said, "but they can make me so uncomfortable that I quit." She was under a lot of stress and taking a natural pill called "Calm Spirit," which claimed to be full of a special blend of B vitamins and amino acids. Marchello had taken the pills during her divorce from Richard and said they had helped. "At my worst, I was probably taking about 16 a day," she said. She was also making preparations for life after the oil field. She was studying to retake an acupuncture test to reapply for her license.

Though Marchello often talked about quitting the oil field, I wondered if she actually would. In April 2014, she told me: "If, by June 1, I don't have my hours back, I'm leaving." Then after June 1 came and went and she didn't have her hours back, she said: "I'm only staying here until August." August came and she was still there. She had to get bone graft surgery on her mouth and wanted to keep her health insurance, she said. Then her plumbing at her house needed to be repaired. I was beginning to think she might never leave.

"Is it really this bad everywhere?" she asked Scott Morgan one day over lunch at Applebee's. Morgan had recently returned from a C&J job in Texas.

"Which part?" Morgan replied. "The drama? The bullshit? The infighting? The babysitting grown-ass men who should know better?"

Marchello sighed. "The instability, I guess. The constant lack of management." C&J had gone through seven operations managers in less than two years.

Morgan said it was similar throughout the oil field.

Marchello had also recently met someone. His name was Dennis Thomas, a widowed veteran who lived in Roy, Utah, a 15-minute drive from her house. She met him through the dating service named It's Just Lunch. She beamed when she talked about him. Thomas respected and admired her for working in the oil field. "It's so cool that she's out there blazing the trail for ladies," he told me later. Marchello bought her first dress in years to wear on their fourth date. "You did not," Morgan said when she told him. "You're Cindy. You don't do anything girly."

Then in late August, Marchello couldn't take it anymore. A C&J

human resources representative traveled to North Dakota to have a meeting with her. The meeting was private, but Marchello claimed the representative told her: "I'm here to tell you to stop it and stop it now," in regard to her EEOC complaints. The man said the company planned to cut her wages to $15 an hour, take away her housing, her rotation home, and her per diem bonuses, and he told her she was not allowed to speak about the case to other C&J employees. "I didn't think he was going to be so hostile and nasty to me," she said later.

"So is this retaliation?" Marchello asked him.

"No, this is an adjustment to what you deserve. This is what everyone else at C&J gets for the job you do," she recalled him saying.

Marchello asked if she could return to field work. She remembered him saying that it wasn't in C&J's best interest to send her back to the field because the company had received complaints about her from her male coworkers. "When he told me that the men refused to work with me, I knew that was an out-and-out lie," Marchello said. "I wanted to see it in writing." The HR representative never filed any paperwork to implement Marchello's wage decrease, but the message was loud and clear: the company was putting up a fight.

After the meeting, Marchello didn't want to spend another day working at C&J, but she couldn't afford to quit outright. She had planned to take a month off using her sick days and vacation time in early September to have surgery on her mouth, so she moved up the appointment a few weeks. She also called the EEOC and told them about C&J's intimidation tactics. "This is the same fight I've had for 40 years," Marchello told me, "wanting to be paid what the guys are being paid."

In early October 2014, C&J's lawyers sent the EEOC their rebuttal to Marchello's allegations. The company denied everything. C&J said it had transferred Marchello to the office because her performance as a coil tubing operator was underwhelming, and after her crew left, there were no other coil tubing positions available. The company transferred her to the office instead of laying her off to keep her productive. It claimed Marchello never received a raise because she wasn't qualified for the coil tubing position to begin with, had limited experience in the oil field, and was already paid an hourly wage higher than normal for her duties as a warehouse coordinator. The company cited an official warning Marchello received in March 2013 for a pump unexpectedly freezing on location as evidence of her subpar performance.

Marchello said plenty of her coworkers—some who were receiving raises—also had citations on their records. In addition, she claimed her citation was unfounded. Scott Morgan was on location with her when the incident happened. "It froze up and [the supervisor] ended up blaming that on Cindy," recalled Morgan. "I remember looking at him, thinkin', 'Cindy was runnin' the nitrogen pump, how is it her fault that the fluid pump froze when the other guys were supposed to winterize it?' It wasn't Cindy's fault. And I know it wasn't Cindy's fault because I saw her runnin' the nitrogen pump and I was watchin' the guys work on the other pump. I think they skipped a step and that's what fucked it up. It was fucking cold and they were trying to get done."

After the company's rebuttal, the EEOC declined to take her case, stating it was "unable to conclude that the information obtained establishes violations of the statutes." If she pleased, she had the right to file a lawsuit under federal law within 90 days of the decision.

On October 5, 2014, just before Marchello was due back at work, she sent in her resignation to C&J. She also contacted a lawyer, Stephen Premo at Halunen Law firm in Minneapolis, and filed a lawsuit. Premo wanted Marchello to detail every time she felt discrimination during her employment at C&J, not just instances she felt she could prove with a paper trail. Marchello had a lot of ammunition. In addition to her claims of unequal pay and being denied for raises and training opportunities, she included the time she overheard her supervisor say "You guys want her to quit? I'll get her to quit; she won't be here by

Halloween." And another time he told her she would "suffer a cruel, slow death" at his hands. She included the time she was called a cunt by a male coworker, and nothing was done about it. She included a claim that her first supervisor refused to allow her restroom breaks on location because she wanted to walk to an outhouse instead of pee behind a truck.

"The allegations are pretty shocking," said Premo. "She was called terrible names. It's just despicable stuff that has no place in a 21st-century workplace. It's sad that in this day and age, women are still fighting for pay equality and to be treated fairly and equally in the workplace."

Premo filed the lawsuit detailing Marchello's claims with the U.S. District Court of North Dakota on February 20, 2015. This initiated a long fact-finding process to corroborate her claims, with the potential for more plaintiffs to come forward and the possibility of going to trial. "We believe there are other women out there in the North Dakota oil shale that have been discriminated against," said Premo. "Plaintiffs are important because they can bring change to the workforce and you have a good ol' boys network that perpetuates discrimination. Our goal is to bring law and order—at least when it comes to employment discrimination—to North Dakota, which appears to have been lacking in it."

Marchello and her lawyers had a lot of challenges ahead of them, however. In Marchello's case, a class action suit with multiple plaintiffs was unlikely. Most class action plaintiffs need to have the same employer and face similar working conditions. But as the only female coil field operator for the company in North Dakota, Marchello was essentially on her own. "Finding a defendant that employed enough women to bring a class action suit in North Dakota would be difficult," said Premo. Without more women coming forward, it was likely Marchello's case would settle—approximately 98 percent of single-plaintiff civil cases like hers settle in federal court. If a settlement couldn't be reached, many cases like hers were thrown out by a judge before they went to trial. In addition, some of Marchello's claims were difficult to prove—in many instances, she had no witnesses or the only witness still worked for the company and therefore might not be forthcoming. But Premo said his law firm was highly selective with the cases it took on and had considered all of these factors before agreeing to represent her. "Cindy's sworn testimony is evidence and we believe her story," he said. "It's just up to us now to prove it."

Meanwhile, Marchello applied for jobs in Utah and tried to figure out what her life post–oil field would look like. "You know, as scary as it was to come here, it's scary to walk away from it too," she said. "Now what am I gonna do? The oil field has ruined my attitude. I would not fit in at the cheese plant. They would fire me. They would—I'm too mouthy. I'm too mouthy."

40. TOM STAKES

In addition to AA meetings, Tom Stakes returned to church. It had been over two years since he stepped foot in one. Rick Sonstegaard attended a congregation called the Church of God north of town and suggested they go together. I tagged along one Sunday. The church was located past Buffalo Trails campground, one of the first campgrounds to fill up when the boom started. Beyond it was the Eagle Ridge golf course and a new housing development called the Meadows where houses were going for over $400,000. On Sunday mornings in Williston, many local radio stations broadcast church sermons. We listened to one on the drive over as a light snow fell.

The church was a one-room chapel built in 1912. It was part of a historical pioneer village and museum, complete with a preserved 1900s-era home, a schoolhouse, and a general store. The chapel was originally a Swedish Lutheran church located in another town, but it had been moved to Williston in the 1960s. Ever since the boom had begun, the museum's board of directors had been losing volunteers. Most were retirees living on fixed incomes and were forced to move out of town when rents soared. Not wanting the chapel to fall into disrepair, the board looked for an active congregation to use and maintain the building. That's when they found Pastor Wayne and his small Church of God congregation.

We walked inside, careful not to slip on the ice on the way in. A pot of steaming coffee was in the lobby, and Stakes filled up a cup, adding two packets of Splenda. We walked down the carpeted aisle, past wooden pews, and slid into a row near the front. There was a pipe organ in the corner, and at the altar was a painting of Jesus, standing in a robe with his arms open, in an ornate white-and-gold frame. Under it were the words "Helig Helig Helig," which means "Holy Holy Holy" in Swedish. Television screens had been installed in the front of the room, and a small heater pumped out warm air. Only six other people had showed up this morning. Stakes set his Bible, encased in its black satchel, down next to him.

The pastor stood at the front of the room. "Well, good morning!" he said as he looked around. "Good to have you with us this morning!" The pastor appeared to be in his mid-40s, tall and slender with a sharp nose, thinning dark brown hair, and a bushy salt-and-pepper mustache cascading down both sides of his mouth. He wore a slightly-too-big white dress shirt with reading glasses tucked into the breast pocket.

"Father, we come to you this morning, thankful for your presence in our lives!" the pastor yelled. "The blessings that you've instilled into our families, God, thank you for giving us this day. This is the day the Lord has made. I will rejoice and be glad!"

The heater in the corner blew hot air directly on us. Stakes wiped sweat from his forehead and took off his jacket.

The pastor asked everyone to stand. The television screens lit up with images of clouds and began playing music. Lyrics popped up on the screen, and the pastor began singing a ballad. "Welcome to this place! Welcome to this bro-ken vessel!" he belted out. The audience sang along softly. When there was a pause in the song, the pastor yelled, "Hallelujah! Lord, thank you! Thank you for your presence this morning!"

After we sang and sat back down, the pastor stood in the center of the aisle and bowed his head. The word REDEMPTION ran across the screen in big white block letters.

"Redemption!" the pastor yelled, jerking his head up. "If it was not for Christ coming, we would be so lost. We only received redemption because of Christ. Because of Him."

Stakes watched the pastor closely, resting his elbow on top of the pew in front of him.

The pastor continued talking for another 30 minutes, putting boisterous emphasis on certain words and sentences. "He came in flesh, so HE KNOWS about everything that you face in your life," Pastor Wayne said. "He is JESUS CHRIST! God with us! GOD! WITH! US! He knows about all those temptations that are out there. He knows about all the sin that's in our lives. He KNOWS the things that you're going through . . . because he loves us so much. He says 'Fear not. FEAR NOT!'"

"Fear not," Stakes repeated quietly under his breath.

After the service, as we walked back to the car, Stakes said he enjoyed the sermon. "I believe they're tryin' to worship in a good way. Of course they have media, a technological approach to the music and the sermon. Hey, a lot of churches do that now. I didn't know any of those songs, but I tried to sing 'em." He laughed. "And the old buildings are just a natural setting for it. You can imagine the spirits that walk amongst that church." He sniffled from the cold. "The things that church has seen through the years." He planned on returning to the church the next Sunday. Rick Sonstegaard had suggested that Stakes talk to Pastor Wayne about possibly filling in for him one day. The idea of preaching excited Stakes. "I always pray to God," Stakes said. "I say 'Lord, You know my life. If You ever want me back in any form of ministry, just open the door and I'll walk through it.' The doors were closed for so long. But now I think He's seein' an effort on my part to try and straighten my life back out, and He's startin' to crack the door open a little bit."

On Christmas Day in 2014, I snuck away from my family after we opened presents to call Stakes. He said he was sitting on the couch at the Sonstegaard house, watching television alone. He had recently returned from an AA meeting and seemed in good spirits. Although he still didn't have a job, he claimed he was staying sober. The previous night, Sonstegaard's sister had invited him over to her house for a holiday dinner party. The house was packed with about 20 people, and they feasted on lasagna and fruit salad. It was the first holiday dinner Stakes had attended in a long time.

After my visit, Stakes went to a Church of God service one more time, but then Sonstegaard stopped going and Stakes didn't have a ride. He still attended AA meetings most days, though not as often as before. Today, he said, a man at the AA meeting broke down in tears. The man announced he was miserable and questioned the point of attending AA. "He was just goin' through a tough time," Stakes said, "it being the holidays and all."

Stakes told me he was watching snowflakes flutter down outside the window. It was in the low 20s that day, but the following week, the temperature was forecast to drop into the negatives. His phone buzzed while we were chatting and Stakes said he had to go. He thought it might be his son calling.

Tom Stakes stayed in North Dakota until the middle of May 2015. Oil prices had hit a low of $43 a barrel in March, and the outlook wasn't promising. Halliburton had laid off 9,000 workers, or about 10 percent of its global workforce, and reported a $643 million loss in the first quarter of 2015. Schlumberger had laid off 20,000 employees, and Baker Hughes laid off 7,000. North Dakota's unemployment rate went from 2.7 percent to 3.1 percent.

Earlier that year, just before his sixtieth birthday in late January, Stakes had reconnected with his old boss, Gary Westerman. Westerman hired Stakes again but warned he'd be fired immediately if he started drinking. Stakes kept his promise until his final night in Williston on May 14. He went to the bars to say good-bye to Greg Mackie and Nate Beatty, and they drank until the early morning. Mackie had been indicted for selling drugs and sentenced to a year in jail. He only had a few nights of freedom remaining. He asked a friend to watch over his little yellow school bus while he was locked up.

Westerman and Stakes left North Dakota because Westerman wanted to grow marijuana and sell it to dispensaries in Denver, Colorado, which had legalized the plant in 2012. They planned to do construction projects while they developed the business, but Westerman estimated they could ultimately make $20,000 a month growing and selling weed. "It's like the new gold rush," Stakes said.

Before he left, Stakes had saved up about $2,000. He needed to get his driver's license back to make the trip to Denver, but in order to do so, he had to pay fines, a reinstatement fee, and pay for two alcohol education courses. He also needed to pay for gas and hotels to get to Colorado. He had come to North Dakota with about $20 in his pocket and left with about $1,000. "Livin' in North Dakota is not for the faint-hearted," he said. "You come up here expectin' to be in paradise, and everythin's gonna be fine, but it's a tough life."

"Was it worth it?" I asked.

He paused. "I guess it's just part of livin'. You make it some places, and some you don't. Then you just gotta move on and try to find a new life."

41. WILLISTON

On one of my drives to Williston from California, I took an empty two-lane road after leaving Rock Springs, Wyoming, cut through old mining lands, and eventually came to the town I was looking for: Jeffrey City.

The "city," if you could call it that, was a cluster of buildings on the side of the highway. I pulled onto an empty street on the outskirts of town. There were no other cars or pedestrians in sight. Along the street was a roped-off gas station, a boarded-up building called Sagebrush Flats Bar, and a phone booth with a broken door and a faded, torn phone book inside. The book was folded open, as if someone had been searching for a number but left in a hurry. I turned down another street and saw a row of long buildings with broken shutters and peeling paint. Decaying steps led to a second-story entrance, and a DANGER: NO TRESPASSING sign was posted out front. I parked my car and walked down what used to be a sidewalk, the cement slabs slowly being swallowed up by prairie grass. Blades crept through the cracks and buckled the cement panels. I walked over to the buildings. They looked like old barracks. I saw another sign: BACHELOR APARTMENT #2. Ah. These were former man camps.

Jeffrey City was once a hub for the uranium mining industry. It was founded during the early 1950s as a company town for the Lost Creek Oil and Uranium Company, and the area boomed during the 1970s as more companies established uranium mines. By 1980, the town had grown to over 4,000 people, with some 1,000 workers employed by the industry. Subdivisions sprang up, new businesses were launched, and the city built a $1.2 million high school gymnasium. But a few years later, as a glut of uranium entered the market and safety concerns rose, the industry went bust. A mass exodus from Jeffrey City soon followed. Within two years, 95 percent of the area's workforce had left. By 1982, only 1,000 residents remained and, soon, fewer than 100. Today, only a handful of people live here. A sign, JEFFREY CITY: THE BIGGEST BUST OF THEM ALL, by Wyoming's Department of State Parks and Cultural Resources, told the story of the town: "The vacant streets still whisper of the thousands who once lived and played here," it read.

As I walked through the overgrown sagebrush, I heard yelling in the distance. It was faint, muffled from the wind. I walked toward the sound and saw a group of men sitting across the highway at a junk shop. One gestured for me to come over. I returned to my car and drove to where they sat. An older man with leathery skin and a potbelly and two men in their late 20s sat on camping chairs and passed a jug of whiskey between them. I exited my car but kept it running in case I needed a quick getaway.

One of the younger guys introduced himself as Bryan. "Whatcha doin' over there?" he asked.

I told him I was a writer passing through. I wanted to learn more about Jeffrey City.

"You wanna go shoot guns with us?" he asked, slurring his words.

I declined the offer and asked if any of them lived in Jeffrey City. They didn't, they said. But they lived nearby. They knew only one guy who still lived in town: His name was J.D., and he was Jeffrey City's sheriff and had been around since the boom days. He was now 88 years old and liked to tell people that he was "just sitting around waiting to die."

I thanked them and turned to leave.

Behind me I heard Bryan slur: "I hate to see you go, but I like to watch you do it." The three of them broke into drunken giggles.

I quickly closed the driver's door and rolled back onto the highway.

Would this be Williston's future?

The story of Williston's boom is not a new one. During the region's bountiful oil years, as the rush for oil and money cast a spell and clouded visions, few in the Bakken region seemed to stop and think that they were pumping millions of new barrels into the world's supply of oil. And when supply spikes and demand stagnates, prices fall. The same thing has happened dozens of times throughout history since oil was discovered in the United States back in 1859. OPEC typically helps regulate fluctuations in the market by holding back production, but this time, feeling threatened by the U.S. oil revival, it sat back and did nothing. OPEC hoped it could cope with dismal oil prices longer than U.S. companies could.

During the boom, oil producers ran into another problem with new fracking and horizontal drilling methods. The wells they drilled were incredibly productive in the beginning—some pumping nearly two thousand barrels a day—but didn't stay that way for long. Oil production from these fracked wells plummeted after only a year. Most wells would fall to half their peak production level by the end of the first year and decline another 30 to 40 percent by the end of the second year. In late 2012, about 90 new producing wells per month were needed just to maintain production levels. To keep output growing and their investors happy, companies had to drill more wells, faster. The drilling intensity was staggering—the number of wells drilled or fracked in U.S. shale formations in 2011 outpaced the total number of oil and gas wells drilled in the rest of the world (excluding Canada) that year. Sustaining such a pace was difficult.

"The shale oil phenomenon will prove merely temporary," wrote Leonardo Maugeri, a researcher with Harvard's Geopolitics of Energy Project, back in June 2013, "a sort of bubble inflated by the very rapid ramp-up of production in the early months . . . but doomed to bust as soon as the best shale areas have gone."

In Williston, as prices fell in late 2014, few residents believed that the state's beloved oil boom might end. No one used the word "bust." Instead they called it a "downturn" or a "temporary slowdown." "It will give the city time to catch up," said one official. "It will rebound soon," another resident said. "We're normalizing," said a local real estate agent.

But prices continued to fall—dropping about 70 percent over the next year and a half. By 2016, the price per barrel was under $35, down from the peak of $145 eight years earlier. Some 10,000 jobs were cut in North Dakota. After a 40-year-old ban on exporting crude, enacted after the 1970s oil crisis created fears of scarcity, the United States repealed that decision in December 2015 in an attempt to stop the bleeding.

I visited Williston in October 2015, when the price per barrel hovered at $45. A year had passed since the downturn began. Cindy Marchello had left the oil field and returned to Utah; Tom Stakes was in Colorado; Jacob Klipsch had lost his job, and he and Chelsea Niehaus had separated; and Donny Nelson had retreated from his activism and media attention. Fighting oil development had taken a toll on him. Jay Reinke was the only person I saw during my trip, and he didn't want to talk about the Overnighters program. He wanted to put that chapter of his life behind him.

Some Williston residents were coming to terms with the possibility of the "temporary downturn" being longer than expected. Rental rates and hotel rates had finally normalized. I found a room at the newly built Aspen Lodge and Suites for $50 a night—less than what most hotel rooms had cost before the boom. A man camp along the highway advertised rooms for "$24.99 and up." New trucks in GMC's car lot collected dust. Shiny new shopping centers stood half empty. The estimated occupancy rate for newly built apartments was at 50 percent—and approximately 5,000 hotel rooms and apartment units were now empty. Trailers and mobile homes sat discarded in open fields. A dump yard called TJ's Salvage could hardly keep up with people abandoning their trailers and skipping town. The yard stretched across the prairie with some 400 discarded vehicles, rusted trailers, and trashed oil field equipment. Melted steel frames twisted around crumbling cement blocks, and dogs roamed through the rubble.

Despite the decline in newcomers, Williston's building frenzy continued. About 1,350 new apartments were still under construction in the fall of 2015 and scheduled to come onto the market, adding to the 10,000 new homes and apartments built during the boom. Many developers had already invested the money and signed the building permits, so they figured they might as well build, hoping occupancy rates would rise. Apartment complexes offered move-in specials, such as two months of free rent or "$1,500 Off First Month + $99 Deposit on approved credit!" One complex slashed its prices and began offering free alcohol in the common lounge. A two-bedroom apartment that once went for $3,200 a month was now a third of the price. Other complexes came up with catchy mottos to attract residents: "Turning a Boomtown into a Hometown" was one development's tagline.

Williston was now a sprawling city with major subdivisions, industrial yards, and expanded highways. A newly constructed shopping center with the chain store Menards was located between two yards filled with oil field tanks and pipes. New high-rise apartment complexes and single-family homes were tucked in between the industrial mess. The small-town charm Williston once had was mostly gone, though a few long-standing local businesses held on. The city was in the process of building a $70 million high school and a larger airport, but now had about $215 million in debt. The city's municipal bonds were downgraded to junk status in March 2016. City officials justified the continued building, reasoning that when the boom came back, they'd be ready. But as more companies shut their doors and layoffs continued, a full rebound looked less likely.

I drove by the old trailer park where I had lived over the summer of 2013. I passed oil pumpjacks that sat dormant, leaning over like surrendered soldiers. My space, number 305, was empty. Many surrounding spots were vacant as well. The trailers that remained looked as if they had been there for years—reinforced, winterized fortresses. Tumbleweeds blew past the empty lots and piled up next to the trailers still standing.

Across from the trailer park, just off of Energy Street, the same developer had built a new neighborhood, with prefabricated modular homes and freshly paved roads with names like Owl Street and Hawk Street. Beyond the homes were more empty square lots, waiting for residents to come. Only one or two homes had lights on, glowing like lone flares on a dark prairie.

AFTERWORD

For the tens of thousands who migrated to Williston and soon left, the boom will likely fade into a distant memory. Many went back to their old lives. Some cleared debts and saved homes—but others overspent during the flush years on new trucks and big houses and found themselves with more debt than when they started. A number of workers parlayed their oil field experience into solid working-class jobs with more manageable hours, but their paychecks weren't anywhere close to oil field money. Few sectors paid as well as the oil field for workers without a college degree—railroads, power utilities, heavy machinery operation—and those industries didn't have nearly enough job openings to absorb the laid-off workers. Many former oil workers turned to minimum-wage jobs to get by. The lucky ones transferred to offshore rigs or oil service jobs in North Dakota and more established areas, such as Texas and Oklahoma. But for the most part, thousands of blue-collar workers were back where they started—struggling to survive. North Dakota's boom helped them keep their heads above water for a few years, but now what?

The worry and uncertainty oil workers felt during this time coincided with the rise of Donald Trump's popularity during the 2016 election. Trump campaigned heavily in oil patch regions and tapped into people's anger. He blamed the struggling oil industry on President Obama's regulatory policies and promised to use his business prowess to unleash a U.S. energy revolution. His message worked, and Trump was elected by a large margin in oil industry states.

LISA DEVILLE AND DONNY NELSON

In December 2016, after months of intense protests, the Army Corps of Engineers denied the easement needed for the Dakota Access Pipeline to cross beneath Lake Oahe near Standing Rock and announced it would explore alternate routes. DeVille was thrilled for the tribe and appreciated the attention their movement brought to pipeline concerns, but with Donald Trump's election, the future of the fight looked bleak. Trump had between $500,000 and $1 million invested in the company building the pipeline as of December 2015 (though he later sold off some of his shares), and one of his first actions as president was to push the Dakota Access Pipeline toward completion. DeVille vowed to continue fighting. Donny Nelson stayed on his farm in Keene and launched a new construction and a custom harvesting business. He drifted away from his political activism.

CINDY MARCHELLO

After Cindy Marchello returned to Utah, she found a job at a salt mine not far from her house. In the spring of 2015, after dating for about 10 months, her boyfriend, Dennis Thomas, proposed. Their wedding was four months later at a campground in the Utah countryside. It was a small ceremony, about 50 people, including Marchello's newest five-week-old granddaughter. Marchello stood next to her daughters as she recited her vows. Afterward, guests ate barbecue and danced inside a small barn. Marchello joked that it was officially "her last wedding."

Marchello quit her job at the salt mine in December 2015 and launched her acupuncture business again—though it was a slow start. For the most part, she and Thomas lived off his income as she built up her client base. In July 2016, she and Thomas separated. According to Marchello, Thomas didn't include her enough in financial decisions and she didn't feel like an equal partner in their marriage. She took a job working the assembly line at the local Lofthouse Cookies factory for $10 an hour to help pay bills.

Her lawsuit against C&J dragged on for over a year and a half, and Marchello eventually told her lawyer, Steven Premo, that she wanted to settle and put it behind her. A few weeks before their meeting to discuss a settlement, C&J filed for bankruptcy. Marchello and her lawyer had to hire a bankruptcy attorney to file additional paperwork, and mediation was delayed for another six months. Finally, in February 2017, Marchello settled the lawsuit for an undisclosed amount and couldn't discuss the details of the meeting publicly.

Mana Kula continued to work for C&J, but mostly in Texas and Oklahoma. Scott Morgan quit his job at C&J but stayed in the oil industry. He rented an apartment near Fort Collins, Colorado, and took jobs closer to home. E, Kula's good friend, passed away from cancer during the summer of 2016.

TOM STAKES

In Colorado, things did not work out as Tom Stakes had hoped. He and Gary Westerman had a falling out one drunken night. After screaming at each other, the fight became physical. Stakes moved out soon after. He found a room in a mobile home in Golden, Colorado, for $440 a month. He took painting jobs when he could, but most paid only $10 to $12 an hour. It was difficult to make ends meet. One night he called me from Denver, sounding panicked. He said he'd lost his job and been thrown out of his place at 6 a.m. He didn't have a place to sleep for the night. The temperature was expected to sink into the single digits that night, and a snowstorm was coming. The local homeless shelters were at capacity and turning people away. "I'm down here with, like, 300 people," he said. "I'm scared. I'm cold. I got no place to be. Denver is not a friendly town." After we hung up, I called a few homeless shelters in Denver to see if anyone could fit Stakes in for the night. I finally found one that said it could take him if he arrived within the hour.

A few days later, per someone's suggestion at the homeless shelter, Stakes applied for a public assistance program in Denver that gave him about $700 a month (he called it "the Old People's Pension"). With the money, he bought a bus ticket back to Georgia to stay with his son Jay. But after a few months, he decided that another place might be a better fit for him: Williston, North Dakota. About a year after he'd left, he returned to live with Rick Sonstegaard and his mother, who welcomed him back.

CHELSEA NIEHAUS

Jacob was laid off in April 2015, and Chelsea and Jacob filed for divorce soon after. Jacob went home to Vincennes, Indiana, to live with his parents, and Chelsea, Will, and Litha moved in with her parents about 10 miles from Jacob. Chelsea and Jacob shared custody of the kids but did their best to avoid talking with each other. "Everything kind of collapsed at the same time," said Chelsea. "The divorce, the job, where we live. It all kind of came down on us. Some days, going back to North Dakota looks good." Chelsea finally sold her house in Louisville in early 2016. Jacob looked for oil field jobs in Indiana but eventually left to join a resistance army in northern Syria to fight ISIS.

Will went to day camp during the summer of their divorce, but Chelsea worried about how the separation was affecting him. That fall, Chelsea enrolled Will in the Catholic school she had attended as a child. Chelsea taught art at a local junior high school and moved into her own apartment. In the fall of 2016, after quitting the high school job, she started teaching English as a Foreign Language classes to Chinese students online. Jacob returned to the United States in late 2016 and reconnected with Chelsea. As of early 2017, he was still looking for employment.

JAY REINKE

Reinke stayed in Williston and worked at Pipeline Supply and Service, though he hoped to find work he was more passionate about. After a wave of layoffs hit Williston, he continued to help downtrodden men by letting them stay in his home.

In early 2017, as oil prices stabilized, there was talk of renewed drilling activity in the Permian Basin in Texas and New Mexico, and the Niobrara Formation in Colorado. Hundreds of men stood by, ready to relocate at a moment's notice. They were eager to see if, this time, it was the boom they'd been waiting for.

ACKNOWLEDGMENTS

I could fill the pages of this book with names of people who helped me along the way. First and foremost I want to thank the people who allowed me to observe their daily lives and welcomed me into their worlds. Cindy Marchello and her family, Tom Stakes, Chelsea Niehaus and Jacob Klipsch, Donny and Rena Nelson, Jay Reinke, Lisa DeVille, Marilyn Hudson, Mana Kula, Scott Morgan—you likely didn't know what you were in for when I introduced myself, but without your patience and openness, this book would not have been possible.

There were many others in North Dakota who helped illuminate issues, connected me to sources, explained complicated mechanics or legal topics, or gave me a place to rest my head—Daryl and Christine Peterson, Theodora Bird Bear, Richard Crows Heart, Sarah Christianson, Doug and Kristie Allard, Wanda and Frank Leppell, Curtis Kenney, Blake Ellis, Chevy, Heidi McCormick, Andy Bikkie, Betsy Wilkinson, Amy Dalrymple, Eric Killelea, Jesse Wellen, Chris Bean, Fintan Dooley, Stephen Premo, Blake Hall, Steph Nelson, Keith and Judy Lytle, and too many others to fit here.

I want to thank my early supporters—the crowdfunders who made my initial research trip possible (particularly Trefor Munn-Venn,

Vaibhav Sinha and Baldy Rakhra, and Di Strachan), and the organizations that provided funding or time and space to write: Mesa Refuge, Blue Mountain Center, the Headlands Center for the Arts, the Barbara Deming Memorial Fund, and the Richard J. Margolis Award. Much of the book was written in beautiful settings that reminded me how important it is to protect our environment.

I also had a support staff that kept me sane throughout the process. Thank you to Ed Neely and Lisa Aldred, whose early readings, commentary, and reassurance were paramount to finishing the manuscript. Thank you to my first reader of the earliest draft, Erin Diebboll. Your edits and suggestions made the book infinitely better. Patrick Dyer Wolf listened to more recordings of my voice than I care to think about—I'd still be transcribing tapes if it weren't for your help. Sarah Stanley fact-checked the toughest sections of the manuscript. Thank you to Ashley Panzera, Brad DeCecco, and Will Christiansen, who, in addition to their friendship, provided a stunning visual element to my work. Thanks to Tom Zoellner for always being so generous with your time and advice, and to Jackie Leo: meeting you changed my life for the better. Thank you for championing me. To my agent, Laura Yorke, and editor, Hannah Braaten: Thank you for believing in this project from the beginning. You improved my work at every stage and pushed me to the finish line. This book would not have happened without you.

My family has been there for me long before I became a writer. My parents, Greg and Carolyn Briody, not only pulled a trailer from California to North Dakota for this project, but told me for as long as I can remember to pursue my dreams despite the odds. My father passed away unexpectedly before I completed this book. He taught me many things but perhaps most important was how to find the humor in life and not take myself too seriously. Dad, I miss you every day. My sisters, Cailin and Alyse, are a constant source of inspiration and strength. My cousin Bill Buck helped me move to North Dakota and cheered me along as I went. My aunt Susie Briody brought much-needed reinforcements to Williston. My friends from California, New York, and North Carolina talked me through many challenges and setbacks. My loving partner and best friend, Daniel Whitesides, has been by my side since day one of this project. He responded with enthusiasm and encouragement when I announced I'd be quitting my stable job and moving to North Dakota. I can't imagine doing this work without his steadfast support and love.

NOTES

CHAPTER 2: A FORGOTTEN PLACE

5 The story about men sleeping at Walmart: Blake Ellis, "Six-Figure Salaries, but Homeless," *CNN Money*, October 26, 2011.

6 Job loss in manufacturing: Economic Policy Institute analysis of Bureau of Labor statistics; Robert E. Scott, "Manufacturing Job Loss," Economic Policy Institute, Issue Brief #402, August 11, 2015.

6 Job loss in construction: Christopher J. Goodman and Steven M. Mance, "Employment Loss and the 2007–09 Recession: An Overview," *Monthly Labor Review*, Bureau of Labor Statistics (April 2011): 5.

CHAPTER 4: TOM STAKES

Interviews: *Tom Stakes, Ward Koeser, Joshua Stansbury*

14 **20 new people arrived to town every day:** Ruth Moon, "Love Isn't Easy in Man Camp Ministry," *Christianity Today* 56 (October 2012):54.

14 Cities with 20 percent unemployment: U.S. Bureau of Labor Statistics, Unemployment Rate in Yuma County, AZ and El Centro, CA, retrieved from FRED, Federal Reserve Bank of St. Louis.

14 **labor market had lost 8.8 million jobs:** Christopher J. Goodman and Steven M. Mance, "Employment Loss and the 2007–09 Recession: An Overview," *Monthly Labor Review*, Bureau of Labor Statistics (April 2011): 3.

14 **14 million people were unemployed:** Bureau of Labor Statistics News Release, "The Employment Situation—September 2011," October 7, 2011.

14 **4 million people had lost their homes:** CoreLogic, " CoreLogic® Reports 57,000 Completed Foreclosures in September," October 31, 2012.

14 **7 million Americans slid into poverty:** By the end of 2008, the poverty rate was 39.1 million: Alemayehu Bishaw and Trudi J. Renwick, "Poverty:

2007 and 2008," *American Community Survey Reports* (September 2009), accessed at https://www.census.gov/prod/2009pubs/acsbr08-1.pdf. In the beginning of 2011, poverty rate was 46.2 million: Alemayehu Bishaw, "Poverty: 2010 and 2011," *American Community Survey Reports* (September 2012).

14 **three-quarters of those 8.8 million jobs lost . . . were lost by men:** Hanna Rosin, "The End of Men," *The Atlantic* (July/August 2010).

16 North Dakota homeless numbers: Michael Carbone, Carol Cohen, "The Tipping Point," the North Dakota Coalition for Homeless People and the Rural Community Assistance Corportation, 2013; North Dakota Interagency Council on Homelessness, "Housing Homeless," October 1, 2008; "Point-in-Time Summary for ND," North Dakota Coalition for Homeless People, January 23, 2013.

CHAPTER 5: CHELSEA NIEHAUS

Interviews: *Chelsea Niehaus, Jacob Klipsch*

17 **54,000 passengers who rode this overnight train:** Curt Brown, "Life in the Boom: Oil Riches Call . . . and Family Life Back Home Waits," (Minneapolis) *Star Tribune*, January 14, 2014.

18 Lake Sakakawea's coastline: Stephen Regenold, "Under Sail, Under Wraps," *The New York Times*, September 22, 2006.

CHAPTER 7: CINDY MARCHELLO

Interviews: *Cindy Marchello, Scott Morgan*

29 25,000 people in man camps: An estimate from Attorney General Wayne Stenehjem's office, reported by Jenny Michael, "Western N.D. Crime Not Disproportionate to Population," *Bismarck Tribune*, July 30, 2013.

29 *Lady Roughnecks in North Dakota Man-Camps*: *CNN Money*, November 1 2011.

30 **85 percent of oil industry jobs are held by men:** IHS Global Inc., "Minority and Female Employment in the Oil & Gas and Petrochemical Industries," prepared for American Petroleum Institute (March 2014): 20.

30 **women hold fewer than 2 percent of the jobs:** Ibid., p. 25.

CHAPTER 8: PASTOR JAY REINKE

Interviews: *Jay Reinke, Gloria Cox*

35 **80 percent of the first homesteaders who relocated:** Kathleen Norris, *Dakota: A Spiritual Geography* (New York: First Mariner Books, 1993), p. 8.

36 **one church for every 400 people:** Association of Religion Data Archives, "State Membership Report: North Dakota" (2010), data collected by the Association of Statisticians of American Religious Bodies.

38 **hardly keep new trucks on the lot:** E. J. Schultz, "Williston: The Town the Recession Forgot," *Ad Age*, October 31, 2011.

38 **average wage in Williston:** James MacPherson, "N.D. Oil Boom Town Reaping Prosperity, Problems," Associated Press, May 22, 2012.

38 **taxpayers reporting a $1 million-plus income:** Kathy Strombeck, a research analyst at the North Dakota Office of State Tax Commissioner, email communication, March 7, 2016.

39 Reinke's newspaper column: Jay Reinke, "Now Is a Time to Hope," *Williston Herald*, December 2, 2011.

CHAPTER 9: WILLISTON

Interviews: *Chuck Wilder*

40 **1887 push:** Elwyn Robinson, *History of North Dakota* (Lincoln: University of Nebraska Press, 1966), p. 142.

40 **10 percent down and seven years to pay the balance:** Ibid., p. 131.

40 **land under the 1862 Homestead Act:** D. Jerome Tweton, "Getting and Living on a Homestead," *North Dakota Studies*.

40 Quote from the railroad land commissioner: Quoted in Robinson, *History of North Dakota*, p. 132.

41 Harper's Monthly 1888 advertisement: *Word and Picture Story of Williston and Area Since 1887: 75th Anniversary & Diamond Jubilee* (Bismarck, North Dakota: Conrad Publishing Company, 1962).

41 **population . . . an increase of more than 1,000 percent:** Ibid., p. 134.

41 **Lumber . . . hauled from 50 miles away:** John Hudson, "Frontier Housing in North Dakota," in Janet Daley Lysengen and Ann M. Rathke, eds., *The Centennial Anthology of North Dakota History: Journal of the Northern Plains* (Bismarck: State Historical Society of North Dakota, 1996), p. 136.

41 **townships . . . more than 90 percent Norwegian:** Robinson, *History of North Dakota*, p. 157.

41 **76,000 Lutherans were living in North Dakota:** Ibid., p. 538.

42 Living conditions of early settlers: Ibid., p. 159.

42 Elwyn Robinson quote: Ibid., p. 168.

42 **A blizzard in 1887:** Valerie Sherer Mathes, "Theodore Roosevelt as a Naturalist and Bad Lands Rancher," in Lysengen and Rathke, *Centennial Anthology of North Dakota History*, p. 174.

42 **another blizzard killed nearly 100 people:** Robinson, *History of North Dakota*, p. 168.

42 **In 1889, a severe drought:** Harold E. Briggs, "The Great Dakota Boom, 1879–1888," in Lysengen and Rathke, *Centennial Anthology of North Dakota History*, p. 125.

42 **a typhoid epidemic nearly wiped out:** "Grand Forks Epidemic," *The Winnipeg Tribune*, January 29, 1894, p. 5.

43 Life for women pioneers: Robinson, *History of North Dakota*, p. 169.

43 **Thousands of pioneers left:** Ibid., p. 135.

43 **4 million acres of land were held by speculators:** Ibid., p. 150.

43 **Army officer wrote to his wife:** Quoted in ibid., p. 131.

43 Robinson quote: Ibid., pp. 135.

44 Mary Dodge Woodward quote: Quoted in ibid., p. 170.

44 Robinson quote: Robinson, *History of North Dakota*, p. 173.

44 **a young man from Virginia:** Warren A. Henke, "Imagery, Immigration, and the Myth of North Dakota: The First Quarter Century," in Lysengen and Rathke, *Centennial Anthology of North Dakota History*, p. 192.

44 Theodore Roosevelt quote: Mathes, "Theodore Roosevelt as a Naturalist and Bad Lands Rancher," in Lysengen and Rathke, *Centennial Anthology of North Dakota History*, p. 177.

44 **the most wildlife refuges of any state in the country:** National Park Service, "Theodore Roosevelt and Conservation," at http://www.nps.gov/thro /learn/historyculture/theodore-roosevelt-and-conservation.htm.

45 Bismarck population growth: "Bismarck–Burleigh County Actual & Projected Population 1920–2040," U.S. Census Bureau and Community Development Department.

45 **The population of urban areas in the state grew:** "Urban and Rural Population for the U.S. and All States: 1900–2000," The State Data Center of Iowa, U.S. Census Bureau.

45 Building boom in the 1920s: Richard Rubin, "Not Far from Forsaken," *The New York Times Magazine*, April 9, 2006.

45 Average rainfall and record temperatures: Robinson, *History of North Dakota*, p. 398.

45 North Dakota per capita income in 1930s: Ibid., p. 400.

45 **one-third of North Dakota's families lost their farms:** Ibid.

45 **80,000 people fled . . . and nearly half of the population lived on government relief:** Ibid., p. 401.

45–46 **Slope County . . . lost 29 percent of its population:** Ibid.

46 **population peaked at 680,845:** Rubin, "Not Far from Forsaken."

46 More income from agriculture and less from manufacturing: Robinson, *History of North Dakota*, p. 451.

46 **highest numbers of nuclear warheads:** "50 Facts About U.S. Nuclear Weapons," The Brookings Institution, 1998.

46 Norris quote: Kathleen Norris, *Dakota: A Spiritual Geography* (New York: First Mariner Books, 1993), p. ix.

CHAPTER 10: IT TAKES A BOOM

Interviews: *Cindy Marchello, Mana Kula, Scott Morgan, Curtis Kenney, Matthew Anderson, Tatum O'Brien Lindbo*

48 **Jobs . . . began to decline in the mid-1980s:** Bureau of Labor Statistics, "Employment, Hours, and Earnings from the Current Employment Statistics Survey," 1980–2016.

48 **The boom coincided with the withdrawal:** "Obama: U.S. to Withdraw Most Iraq Troops by August 2010," CNN, February 27, 2009.

48 **Bakken region "the next deployment":** Curt Brown, "Life in the Boom: Battlefield to Oil Field," (Minneapolis) *Star Tribune,* January 14, 2014.

49 **ShaleNet, a $20 million federally funded program:** ShaleNET, "About ShaleNet," accessed at https://www.shalenet.org/about.

49 **Only 12 percent of oil and gas workers in Williston had a bachelor's degree or higher:** "Williston's WIB's Beginning of Quarter Employment: Counts by Worker Education," QWI Explorer application, U.S. Census Bureau.

49 **for every drilling rig, some 120 workers:** From Alison Ritter, public information officer at the North Dakota Department of Mineral Resources, email communication, May 22, 2017.

49 **an average of 100 new wells drilled or fracked every month:** Leonardo Maugeri, "The Shale Oil Boom: A U.S. Phenomenon," Geopolitics of Energy Project, Discussion Paper #2013-05, Harvard Kennedy School, June 2013, p. 6.

49 **recruit potential dropouts:** Jack Healy, "Pay in Oil Fields Is Luring Youths in Montana," *The New York Times,* December 25, 2012.

49 Average wage for oil field workers: 2012 annual average from the Covered Employment and Wages program for code 211 Oil & Gas Extraction, U.S. Census Bureau, from Michael D. Ziesch, research analyst at Job Service North Dakota, email communication, October 24, 2013.

50 Average wages for high school graduates, dropouts, and college graduates: "Education Attainment," 2008–2012 American Community Survey 5-Year Estimates, U.S. Census Bureau.

52 **North Dakota became the most dangerous state to work in:** American Federation of Labor and Congress of Industrial Organizations, "Death on the Job: The Toll of Neglect," May 2014, p. 131.

52 2007 state job fatality rate: American Federation of Labor and Congress of Industrial Organizations, "Death on the Job: The Toll of Neglect," April 2009, p. 82.

52 2012 state job fatality rate: "Death on the Job," May 2014, p. 131.

52 **104 deaths per 100,000 workers:** Ibid., p. 32.

52 **Burn injuries among workers:** Maya Rao, "Twin Cities Hospitals Are Front Line in Treating Bakken Burn Victims," (Minneapolis) *Star Tribune,* February 15, 2015.

52 **342 workers died on the job in North Dakota:** "Death on the Job," May 2014, p. 134.

52 **At least 74 . . . from an accident in the Bakken:** Jennifer Gollan, "In North Dakota's Bakken Oil Boom, There Will Be Blood," *Reveal* from The Center for Investigative Reporting, June 13, 2015.

52–53 **OSHA field investigators . . . in western North Dakota:** Ibid.

53 **median OSHA fine in cases involving a death:** "Death on the Job," p. 118.

53 **one oil exploration company . . . was fined for a worker death:** Gollan, "In North Dakota's Bakken Oil Boom," *Reveal.*

53 **workers' compensation claims have more than quadrupled:** Tim McDonnell and James West, "It's the Wild F*ing West Out There," *Mother Jones* (November/December 2012).

53 **employers . . . paid the least among the states toward workers' compensation:** Michael Grabell and Howard Berkes, "The Demolition of Workers' Comp," *ProPublica*, March 4, 2015.

54 **higher-than-recommended levels of silica:** Eric Esswein, Max Kiefer, John Snawder, and Michael Breitenstein, "Worker Exposure to Cystalline Silica During Hydraulic Fracturing," National Institute for Occupational Safety and Health at the Centers for Disease Control and Prevention, May 23, 2012.

55 **ruled against injured workers most of the time:** Yue Qiu and Michael Grabell, "Workers' Compensation Reforms by State," *ProPublica*, March 4, 2015.

55 **labor union membership had fallen by half:** Drew Desilver, "Job Categories Where Union Membership Has Fallen Off Most," Pew Research Center, April 27, 2015.

CHAPTER 12: DONNY NELSON

Interviews: *Donny Nelson, Rena Nelson, Charles Neff*

63 **8,500 wells that were drilled:** Lynn Helms, "Director's Cut," North Dakota Industrial Commission's Department of Mineral Resources, Oil and Gas Division, December 12, 2014.

63–64 **244 million barrels of oil had been recovered:** Matthew Rocco, "North Dakota Oil Boom Driving Economic Development," FOXBusiness, February 11, 2013.

64 The state's mineral laws: Charles L. Neff, attorney at law at Neff Eiken & Neff, PC., personal communication, January 30, 2017.

64 **one in five surface owners:** A. G. Sulzberger, "A Great Divide over Oil Riches," *The New York Times*, December 27, 2011.

65 **retired farmer and rancher Lenin Dibble:** Ibid.

68 **The average rainfall:** "Total Precipitation in Inches by Month," Earth System Research Laboratory at the National Oceanic & Atmospheric Administration, 1971–2000.

CHAPTER 13: CINDY MARCHELLO

Interviews: *Cindy Marchello, Scott Morgan, Mana Kula, Curtis Kenney, Joanna Thamke*

69 Water aquifer depths in North Dakota: Joanna Thamke, hydrologist at the USGS Wyoming–Montana Water Science Center, personal communication, April 4, 2016.

70 **staying within 10 feet of the target path:** Mason Inman, "Adventures in Mapmaking: Mapping a Fracking Boom in North Dakota," *Wired*, January 7, 2015.

70 **It took about 40 to 60 days to drill:** Leonardo Maugeri, "The Shale Oil Boom: A U.S. Phenomenon," Geopolitics of Energy Project, Discussion Paper #2013-05, Harvard Kennedy School, June 2013, p. 8.

70 **2,000 truck trips:** Edwin Dobb, "The New Oil Landscape," *National Geographic*, March 2013.

70 **1.5 million to 6 million pounds of sand:** Sally Younger, "Sand Rush: Fracking Boom Spurs Rush on Wisconsin Silica," *National Geographic*, July 4, 2013.

71 **9,000 pounds of pressure per square inch:** Seamus McGraw, *The End of Country: Dispatches from the Frack Zone* (New York: Random House, 2011), p. 101.

CHAPTER 14: TIOGA

Interviews: *Chuck Wilder*

76 **Pioneer Oil & Gas, drilled in the Williston area in 1916:** John P. Bluemle, "The 50th Anniversary of the Discovery of Oil in North Dakota," North Dakota Geological Survey, Miscellaneous Series No. 89 (2001): 3.

76 "Possible Oil & Gas in North Dakota" press notice: Ibid., p. 1.

76 **One well achieved the shocking depth:** Sidney B. Anderson and John P. Bluemle, "Oil Exploration and Development in the North Dakota Williston Basin: 1982–1983 Update," North Dakota Geological Survey, Miscellaneous Series No. 65 (1984): 2.

77 The drilling of Clarence Iverson No. 1: Bluemle, "The 50th Anniversary of the Discovery of Oil in North Dakota," pp. 23–35.

77 **300 barrels in 17 hours:** Ibid., p. 29.

77 Charles S. Agey quote: Ibid.

77 **largest gas flares:** Bluemle, "The 50th Anniversary of the Discovery of Oil in North Dakota," p. 35.

77 Bill Shemorry quote: William E. Shemorry, "Mud, Sweat and Oil: The Early Years of the Williston Basin," 1991, quoted in Bluemle, "The 50th Anniversary of the Discovery of Oil in North Dakota," p. 25.

78 **The location continued to produce oil for 28 years:** Bluemle, "The 50th Anniversary of the Discovery of Oil in North Dakota," p. 30.

78 **Leon "Tude" Gordon . . . later created:** Ibid., pp. 32–33.

78 **150 oil operators:** Elwyn Robinson, *History of North Dakota* (Lincoln: University of Nebraska Press, 1966), p. 459.

78 Robinson quote: Ibid.

78 **800 people were living in trailers in Williston:** Ibid.

78 **Tioga, grew 250 percent:** Ibid.

78 **landowners sold their rights for as little as 62 cents an acre:** Ibid.

79 **tenth highest-producing state in the United States:** Ibid., p. 460.

79 Discovery of Charlson-Silurian Pool and the Little Knife Field: Bluemle, "The 50th Anniversary of the Discovery of Oil in North Dakota," p. 44.

79 **834 wells . . . and production peaked . . . 52.6 million barrels:** Ibid., p. 45.

79 **Williston was stuck with a mountain of debt:** Mike Soraghan, "Big Mac Is King in N.D. Energy Boom, but Other Businesses Struggle to Keep Up," *E&E News,* June 29, 2011.

80 **Halliburton . . . experimented with fracturing rock:** Seamus Mc-Graw, *The End of Country: Dispatches from the Frack Zone* (New York: Random House, 2011), p. 48.

81 **Oryx Energy was experimenting with horizontal drilling:** Gregory Zuckerman, *The Frackers: The Outrageous Inside Story of the New Billionaire Wildcatters* (New York: Portfolio, 2013), p. 56.

81 Kenneth Bowdon quote: Ibid., p. 63.

82 **413 billion barrels of oil:** Zuckerman, *The Frackers*, p. 230.

82 Bluemle prediction: Bluemle, "The 50th Anniversary of the Discovery of Oil in North Dakota," p. 54.

82 Continental Resources' first well: Zuckerman, *The Frackers*, pp. 231–232.

82 **experimented with fracking wells in stages:** Ibid., pp. 252–254.

83 Hamm's net worth: David Segal, "An Oklahoma Oilman's Billion-Dollar Divorce," *The New York Times*, November 10, 2014.

83 **owned more oil under U.S. soil than any other American:** Zuckerman, *The Frackers*, p. 6.

83 **EOG drilled its first well in April 2006:** Ibid., p. 234.

84 U.S. deployment in Iraq: Barbara Salazar Torreon, "U.S. Periods of War and Dates of Recent Conflicts," Congressional Research Service, September 29, 2016, p. 8.

84 Cheney meeting with oil representatives: Thaddeus Herrick, "U.S. Oil Wants to Work in Iraq," *The Wall Street Journal,* January 17, 2003.

84 General John Abizaid quote: "Courting Disaster: The Fight for Oil, Water and a Healthy Planet," 2007 Roundtable, Stanford University, October 13, 2007.

84 **3,500 U.S. soldiers lost their lives in Iraq:** "A Timeline of the Iraq War," *ThinkProgress*, March 17, 2006.

84 **In 2007, the United States consumed:** "Data 5: Finished Products," U.S. Supply and Disposition, U.S. Energy Information Administration.

84 **U.S. gasoline prices reached a record high:** "Gas Prices Hit Record High," *CNN Money*, May 7, 2007.

84 2008 USGS survey: U.S. Geological Survey, "3 to 4.3 Billion Barrels of Technically Recoverable Oil Assessed in North Dakota and Montana's Bakken Formation—25 Times More Than 1995 Estimate," press release, April 10, 2008.

85 **9 out of 10 oil and gas wells . . . use hydraulic fracturing:** Leonardo

Maugeri, "The Shale Oil Boom: A U.S. Phenomenon," Geopolitics of Energy Project, Discussion Paper #2013-05, Harvard Kennedy School, June 2013, p. 25.

85 **15 million Americans live within a mile:** Russell Gold, *The Boom: How Fracking Ignited the American Energy Revolution and Changed the World* (New York: Simon & Schuster, 2014), p. 19.

85 Harold Hamm quote: Quoted in Chico Harlan, "How the Plunging Price of Oil Has Set off a new Global Contest," *The Washington Post*, July 15, 2015.

85 Hamm estimate of 900 billion barrels: Christopher Helman, "Oil Billionaire Harold Hamm on the 40th Anniversary of the OPEC Embargo," *Forbes*, October 16, 2013.

85 **Between 2007 and 2014, oil production skyrocketed:** U.S. Energy Information Administration, "North Dakota Field Production of Crude Oil."

86 David Petraeus quote: Quoted in Eric Killelea, "Wardner: Petraeus Called Oil Patch a 'War Zone,'" *The Williston Herald*, September 26, 2014.

CHAPTER 15: DONNY NELSON

Interviews: *Donny Nelson, Frank and Wanda Leppell, Brenda and Richard Jorgenson, and Theodora Bird Bear*

87 **oil companies in North Dakota burned away:** U.S. Energy Information Administration, "North Dakota Natural Gas Flaring Targets Challenged by Rapid Production Growth," November 13, 2015.

87 **$100 million of it every month:** Ernest Scheyder, "Exclusive: Bakken Flaring Burns more than $100 Million a Month," *Reuters*, July 29, 2013.

87 **as much carbon dioxide a year as a million cars:** Ryan Salmon and Andrew Logan, "Flaring Up: North Dakota Natural Gas Flaring More than Doubles in Two Years," *Ceres*, July 2013.

87 **60 types of pollutants:** Douglas M. Leahey, Katherine Preston, Mel Strosher, "Theoretical and Observational Assessments of Flare Efficiencies," *Journal of the Air & Waste Management Association* 51, no. 12 (2001): 1610–1616.

87 **benzene, methane, propylene, and butane:** Eman A. Emam, "Gas Flaring in Industry: An Overview," *Petroleum & Coal*, December 3, 2015.

88 University of Michigan study: E. A. Kort et al., "Fugitive Emissions from the Bakken Shale Illustrate Role of Shale Production in Global Ethane Shift," *Geophysical Research Letters* 43, no. 9, May 7, 2016.

88 **1993 Environmental Protection Agency (EPA) report:** Environmental Protection Agency, Office of Air Quality Planning and Standards, "Report to Congress on Hydrogen Sulfide Air Emissions Associated with the Extraction of Oil and Natural Gas," October 1993, pp. 24–66.

89 George P. Mitchell quote: Quoted in Michael R. Bloomberg and George P. Mitchell, "Fracking Is Too Important to Foul Up," *The Washington Post*, August 23, 2012.

89–90 Lynn Helms quote: Quoted in "Hydraulic Fracturing on Public Lands

Forum" transcript, forum hosted by the Bureau of Land Management, Bismarck, North Dakota, April 20, 2011, p. 212.

90 **A nationwide 2015 study:** Environmental Protection Agency, Office of Research and Development, "Hydraulic Fracturing for Oil and Gas: Impacts from the Hydraulic Fracturing Water Cycle on Drinking Water Resources in the United States," Washington, DC: EPA/600/R-16/236F, 2016.

90 **drinking water systems for more than 8.6 million . . . within a mile of at least one fracked well:** Ibid., p. 44.

90 Anthony Ingraffea's cement study: Anthony R. Ingraffea, Martin T. Wells, Renee L. Santoro, and Seth B. C. Shonkoff, "Assessment and Risk Analysis of Casing and Cement Impairment in Oil and Gas Wells in Pennsylvania, 2000–2012," *Proceedings of the National Academy of Sciences* 111, no. 30 (2014).

90 **nearly 300 cases of pollution:** Pennsylvania Department of Environmental Protection, "Water Supply Determination Letters," February 3, 2017.

90 Fines to Pennsylvania gas companies: Susan Phillips, "Marcellus Shale Drillers Fined for Methane Migration," StateImpact, NPR, August 25, 2015.

91 Recoverable gas in Marcellus compared to Bakken: U.S. Energy Information Administration, "Assumptions to the Annual Energy Outlook 2016," p. 136.

91 Edwin Dobb quote: Dobb, "The New Oil Landscape," *National Geographic* (March 2013).

93 2013 State Senate hearing on setback bill: Senate Natural Resources Committee, "2013 Senate Standing Committee Minutes," SB 2206, Fort Lincoln Room, North Dakota State Capital, January 24, 2013.

CHAPTER 16: TOM STAKES

Interviews: *Tom Stakes*

95 Tom Stakes's DUI charge: Michael R. Wald, "Case/Incident Report," North Dakota Highway Patrol, July 26, 2013.

95 **DUI arrests had increased by over 1,000 percent:** 15 in 2008, 205 in 2012: Eric Killelea and Jerry Burnes, "Police Playing Catch Up to Oil Patch Crime Increases," *The Williston Herald*, February 15, 2014.

CHAPTER 17: WILLISTON

101–102 **$353 million worth of building permits:** "Williston Impact Statement, 2014," Williston Economic Development, 2014, pp. 18-19.

102 **9,000 man camp units:** Bartley Kives, "Welcome to Williston, North Dakota: America's New Gold Rush City," *The Guardian* (UK), July 28, 2014.

CHAPTER 20: FORT BERTHOLD

Interviews: *Marilyn Hudson, Lisa DeVille*

121 **40 percent of the tribe's workforce was unemployed:** Sierra Crane-Murdoch, "The Other Bakken Boom: America's Biggest Oil Rush Brings Tribal Conflict," *High Country News*, April 23, 2012.

121 **crammed with three or more families:** James William Gibson, "Shale Oil Boom in North Dakota Is Impacting Native Americans Especially Hard," *Earth Island Journal*, December 3, 2012.

121 **Life expectancy on the reservation was 57 years:** Deborah Sontag and Brent McDonald, "In North Dakota, a Tale of Oil, Corruption and Death," *The New York Times*, December 28, 2014.

121–122 Tex Hall quote: YouTube, "Chief Tex Hall," Robin Bossert from Bossert and Company, August 3, 2013, accessed at https://www.youtube.com/watch?v=kMA9AgVnfNQ.

122 **tribal government set aside $421 million:** "Tribal Business Council [TBC] Four Bears News Letter," December 2013, Publication No. 13-6, p. 3.

122 **$2.5 million yacht:** According to a senior tribal official, reported by Sontag and McDonald, "In North Dakota, a Tale of Oil, Corruption and Death."

123 **"70 percent of our community is living in overcrowded conditions":** Lisa DeVille and Walter DeVille, personal communication and "The Mandaree Community Volunteers Needs Assessment," August 9, 2012.

124 First case of heroin on the reservation in 2012: Cindy Carcamo, "Drug Explosion Follows Oil Boom on North Dakota Indian Reservation, *Los Angeles Times*, February 22, 2015.

125 **evidence of sex trafficking on the reservation:** Kayla Webley and Christa Hillstrom, "Sex Trafficking on the Reservation: One Native American Nation's Struggle Against the Trade," *Marie Claire*, September 22, 2015.

125 **white mechanic on the reservation:** Sierra Crane-Murdoch, "On Indian Land, Criminals Can Get Away With Almost Anything," *The Atlantic*, February 22, 2013.

126 **smallpox outbreak tore through the area:** Paul VanDevelder, *Coyote Warrior: One Man, Three Tribes, and the Trial That Forged A Nation* (Boston: Little, Brown, 2004), p. 59.

126 **official reservation borders were drawn in 1870:** Horwitz, "Dark Side of the Boom."

126 **1.6 million acres of reservation land:** "Tribal Historical Overview—Change," The History and Culture of the Mandan, Hidatsa, and Sahnish, *North Dakota Studies*, State Historical Society of North Dakota.

126 **By the early 1910s, fewer than 3 million acres:** "Tribal Historical Overview—1900s—Garrison Dam," The History and Culture of the Mandan, Hidatsa, and Sahnish, *North Dakota Studies*, State Historical Society of North Dakota.

127 **fewer than 3 percent of those living on the reservation:** VanDevelder, *Coyote Warrior*, p. 112.

127 Martin Cross's efforts to stop the Garrison Dam: Ibid., p. 114–121.

127 **some 155,000 acres of land:** "Indians Lose Land in Path of Big Dam," *The New York Times*, June 10, 1952.

127 **436 properties:** VanDevelder, *Coyote Warrior*, p. 116.

127 **The tribes received only $12.5 million in compensation:** "3 Indian Tribes Sell Land for Dam, but Reluctantly," *The New York Times*, March 17, 1950.

128 Louise Holding Eagle's home: VanDevelder, *Coyote Warrior*, pp. 139–140.

128 **former high school basketball players:** Ibid., p. 159.

129 **study by the Bureau of Indian Affairs in 1964:** U.S. House, *Report on House Resolution 108 Authorizing the Committee on Interior and Insular Affairs*, cited in VanDevelder, *Coyote Warrior*, p. 173.

130 Paul VanDevelder quote: VanDevelder, *Coyote Warrior*, p. 183.

130 **unemployment on the reservation fell to the single digits:** Joe Cicha at North Dakota Department of Commerce, "Growing ND by the Numbers," North Dakota Census Office, December 2015.

CHAPTER 21: CHELSEA NIEHAUS

Interviews: *Chelsea Niehaus, Jacob Klipsch*

140 **average income . . . had doubled:** David Bailey, "In North Dakota, Hard to Tell an Oil Millionaire from Regular Joe," *Reuters*, October 3, 2012.

140 **five millionaires were made every day:** Bruce Gjovig of the University of North Dakota's Center for Innovation, reported in ibid.

CHAPTER 22: PASTOR JAY REINKE

Interviews: *Jay Reinke, Stuart Bondurant, Gloria Cox, Caleb Fry, Blake Hall, Stephanie Nelson*

144 Donna Sieg quote: Quoted in Hank Stephenson, "Love Thy Neighbor," *The Williston Herald*, June 18, 2012.

145 Homicides at highest level; rapes highest: Wayne Stenehjem, Office of Attorney General, Bureau of Criminal Investigation, "Crime in North Dakota, 2012: A Summary of Uniform Crime Report Data," prepared by Colleen Weltz, 2013, p. 5.

145 **drug-related arrests in the state:** Ibid.

145 **alcohol was a factor in more than half of the deadly traffic accidents:** "GOP Bill Imposes 4 Days in Jail for First-Time DUIs," *Grand Forks Herald*, December 18, 2012.

145 Andy Anderson quote: Quoted in James MacPherson, "Firearm Permits Rise in ND's Booming Oil Patch," Associated Press, April 7, 2012.

145 *Williston Herald* editorial about sex offender list: "Here's Why We Ran the List," *Williston Herald*, February 18, 2012.

146 **The Williston Police Department went from receiving:** Williston Police Chief Jim Lokken, cited in Jenna Ebersole, "Emergency Responders Struggle to Keep Up," *The Williston Herald*, November 6, 2012.

146 Scott Busching quote: Quoted in "Bursting at the Bars," *The Williston Herald*, November 15, 2014.

CHAPTER 26: DONNY NELSON

Interviews: *Donny Nelson, Jim Fuglie*

179 **$550,000 from oil-related groups:** Deborah Sontag, "Where Oil and Politics Mix," *The New York Times,* November 23, 2014.

179 Dalrymple's ExxonMobil stock: Lauren Donovan, "N.D. Gov. Dalrymple Owns Stock in Company That Plans to Drill Near Elkhorn Site," *Bismarck Tribune,* March 22, 2013.

179 *New York Times* review of Industrial Commission minutes: Sontag, "Where Oil and Politics Mix."

179 **fewer than 50 disciplinary fines for all drilling violations:** Nicholas Kusnetz, "North Dakota's Oil Boom Brings Damage Along with Prosperity," *ProPublica,* June 7, 2012.

180 **19 inspectors in 2012:** Ibid.

180 Lynn Helms quote about EPA involvement: "Hydraulic Fracturing on Public Lands Forum" transcript, forum hosted by the Bureau of Land Management, Bismarck, ND, April 20, 2011, p. 47.

180 Kathleen Norris quote: Norris, *Dakota: A Spiritual Geography* (New York: First Mariner Books, 1993), p. 18.

180 **Unitization was promoted in the early 1990s:** John P. Bluemle, "The 50th Anniversary of the Discovery of Oil in North Dakota," *North Dakota Geological Survey,* Miscellaneous Series No. 89 (2001): 50.

181 **ConocoPhillips revised that number to 200 wells:** Lauren Donovan, "Lots of Unknowns Surround Corral Creek Unit," *Bismarck Tribune,* December 16, 2012.

CHAPTER 28: TOM STAKES

Interviews: *Tom Stakes, Jay Stakes, Gary Westerman, Eddie Bergeson*

191 **On May 29, 2014, Stakes was arrested:** "Williston Municipal Case Summary," Case no. WI-2014-CR-01365.

198 **The roommate pulled out a knife:** Cynthia Hubert and Phillip Reese, "Mental Patients Bused—and Crime Followed," *The Sacramento Bee,* December 15, 2013.

CHAPTER 33: FORT BERTHOLD

Interviews: *Edmund Baker, Josh Wood, Lisa DeVille, Marilyn Hudson, Donny Nelson, Dr. Avner Vengosh, Theodora Bird Bear*

237 **pipeline had been built in 2010:** Amy Dalrymple, Forum News Service, "EPA Involved in 2014 Bakken Pipeline Leak Investigation," *The Billings Gazette,* May 18, 2015.

237 **and didn't have monitoring equipment:** Associated Press, "EPA Trying to Confirm North Dakota Spill Didn't Reach Lake," *Rapid City Journal,* July 10, 2014.

237 **not required under North Dakota law:** Chester Dawson, "Farmers Fight a New Kind of Pipeline Spill—Salty Wastewater," *The Wall Street Journal*, May 15, 2015.

237 **The spill was discovered only as the company:** Associated Press, "EPA Trying to Confirm North Dakota Spill Didn't Reach Lake."

238 **path of the brine:** Associated Press, "Cleanup Area Extends Nearly 2 miles After N.D. spill," *USA Today*, July 10, 2014.

238 **fracking wastewater laced with chemicals:** Theo Colborn, Carol Kwiatkowski, Kim Schultz, Mary Bachran, "Natural Gas Operations from a Public Health Perspective," *Human and Ecological Risk Assessment: An International Journal* 17, no. 5 (2011).

238 **10 times saltier than ocean water:** Neela Banerjee, "Wetland Contamination Can Be Predicted in Oil Boom States, Study Finds," *The Los Angeles Times*, January 8, 2014.

238 **Some batches even contain traces of radium:** Lisa Song, "'Saltwater' from North Dakota Fracking Spill Is Not What's Found in the Ocean," *Inside Climate News*, July 16, 2014.

238 **10 barrels of wastewater brine:** Banerjee, "Wetland Contamination Can Be Predicted in Oil Boom States."

242 4,000 brine spills in the state: North Dakota Department of Health Environmental Health, "Oilfield Environmental Incidents Older Than 12 Months," accessed at http://www.ndhealth.gov/ehs/spills/.

242 Kris Roberts quote: Quoted in Nicholas Kusnetz, "North Dakota's Oil Boom Brings Damage Along with Prosperity," *ProPublica*, June 7, 2012.

242 **spills totaling about 1.7 million gallons of brine:** Jeff Larson and Nicholas Kusnetz, "North Dakota Spills," *ProPublica*, June 7, 2012.

242 **many companies report zero barrels spilled:** North Dakota Department of Health, Environmental Health, "Oilfield Environmental Incidents," accessed at http://www.ndhealth.gov/ehs/spills/.

243 **an estimated 75 tons of those filter socks are generated:** Lauren Donovan, "North Dakota Takes Slow, Historic Step toward Radioactive Waste," *Bismarck Tribune*, February 15, 2013.

243 **filter socks can contain as high as 70 picocuries:** Lauren Donovan, "Study to Look at Raising Radioactive Waste Limits," *Bismarck Tribune*, November 15, 2013.

243 Timeline of when Tesoro reported the spill: Dan Frosch, "Oil Spill in North Dakota Raises Detection Concerns," *The New York Times*, October 23, 2013.

243 **The spill contaminated about 15 acres:** Amy Dalrymple, "Two Years after North Dakota Oil Spill, Dirty Pile Still Dwarfs Clean Pile," Forum News Service, September 26, 2015.

244 **only a few pipeline inspectors and didn't require companies to**

reveal any data . . . until April 2014: Dawson, "Farmers Fight a New Kind of Pipeline Spill—Salty Wastewater."

244 **Fines . . . are limited to $12,500 a day:** Ibid.

244 **More than 50 percent of pipeline incidents:** Carl Weimer, "Testimony of The Pipeline Safety Trust," Subcommittee on Energy and Power of the Committee on Energy and Commerce, U.S. House of Representatives, July 14, 2015.

244 Mark Fox quote: Quoted in George Lerner and Christof Putzel, "Tribal Environmental Director: 'We Are Not Equipped' for N.D. Oil Boom," *America Tonight,* May 16, 2015.

245 **checkpoint manned by a single guard:** According to Lisa DeVille. The checkpoint was there before the spill, according to Josh Wood (though, in general, checkpoints are rare at oil drilling sites in North Dakota).

245 **North Dakota's largest brine spill to date:** Ernest Scheyder, "Millions of Gallons of Saltwater Leak into North Dakota Creek," Reuters, January 22, 2015.

245 **The pipeline was only six months old and had a monitoring system:** Amy Dalrymple, "Pipeline Company Didn't Use Remote Sensors Before Leak," Forum News Service, February 28, 2015.

245 **Energy Transfer Partners, claimed it would create:** Holly Yan, "Dakota Access Pipeline: What's at Stake?" CNN, October 28, 2016.

245 **original path was closer to Bismarck:** Amy Dalrymple, "Pipeline Route Plan First Called for Crossing North of Bismarck," *The Bismarck Tribune,* August 18, 2016.

246 DeVille's testimony in June 2015: North Dakota Public Service Commission Public Hearing at Killdeer, ND, at the High Plains Cultural Center on June 15, 2015.

247 Dr. Vengosh's report on water contamination: Nancy E. Lauer, Jennifer S. Harkness, and Avner Vengosh, "Brine Spills Associated with Unconventional Oil Development in North Dakota," *Environmental Science & Technology* 50, no. 10 (2016): 5389–5397.

CHAPTER 40: TOM STAKES
Interviews: *Tom Stakes, Rick Sonstegaard, Darin Henderson*
263 Oil company layoffs and first-quarter losses: Christopher S. Rugaber, "Layoffs by Energy Companies Drag Down Job Growth in Oil Patch States in April," Associated Press, May 27, 2015.

CHAPTER 41: WILLISTON
307 Jeffrey City population and $1.2 million gym: Dale D. Buss, "Uranium Industry Boom Goes Bust As Growth of Nuclear Power Falters," *The Wall Street Journal,* November 3, 1981.
307 **95 percent of the area's workforce had left:** Michael A. Amundson,

"Home on the Range No More: The Boom and Bust of A Wyoming Uranium Mining Town, 1957–1988," *Western Historical Quarterly* (Winter 1995): 484.

308 **some pumping nearly two thousand barrels a day:** Continental Resources press release, "Continental Resources Continues to Improve Initial Well Production Rates in the North Dakota Bakken," January 6, 2010.

308 Well production declined by half in first year, 30 to 40 percent in second year: Leonardo Maugeri, "The Shale Oil Boom: A U.S. Phenomenon," Geopolitics of Energy Project, Discussion Paper #2013-05, Harvard Kennedy School, June 2013, p. 3.

308 **90 new producing wells per month were needed:** Ibid., p. 1.

308 **wells . . . in U.S. shale formations:** Ibid., p. 1.

309 Leonardo Maugeri quote: Ibid., p. 3.

309 Williston real estate agent quote: Melissa Krause, "Home Ownership Could Be Boosted by Decision," *The Williston Herald*, March 13, 2016.

309 **10,000 jobs were cut in North Dakota:** Debbie Carlson, "North Dakota's Oil-Heavy Economy Is Hanging On, but for How Long?" *The Guardian* (UK), December 27, 2015.

310 **occupancy rate for newly built apartments:** Amy Dalrymple, "Apartment Developers Trying to Ride Out Oil Slump," Forum News Service, March 28, 2016.

310 **5,000 hotel rooms and apartment units:** Kevin Wallevand, "'After the Boom'—Part One," WDAY-TV, May 1, 2016.

310 **1,350 new apartments were still under construction:** Jennifer Oldham, "The Real Estate Crisis in North Dakota's Man Camps," Bloomberg, September 29, 2015.

310 **10,000 new homes and apartments built during the boom:** William Yardley, "In North Dakota, an Oil Boomtown Doesn't Want to Go Bust," *Los Angeles Times*, January 11, 2016.

311 **about $215 million in debt:** Jack Healy, "Built Up by Oil Boom, North Dakota Now Has Emptier Feeling," *The New York Times*, February 7, 2016.

311 **municipal bonds were downgraded to junk status:** Ernest Scheyder, "In North Dakota's Oil Patch, a Humbling Comedown," Reuters, May 18, 2016.

AFTERWORD

Interviews: *Lisa DeVille, Donny Nelson, Cindy Marchello, Tom Stakes, Chelsea Niehaus, Jay Reinke, Scott Morgan*

313 **Trump had between $500,000 and $1 million invested:** Associated Press, "Donald Trump's Stock in Dakota Access Oil Pipeline Raises Concerns," November 25, 2016.